Only The Lonely

The Life and Artistic Legacy of Roy Orbison

D1325198

Also by Alan Clayson:

Call up the Groups: The Golden Age of British Beat, 1962–67

Back in the High Life: A Biography of Steve Winwood

Alan Clayson has been involved in the British music business for nearly twenty years. Born in 1951, he played with various bands before forming his own band, Alan Clayson and the Argonauts, in 1975. Their latest album was released in 1985. More recently he has played keyboards for Dave Berry, as well as producing his latest album and single. He lives in Berkshire with his wife and children.

Alan Clayson

Only the
Lonely

PAN BOOKS
London, Sydney and Auckland

First published in Great Britain 1989 by Sidgwick & Jackson Limited
This edition published 1990 by Pan Books Limited
Cavaye Place, London SW10 9PG

9 8 7 6 5 4 3 2 1
© Alan Clayson 1990
ISBN 0 330 31484 X

Photoset by Rowland Phototypesetting Limited
Bury St Edmunds, Suffolk
Printed and bound in Great Britain by
Richard Clay Limited, Bungay, Suffolk

Contents

TO THE FAMILIES OF KAREN,
SAM AND MIRIAM

'By Hercules! The man was greater than Caesar or Cromwell – nay, nearly equal to Odin or Thor! The Texans ought to build him an altar!'

Thomas Carlyle, speaking of Jim Bowie

Acknowledgements

Firstly, I wish to express my deepest gratitude to Oliver Johnson, Caroline Freyer and Charlotte Stone for assistance that went beyond the call of duty. Thanks also to Susan Hill, Carys Thomas and the rest of the team in Museum Street.

I owe a particular debt to the following for their encouragement and for trusting me with archive material: David Cox, Roger Dopson, Stuart Hobday, Martin Hawkins, Allan Jones, Spencer Leigh, Steve Maggs, Steve Rowley, Charles Salt, John Tobler and Michael Towers.

I have also drawn from conversations with Chet Atkins, Cliff Bennett, Bill Dees, Fred Foster, Paul Munday, Joe Melson, Gordon Stoker and Kay Vasquez, and I thank them for their candour. In this respect, I am even more in the debt of Barry Booth, Brian and Pam Poole and, of course, Steve and Michael Howe.

Thanks is also due in varying degrees to Evie Baldwin, B & T printers, Rowland Phototypesetting, Roger Barnes, Dave Berry, Stuart and Kathryn Booth, Rob Bradford, Trevor Burrows, Terry Clarke, Gordon and Rosemary Clayson, Ron Cooper, Pete Cox, Greg and Debi Daniels, Kevin Delaney, Peter Doggett, Tim Fagan, Pete Frame, Anne Freer, Bernard Futter, Eric Goulden, Paul Hearne, David Horn, Graham Larkbey, Graham and Yvonne Lambourne, Brian Leafe, Fraser Massey, Jim McCarty, Colin Miles, David Nicolle of the *Reading Evening Post*, Peter O'Brian, Darrell Paddick, Sarah Parish, Tony Peters of Acuff-Rose, Ray Phillips, Athenia Pierce of the Wink Chamber of Commerce, Denis Reed, Patsy Riches, Geoff Taggart, Andy

Taylor, Paul Tucker, Marion Vause and Chris Warman –
plus Inese, who shielded me as far as possible from the real
world, as well as Jack and Harry who like to be included.

Note to the reader
Numbers in the body of the text refer to notes at the end of
each chapter. Some numbers will recur when the same article
or interview cited before is referred to again.

1

The Eyes of Texas
are Upon You

'I always wanted to be a millionaire,' reckoned Roy Orbison in 1965, 'even when I was thirteen. I'd made up my mind to be one by the time I reached thirty.'[1] This dream would come true well before he reached that age, but Orbison never forgot the struggle. They weren't empty words, therefore, when the 52-year-old singer told the capacity crowd at his last performance, 4 December 1988, that they made him feel young again. His latest single, 'You Got It', had been received as ecstatically as any of the old hits of the sixties that Sunday. Once again, Roy Orbison was back in favour.

His long-standing fame was exemplified by the municipal two-thousand seater where he'd booked for that final show in Akron, Ohio. When the breaks had come, however, Roy had never deserted the network of one-horse-town halls, glum high school gyms and army messes that had sustained him through leaner years. 'If I get to be a star,' he'd declared as a teenager, 'I'm going to play smaller places – anywhere that wants to hear me.'[2]

You couldn't get much closer to the heart of the American South than west Texas, where Roy Orbison grew up. It was indeed far beyond the pale of mainstream show business – apart from its intermittent use by Hollywood film directors for location westerns. In 1948, for example, Howard Hawks shot a John Wayne cattle-drive drama, *Red River*, on the east side of the Panhandle. Only two miles from the actual river of the film's title, the Chisholm Trail to Missouri had passed along the main street of Vernon, the Wilbarger county town where Roy Kelton Orbison was born on 23 April 1936.

The Texas Centennial Exposition, proclaiming 100 years of proud independence from Mexico, was in full swing in the year of Roy's birth, and the rich drawl he acquired as a toddler would forever betray his upbringing. Yet in spite of their cowboy accents, Texans born in the twentieth century were more likely to be oilmen than gunslingers or bronco busters. Although the 'black gold' had been discovered near Nacodoches in 1866, it had taken nearly fifty years for full-scale production to become feasible. Meanwhile, other deposits had been uncovered all over Texas, often spurting for days as entrepreneurs overcame legal, mechanical and personnel hurdles.

It is difficult to appreciate how suddenly modern Texas came into being and yet how much of the Old West lingers there still. The demise of the Pony Express in lieu of the telegraph, for example, was not too distant a memory for families like the Orbisons who had been settled in Texas for more than two generations. Theirs was a close-knit family which had embraced the innately decent virtues of small-town America and that could smell haughtiness and affectation a mile off. Marrying in 1932 when they were both nineteen, Orbie Lee and Nadine Orbison would produce, by the onset of the Second World War, two sons – Grady and the remarkable Roy. Nadine, a former nurse, was well equipped to cope with her youngsters' ailments – such as Roy's biannual attacks of flu – while Orbie Lee worked as a car mechanic. Years later, Roy would cite his parents as the biggest single influence upon his life. He would spend all day in the garage under his dad's feet, watching him fit brake linings and change tyres. So began Roy's life-long love affair with automobiles: how they worked; the differences between them; the sheer magic of their whizzing springs and pistons. From earliest youth, he could take a small engine to bits and put it back together again. Mr Orbison would also allow his sons to shunt vehicles around in first gear when they came in for repair. Long before they were officially entitled to take a car onto the public highway, the hand and foot co-ordination needed to drive had become second nature to the Orbison children.

A less fortunate legacy of those years was that, like their father, Roy and Sammy would be unable to stop smoking – though Roy 'had a big drink of whiskey once. I asked my father what it was. I said, "Can I have some?" and he said, "Sure." So I slugged back a big shot of whiskey, and I think I was sick for days. So that turned me off drink forever. I still don't drink.'[3] Neither did any of the Orbisons use bad language beyond the mildest expletives.

All the males on Orbie Lee's side were inclined to suffer from poor eyesight, which necessitated the wearing of spectacles – from the age of four in Roy's case. By any standards, the Orbisons weren't a very comely brood either. With a preponderance of receding chins, jug-handle ears and pouchy jowls, they made you think of a family grouping of a cageful of ruminating hamsters. From their father, Grady and Sammy, the youngest, born in 1947, had inherited greater height and more robust constitutions than Roy, whose slighter build and washed-out complexion – from a childhood bout of jaundice – were coupled with an unimposing presence: 'I was totally anonymous – I mean, I was unknown even at my home.'[4]

True to his upbringing, Roy was unswervingly polite; even if the others guffawed and slapped their thighs, he would only smile placidly. At the breakfast table, he'd listen quietly; his deliberated replies to questions unfailingly to the point. Yet he was a likeable, if self-contained, little boy ever eager to please. When playing Cowboys and Indians, Roy would never object if persistently chosen to be the bad guy – although he never looked the part until he'd outgrown the game. When he started school at six, he tried hard at football – but he 'just never was good enough'.

Roy would retain that look of child-like innocence all his

life. His soft, blue-grey eyes would forever be as guileless as a schoolboy's: 'I am very much the same person I was when I was six years of age,' he once admitted. 'It's hard to say and almost impossible to explain. I knew then about religion; I knew then about history – and I could play the guitar.'[5]

Before television became an indispensable domestic fixture in the rural south, musical evenings were a frequent occurrence in many homesteads. Stately colonial mansions may have tinkled to the strains of Debussy and Handel, but at the Orbisons' bungalow with its pot-bellied stove, the backbone of this entertainment issued from the guitars of Dad and Nadine's brother, Uncle Kenneth. Of these most common folk instruments of the South, models etched with Gene Autry on a rearing horse had been available on the Sears-Roebuck mail-order catalogue since the early thirties.

Home-made Southern folk music lay at the bedrock of 'Country and Western' music. At its worst, C & W was a breeding ground for blue-collar, right-wing sloganizing, encouraging suspicion of labour unions, minority groups and foreigners: the Yellow Rose of Texas is the only girl for me. This mixture was alternately laced with pious fear of and matey camaraderie towards not so much God as 'the Man in the Sky' or 'the Lord', who was entreated (as the need arose) as either a militant enforcer of redneck prejudices or a homespun prairie Plato. Above all, the Lord was a Man. He had a crew cut, a Charles Atlas physique and an amused tolerance of boozing and womanizing. Like any right-thinkin' Man, he sure hated queers, commies and niggers. Even as late as 1966, Roy Orbison would say, 'As a male, I personally don't like feminine hair on men. And I imagine women don't like it either.' He added, however, 'if fellows are wearing their hair, not just to be different, but because they like it, then I say that's great. The important thing is to be yourself.'[6]

In 1970, a Houston radio station was twice firebombed by some good ol' boys who begged to differ over its radical anti-Vietnam War policy. Of more abiding sensitivity, airplay problems for what had once been classified as 'sepia' or 'race' music was an important aspect of ingrained racial tension in the Deep South. Negroes as slaves had been cattle. Free and human, they were a nuisance – undesirable and embarrassing. Especially so were the more uppity ones like singer Nat 'King' Cole who was worked over by anti-black extremists midway through his act before a mixed Southern audience in a packed auditorium.

Though nowhere as colour-prejudiced as other states, even those Texan whites who bought Cole's records were similar in style to Caucasian crooners like Bing Crosby or Perry Como and might well have been appalled when compulsory segregation in schools was declared unconstitutional in 1958. Any admixture of negro blood was deemed sufficient to restrict its owner to 'colored' public conveniences and launderettes not displaying the sign 'Whites Only Or Maids In Uniform'. Quite legally, a well-known C & W entertainer, under the pseudonym 'Johnny Freedom', cut several blatantly racist singles during what must have been the lowest point of his career. Paradoxically, it was when the distinction between C & W and black music dissolved that Freedom and many other white Texan performers were able to venture beyond regional popularity.

Unlike his younger brother-in-law, Orbie Lee Orbison hadn't been directly acquainted with black music. But following the fretboard symbols on sheet music, he had taught himself to get by with a few chords in a plain strumming fashion reminiscent of folk-blues exponent, Huddie Ledbetter – 'Leadbelly'. Furthermore, Orbie Lee liked Jimmie Rodgers, a country singer whose songs were couched in rural black phrasing and imagery, complete with yodelled refrains. Little made Orbie Lee happier than copying 'T for Texas', 'Muleskinner Blues' and other 78 rpm records by the ol' Blue Yodeller, as the late Jimmie was known. It was fortunate for his family that Orbie Lee's singing matched his enthusiasm; strong yet soothing, age would never deepen his voice below a youthful-sounding baritone.

Sensibly, neither father nor uncle tried to goad the boys to learn the guitar. Of the three, it was the unobtrusive Roy who seemed the most musical. At first, it was hard to believe that a voice so like his dad's could come from such a pale slip of a child, but 'once I started singing, it was sort of a wonder, and it didn't hurt anybody, and it made me feel good, and some people even said, "Roy, that's nice".'[7] When questioned, Roy would answer that he wanted to be a singer when he grew up, although 'I didn't know then that you could actually make a living out of it.'[8]

A fascinated listener while Orbie Lee practised, Roy as usual waited until he was asked: 'It all started with me walking down a dusty road with my father, and him asking what I wanted for my [sixth] birthday, and me saying, "I want a mouth organ." He asked me if I wouldn't rather have a guitar and, well, I jumped at the guitar.' The knowledge was passed from father to son in the highest oral tradition. 'He taught me the basic chords on the guitar – nothing intricate.' His left hand not yet big enough to fully shape the chords, the first song he could manage was 'You are My Sunshine', a whimsical piece from the Great War which walked a tightrope between joy and despair: still, it was enough for Roy. 'From the very first moment, it was me *and* the guitar playing *and* singing.'[3]

Roy's new-found skills became a passport for staying up late when his family moved from Vernon to an apartment above a chemist's in Fort Worth at the outbreak of hostilities. The US War Office, concerned about the stalemate its forces supporting the Allies had reached against the Axis powers and Japan, had sent for Orbie Lee Orbison. At the defence plant where giant chimneys were trained on the sky like anti-aircraft guns, he – and later Nadine, too – became an infinitesimal cog in the machine provisioning the distant bloodshed with B-24 bombers.

His daily patriotic chore of cranking and riveting done, Mr Orbison would walk back to his evening meal through a tangle of lugubrious streets – modern buildings caked in grime and soot from the plant, oil refineries and the army chemical corps. In the fever of mobilization, long black trains transported the brand-new flying weapons towards Dyers air base in Abilene.

Amid clusters of passing soldiers, he'd even recognize a face or two, for many would be billeted on the Orbisons during those dangerous years. Most welcome were Uncle Kenneth and the various cousins on leave from Europe or the Pacific. 'They didn't know whether they were coming back or not, so the level of intensity and the singing and partying just for right now was very high.'[8] Roy would vamp his handful of chords alongside his father and uncle during these evenings of boozy war hysteria. There were even songs to suit the troubled times – Harold Adamson's 'Comin' in on a Wing and a Prayer' and 'You're in the Army Now' from the Andrews Sisters. During a lull in the yee-hah exuberance, little Roy might even be led forth for a solo turn before being packed off to bed – where his brothers were already soundly asleep. The heart-and-soul exhilaration of those nights left their mark on the young performer too. 'And still, today, that's how I do it – with everything I have. That spirit . . . the easy camaraderie of musicians, that lifestyle is ingrained in me.' There would be moments of doubt, but 'by the time I was seven, I was finished, you know, for anything else'.[4]

Preferences in Roy's growing repertoire included 'Born to Lose' and the topical 'No Letter Today', by Ted Daffan and his Texans, a versatile 'western swing' band whose stamping ground during these years was the Dallas/Fort Worth/Houston triangle. Another favourite was 'Eternally', a ballad written by Charlie Chaplin. Other songs likewise figured in the record sales charts, first published in North America's *Billboard* magazine in 1940. Bestsellers would be assigned to one of three categories – popular, country-and-western and 'sepia' (or 'rhythm-and-blues' as it came to be known). This meant that you could top, say, the 'sepia' chart without figuring at all in the parallel dimensions of pop – unless your disc picked up enough spins on pop-orientated radio to stimulate sales in the chart-return shops. As Roy Orbison would observe later, 'a huge country can sell sixty thousand, whereas you have to sell three to four hundred thousand to get in the pop charts'.[9] Only on rare occasions could you score in all three.

Though there were many varieties of C & W, you knew it when you heard it – whether at its purest in the rootin'-tootin' narrative and abrupt instrumental breaks of blue-grass, or the melancholy schmaltz epitomised by such songs as Red Foley's 'Thank You For Calling', composed by Cindy Walker. Other examples of country kitsch like 'Tragic Romance' by Cowboy Copas, a very early 'death disc', proved popular because, as Hank Williams – the genre's greatest figure – pontificated, 'the tunes are simple and easy to remember, and the singers – they're *sincere* about them.'[10]

The 'sincerity' of vocalists of the Johnny Freedom persuasion, together with the general lowbrow stylistic determination, ensured that if a C & W show hit town, though aimed at an adult audience, it would be disregarded by the liberal local media. Besides, C & W had not been thought a significant market when record companies began investigating specialist regional music in the twenties. Until Lubbock in west Texas launched the nation's first full-time C & W station in 1953, 'you didn't have stations that played just country or just anything else,' recalled Roy Orbison. 'There weren't so many records then, so they played everything.'[8]

Perhaps the most significant breakthrough, however, came in 1925. Through the machinations of an insurance company that owned a Nashville radio station, an 'in-person' C & W presentation entitled 'Barn Dance' went out on the air, and it was from this that sprang the renowned 'Grand Ole Opry', later to be broadcast from the city's Ryman theatre.

A trace element in America's musical melting pot was that fusion of blues accordion and Frenchified patois (Creole), with added washboard and fiddle, called 'Cajun' in Louisiana and 'Zydeco' in Texas. Its influence was felt by, amongst others, the celebrated Jimmie Rodgers and his protégé, Ernest Tubb, as well as the 'King of the Hillbilly Piano Players', Moon Mullican, who carried it into the C & W mainstream. In 1947, Mullican's first million-seller was inspired by Harry Choates' 'Jole Blon' ('pretty blonde'), the Cajun 'national anthem' – which happened to be an all-time favourite of Roy Orbison's. Unfortunately, he never really mastered it. 'I could only learn it by slowing down the record. I would put my finger on the record and slow it down, and even then just word for word . . . the words that were so painfully put together have fallen by the wayside and I don't remember it. I remember the melody and some of the expressions in it, but it made no sense.'³

Those distracted years at Fort Worth also nurtured in him an abiding passion for history which grew into an encyclopaedic understanding of people, places, interactions, and outcomes: 'that's how I correlate things. I get one thing that makes me think of another.'³ Connecting favourite pastimes included collecting war memorabilia and building miniature military aeroplanes. Being something of a loner by nature, his diversions included swimming, fishing and sketching. Still a creature of habit when older, he said, 'I never get interested in any new thing all of a sudden, I've had many long-term interests and I'm happy with those.'⁶

These pursuits had little bearing on his sojourn at elementary school where his teachers had to struggle to write anything out of the ordinary on termly reports about Roy's academic progress. He was solid enough in most subjects. As well as a sound conceptual grasp of mathematics, there were hints of a flair for creative writing and art, but there was always the feeling that he was afraid to take literary risks for fear of getting into trouble. That might also explain why he rarely participated in formal discussions either – unless he was pushed. All that made him remotely extraordinary was that, unlike most other children, he did not need much coaxing to sing solo for class assemblies, 'even if I didn't

want to, I'd be the single source of attention. It grew on me,
I guess.'[2] Roy was never conceited about applause that
was often more than just cursory. Back in class, he'd be
nondescript once more – like Superman reverting to his
Clark Kent persona.

In 1944, the education of Grady and Roy was disrupted
when a polio epidemic in the Fort Worth area made it
necessary for them to move to their grandmother's home in
Vernon. There they would stay until peace was declared and
the whole family could go home. It was during this hiatus
that Roy Orbison's slow transition to pop stardom began.
Rather than a series of close shaves and lucky breaks, it was
a gradual development of a natural aptitude in tandem with
unconscious forces within his background.

Fort Worth in wartime wasn't exactly Al Capone's
Chicago, but living in its crowded, rip-roaring ferment had
brought to Roy an abstracted worldliness. Much of his old
shy self remained, but it was with a new inner confidence
that the eight-year-old singer and guitarist made himself
conspicuous on a Saturday morning 'Amateur Hour' radio
programme on Vernon's KVWC station. So often did he
bicycle to its studio to wow listeners with selections born of
those late nights in Fort Worth that he was granted a regular
non-competitive spot as 'featured popular vocalist'. By the
time his kin came back – with, incidentally, not a single war
fatality – Roy was the show's host.

On regional commercial radio – and, later, television –
throughout the United States, slots would be blockbooked
for a certain period each week. During this time, plugs for
a sponsor's product would be interspersed with entertainment of one kind or another, be it records, talent contests,
drama or 'live' music. In those days, Roy listened to the
radio all the time: 'and that was the big thing when I was
growing up. We didn't have the telly and things like that for
relaxing. And even if *I* wasn't, someone else in our house
was playing the radio. I learned all the songs.' With C &
W, pop and western swing, rhythm-and-blues, Zydeco,

Spanish/Mexican sounds and dog 'classical music' clogging the ether for almost every waking hour in the family home, 'all of those influences probably settled into one thing and I'm the result of whatever it was.'[11]

Following in the footsteps of older performers such as Jim Reeves and Webb Pierce, Roy was not the only musical Texan to reach a wider public via local radio. The career of the incredible P. J. Proby, for example, started on a Houston station in 1949, while Waylon Jennings, 'youngest DJ in the USA', appeared on KDAV – which also hosted a thirty-minute showcase on Sundays by a trio of Lubbock school-boys, 'Buddy, Bob and Larry'. Neither 'Buddy' nor KTRM Beaumont's portly programme director, J. P. Richardson, knew then to what extent their lives – and deaths – would interweave.

As a part-time occupation, Roy's stint on KVWC beat paper rounds and car washing – except that, in keeping with the show's title, no one ever received payment for their gladly given services. Roy's first cash-in-hand engagement took place one weekend in the spring of 1946. Who would ever forget the day that the medicine show came to town? Straight from the pages of a Buffalo Bill annual, the horse-drawn covered wagon came to its groaning halt in the dusty main street . . .

Such a sight was not, however, a twitch in the death throes of the Wild West. Indeed, as the oil business slid more rapidly into recession, medicine shows and similar tourist attractions would become more common. Dude ranches, restored frontier forts, rattlesnake round-ups and establishments like Abilene's Old Betsy Muzzle Loading Shop added to the mythologizing of the recent cowboys-and-injuns past by feature film, musical and TV series. Some organizations – such as the Texas Cowboy Reunion Association – would seek to preserve True West culture, irrespective of financial gain – it was not always simply a matter of sporting a stetson as part of everyday dress. This was not, however, the case with the pageant that trundled into Vernon that day. Behind

its façade of antiquity chugged a pantechnicon transporting
the electricity generator for its coloured lights and public
address system. Wooden benches were set out on the dirt in
front of the makeshift stage. Directly after lunch, the huck-
ster in his card-sharp finery yapped his spiel for the snake-
bite tonics and cure-all elixirs for sale. As the planting of a
'feed' amongst the onlookers was too crass a ploy in such a
smallish community, attention was held with random skits,
comedy routines – and a talent competition with a first prize
of fifteen dollars.

Carried away by the impromptu carnival atmosphere of
this visitation, radio star Roy Orbison agreed to mount the
platform. With the frozen faces of his own parents among
the mob staring up at him, he stood motionless before the
lowered microphone, bar one knee trembling with nerves.
This wasn't the privacy of his own home, nor was he confined
within the protective bubble of KVWC this time or the
lower expectations of an elementary school assembly. Those
closest to him knew that for Roy to be a slouch, after all the
Amateur Hour fuss, might reduce him to the reclusive
mediocrity of old.

For the first of his two numbers, he played it safe with
'Morning Dew', a semi-comic hillbilly excursion that always
went down well whenever its composer, 'Grandpa' Louis
Jones, did it on the Grand Ole Opry. Furthermore, Roy had
already tried it out both on the radio and at a school concert.
Led by the classmate who'd badgered him to go up there,
the clapping that burst forth after he'd finished so embold-
ened Roy that he felt courageous enough to try something a
bit more racy. After the levity of 'Grandpa' Jones, the smart-
alec gabble of 'Jole Blon' transported his audience from
Vernon in the bright sunshine to the witching hour in a
Creole dance hall. 'That was the song that did it for me.'[3]

In spite of his KVWC reputation and the protracted
cheering after 'Jole Blon', there was a split decision, and Roy
had to share the princely purse with a fifteen-year-old who'd
played last. Even then, he ended up with only three dollars

and a quarter because 'my buddy went with me and carried my guitar and rooted for me, so he figured he ought to have half. That was my first taste of a manager.'[7]

This win was the limit of the young Roy Orbison's impact on Vernon. A few months later, the family travelled 300 miles west to Winkler County where Orbie Lee had obtained better paid employment as general mechanical factotum – a 'roustabout' – on an oil field. As Wilbarger had been the setting for *Red River*, so Winkler would be for *Giant*, the James Dean film of 1956 that depicted the entrenchment of the oil barons on the Llano Estacado farming enclosures. Thirty miles from the Mexican border, and equidistant from Odessa and El Paso, the dreary oil town of Wink would be Roy's home for the period of his adolescence when 'the intensity of your emotions . . . is something awe-inspiring, no matter how painful it might sometimes seem. I believe that none of us ever really grows out of that.'[4]

The semi-tropical climate of this part of Texas is so dry that there were few settlers before 1800. During the worst droughts, the clayey soil was borne away by gales strong enough for a character in Marty Robbins' 'El Paso' to be described as 'wild as the west Texas wind'. Irrigation from the mud-brown Pecos flowing between banks of cottonwood would transform the scrubby grassland into soil fertile enough to yield pumpkins, chile and the excellent wine of El Paso. To the east where the Orbisons lived, 'there's nothing. No trees, no lakes, no creeks, a few bushes.'[7]

A few saplings sprouted round the Orbisons' freshly built bungalow at 100 Langley Drive – and even in residential areas in Notrees – on the road to Odessa. For those who viewed it in travelogues, west Texas could seem a place of true abundance, with its 'spacious skies' and 'amber waves of grain' – an epitome, in fact, of 'America the Beautiful'; and even some who lived there were elated by an unbroken terrain 'so flat you can see today going and tomorrow coming by merely looking in the other direction.'

Roy Orbison, on the other hand, 'got out of there as quick

as I could, and I resented being there, but it was a great education. It was as tough as could be, but no illusions, you know. No mysteries in Wink.'[7] It would be a mistake to envisage the thousand-odd souls who populated what was then little more than a village as brutish yokels dwelling in broken-down shacks beside a rutted track. They may have been once, but by the late forties the thirties had touched Wink. In the year of Orbison's coming, Wink's stature had become such that a branch of the County State Bank had opened on Hendricks Boulevard. Soon afterwards, the wooden Wink Wildcats stadium would be torn down to make way for a modern steel-based structure in readiness for the 1949 football season. Feelers to the world of *haute couture* could be put out via the town's Sears-Roebuck office.

Although he'd become quite handy with a cue in Vernon, Roy immediately found Wink's pool hall intimidating. In this stronghold of cool, 'macho guys from the oil field'[7] glared menacingly at weedy, four-eyed interlopers. At least there was a cinema – albeit one of the theatre type rather than a new-fangled drive-in of the kind you'd get in Odessa. Rather than vegetate at home in the weeks prior to his and Grady's enrolment at Wink High School, Roy became addicted to films. With quiet pride, he'd mention how he'd 'give up a good meal even when I'm hungry to see a movie I've looked forward to. I like the kind of picture that entertains without necessarily showing life at its realest and rawest.'[6]

Hollywood was at its most cynical and neurotic during these years: all platinum blondes in sleazy dives; rain-sodden nights lit by neon advertisements; and lonesome anti-heroes, narcissistic and defeatist, like James Cagney. Though espionage thrillers like *Pickup on South Street* would reveal preoccupations with anti-Communism, the film industry was yet to alienate sections of its public with any real criticism of the aggressive redneck populism of the fifties.

In a lighter vein, there was much to please Roy in the escapism of the post-war era, with its 'Things' from outer space and the Saturday morning Western epics which often strayed into the realms of musical comedy, as did Paramount's *Son of Paleface* in 1952. While identifying with Roy Rogers, the 'Singing Cowboy', and slobbering over Jane Russell, the teenage moviegoer was so taken when Bob Hope 'looked into the mirror and went "grrr"'[4] that for weeks after, he sickened his family with his efforts at mimicry.

Roy now had his own bedroom from which, according to his mother, issued 'many hours of mad twanging and singing and howling'[12] – much of it before the mirror no doubt. The confidential record cards from Vernon had already given the junior high school some inkling that Orbison Minor was musical if nothing else. He made a brief attempt to play the baritone saxophone, but was put off by its unpredictable harmonics and, compared to guitar, illogical learning process. He looked in at the school choir which, under the baton of some musical archivist, delved into traditions derived largely from Anglo-Celtic sources. Such stirring songs of the old frontier as 'The Old Chisholm Trail', 'Sam Bass' and 'Bill Was a Texas Lad', had been forged in cow camps, wagon trains and shotgun shacks, to be ranted to available violin or banjo accompaniment. However, after the West was won, and the likes of Geronimo had spent their last days as tourist attractions, such songs as these were seldom heard formally outside school concerts, folk festivals and Lions Club functions.

The choir blended Roy's historical and musical concerns, but he wearied of its hearty clubbism. 'To be with someone else is a bit inhibiting,' he said later. 'It's foreign to me.'[2] Not entailing quite so much active participation was an after-school class in 'musical appreciation'. Teachers tried to arouse adolescent interest in 'classical music' via Brahms' *German Requiem*; but less highbrow were Brooklyn composer Aaron Copland's ballets, *Billy the Kid* and *Rodeo*, incorporating folk themes, dance rhythms and harmonies that invoked the Old West.

Roy was especially fond of the string-laden Mantovani, then perhaps the most popular light orchestra conductor in the world. To Roy, Mantovani, a James Last of his day, was 'my kind of artist. He seems to want to satisfy something in everyone. He's quite the same each time you hear him, dependable you might say. I've never liked too many severe changes. He fits in well with me.'[6]

Wink High knew what to expect from Roy too. Becoming as well-known for his guitar playing and 'good' voice as the volleyball captain and school bully were in their chosen spheres, he was a reliable stand-in between acts at the school play. All the same, the likes of 'Jole Blon' and 'Tennessee Waltz' were frowned upon by the Church of Christ in Texas where the Orbisons worshipped. Though he would always be a Christian by instinct, Roy drifted away from this Church's hell-fire fundamentalism that forbade dancing and secular music.

It may have lacked other facilities, but there was no shortage of religious denominations in Wink. In addition to the Church of Christ, there were four non-conformist ministries whose service schedules were published each Thursday in the *Wink Bulletin* – 'the only newspaper in the world that cares about Wink'. The *Bulletin*, conservatively Democrat in its editorial leanings, devoted a lot of space to goings-on at the 'Wink-loving' High School, especially its sporting activities and Monday meetings of the Lions Club at the community centre.

Social secretary of the Wink wing was a Mr J. A. Moultrie, who also happened to be the High School principal. One day he was looking for a local band to play at the next dinner-and-dance, which was to be given in the school auditorium. No professional bands of import would travel as far out as Wink for less than a king's ransom, so he decided to check if there was anything cheaper locally. That Orbison boy played in the popular style, didn't he? Perhaps he could lead some sort of combo . . .

With such a brainwave, Mr Moultrie would not be opening

a floodgate to an evening of interminable teenage noise. In the late forties, the young had to put up with pretty much the same sort of music that their parents liked. The petrification of the entertainments industry following the war ensured that popular musicians in all fields were generally well into their thirties before achieving recognition. Hank Williams and Johnnie Ray were exceptions, but usually it was a case of either humble servitude in the ranks of an established band or getting work by singing the old standards. You jumped from nursery rhymes to Bing Crosby as if there was nothing in between.

Unless you'd been born into show business, you were not encouraged to think of it as a viable career. C & W – and even jazz – was harmless enough as long as it didn't interfere with school. The variety of popular music most easily accessible to the ordinary people of Wink was the 'western swing' that Roy had encountered in Fort Worth. Originating in the Texas of the mid-twenties, western swing was as curious a hybrid as Zydeco. Merging musical virtuosity and a swinging, infectious dance beat, this 'hillbilly jazz' was a curious potpourri of bluegrass breakdowns, Tin Pan Alley standards, jump blues and adapted urban jazz, spiced with the occasional heel-clattering Mexican fandango. Much more common in the front line than horns were pedal steel guitar and at least two fiddles, plus novelties like the jew's harp or even mouthorgan if you wanted to give it a Spike Jones touch. In the course of a set, an outfit might veer fitfully from Duke Ellington's 'Satin Doll' to 'Steel Guitar Rag', from Louis Jordan's 'Choo Choo Ch'boogie' to 'When You're Smilin'', and then on to originals like Bob Wills and his Texas Playboys' 'My Window Faces the South', complete with 'honky-tonk' vocal refrain. The popularity of western swing peaked in World War Two, but the sound lives on in such groups as Asleep At The Wheel – high on the bill at Wembley's 1989 Country Festival – and Britain's Drew's Brew and Jive Alive.

However, in the hick towns of Texas in the forties, the

form was often adulterated as parochial bands made do.
While bull fiddle, Sears drum kit and yellow-keyed piano
took a bashing, Bob Wills' horn section or Ted Daffan's slick
phalanx of fiddlers might be rearranged for piano accordion
and crudely amplified guitar: 'We would undo the strings
. . . and put the microphone inside then put the strings back
on . . . and we had an amplifier.'[8]

Such ingenuity was not new to the blues which, however,
hovered only as distant thunder in white west Texas. Born
in 1933 in Happy, less than a day's drive from Wink, Buddy
Knox couldn't recall hearing a single record by a black artist
until he visited New York.[13] Measuring his own artistic
development against that of a Tennessean youth of about
the same age, Roy Orbison felt that 'the basic difference was
that Elvis was surrounded by black music almost exclusively;
black music and country music was just beamed every day
in his area. But in my area, no, that wasn't the case.'[3]

Unlike Elvis Aron Presley in the blues city of Memphis,
only the most free-spirited white teenager was likely to
gravitate to juke joints in run-down districts of Odessa,
Midland or Fort Worth to fraternize with the state's most
shunned sub-culture. Through the static, a Wink listener
might tune in by accident to muffled bursts of what segrega-
tionalists heard as 'the screaming idiotic words and savage
music' of faraway Shreveport's rhythm-and-blues station
KWKH where Stan the Man and his No-Name Record Jive
punctuated the likes of the Midnighters' 'Sexy Ways', the
Dominoes' 'Sixty Minute Man', and 'Too Many Drivers'
from Smiley Lewis – all about sex and all banned by white
radio. 'If you don't want to serve Negroes in your place of
business,' ran one racialist handbill, 'then do not have negro
records on your jukebox.'

Instead, for the people of west Texas there was *nice* music,
including records by Doris Day, Eddie Fisher, Horace Heidt
and his Musical Knights, or a 'Xmas Singalong With Mitch
Murray' . . . And 'real' singing was represented by the likes
of 'The Loveliest Night of the Year' from *The Great Caruso*

movie, the song that put Mario Lanza in the pop charts in
1950. If that sounds a bit 'square', there was always Johnnie
Ray, 'Prince of Wails', to fall back on, the man of whom
Hank Williams once said: 'He's sincere and he shows he's
sincere. That's the reason he's popular.'[10]

Through his hammy cry-guy act, Ray introduced an
exhibitionism long prevalent in rhythm-and-blues – a big
on-stage moment was when he launched into his hit cover
version of the Drifters' 'Such a Night'. Such a whitewashing
of an R & B smash for the pop charts was always anticipated
– even welcomed – by black recording artists of the early
fifties as it brought their music, if not their performances,
to a world with money to waste. Some like the Platters and
their role model, the Ink Spots, were even smooth enough
to cross over completely.

Artists who crossed over from C & W to pop included
Slim Whitman and Jim Reeves – but both favoured a light,
'sweetcorn' approach as opposed to the 'hard country' of
Hank Williams. As with R & B, pop stars freely plundered
the C & W exemplified in 1948 when both Patti Page
('the Singing Rage') and electric guitarist Les Paul recorded
Cowboy Copas' 'Tennessee Waltz'. Furthermore, jobbing
Tin Pan Alley tunesmiths were more at home with C & W
than R & B, as witnessed by the clippety-clop offerings of
Frankie Laine, Tennessee Ernie Ford and Vaughan 'Riders
in the Sky' Monroe – all sounding as if they'd cut their teeth
on a branding iron. Perhaps less palatable to a redneck
were such silver screen gems as Bill Hayes' 'Ballad of Davy
Crockett' and Doris Day's whip-crack-away highlights from
'Calamity Jane'.

Falling meekly into line, Roy Orbison at thirteen did not
resent having to conform to adult taste. Not knowing any
better, and having reached the stage where he could 'step
out in front of an audience and not be scared to death',[8] he
was excited by any opportunity to extend himself outside
the usual round of assemblies, intermissions and parents'
evenings. Without his musical prowess, Roy – who wasn't

much of a scrapper – might have had to resign himself to years of misery as the unprepossessing outsider of Wink High. Instead, he was adopted as a sort of mascot by those broad-shouldered shower-room studs who liked his singing but saw him as no rival for female favours.

Roy, however, hormones raging, thought that his prime position in the school band might give him licence to talk to girls, a sex that had been untouchable thus far. Even so, many never seemed to care about humiliating him. With raw physical beauty as their only assets, they'd torment him with their indifference, or with coquettish malice attempt to lead him into some blushing *faux pas*. Others less spiritually ugly would confide in him like a brother about their romantic trials and tribulations, thereby dashing any hopes Roy himself might have had in that direction. 'Every relationship I'd ever been in, the girl already had one going when we first met – even as far back as kindergarten,'[4] he confessed on one occasion.

Similarly motivated, perhaps, were Roy's first band recruits. Alongside Charles Evans, a short, plump Wink High pupil who plucked the double bass, was the lanky James Morrow, a mandolin player. Both Morrow and Orbison now possessed solid-body electric instruments. With a matching amplifier, Roy's was a red Gibson Les Paul, 'cutaway' to give easier access to the higher frets. He no longer confined himself to stroking chords these days. 'At fifteen, I tried to be a lead guitar player, playing intricate melody lines and such. I didn't get very far, so by sixteen, I'd set my mind to playing just rhythm guitar to accompany my voice.'[4] There were other musicians too; and Roy never failed to marshal some kind of a backing band for Lions Club knees-ups in the school hall.

When the ambitious Mr Moultrie was up for election to the Club's district presidency, however, Roy's boys were required to play at his campaign gatherings throughout west Texas. Finding the rapid turnover of personnel prohibitive for this itinerary, Roy whittled down the group to a nucleus of five. The regular line-up of Morrow and Evans was completed by pianist Richard West and drummer Billy Parr Ellis, who thwacked his snare drum with brush sticks so as not to drown the others.

The empire-building Moultrie christened the new quintet 'The Wink Westerners' because 'we had to have the name "Wink" in there, and "Westerners" was meant to represent west Texas which he was running for. So it was "west Texas" as opposed to "western" music because we played all kinds.'[14]

Loosely categorizing themselves as western swing, amongst the dozen or so numbers at the Wink Westerners' command were smooth approximations of 'Jersey Bounce', 'Moonlight in Vermont' and other more sober big band numbers. These were interspersed with current C & W and pop favourites, which ranged from Webb Pierce to Hoagy Carmichael – who was reputed to have 'discovered' Frankie Laine, another repertory source. As well as customary requests for 'Georgia on My Mind' and 'Jezabel', there was always some clever one who wanted to hear 'Cry' or some other Johnnie Ray number, abhorrent to those no longer young. Roy never minded singing them – or any numbers by Frank Sinatra for that matter, who was admired as 'a go-getter all the way'.[6]

At the drop of a hat he'd also pitch into 'Long Black Veil', a murder ballad recorded in 1949 by fellow Texan, Lefty Frizzell, 'the first singer I heard on the radio that really blew me away'. Though not as widely influential as Hank Williams, Frizzell – born in 1928 – left a mark on Roy Orbison for his techniques of 'sliding the syllables together – that just about used to slay me'.[4]

At first almost all the Wink Westerners' bookings came about either through the Lions Club or school. As an amateur group formed by schoolboys, they were content then merely to have somewhere to perform. The next step – if there was to be a next step – would be to play to an audience for money.

In collaboration with club owners and impresarios, radio

stations would also promote country-and-western jamborees, square dances and other Saturday night entertainments featuring local heroes only a rung higher up the ladder than the Wink Westerners. Many of them would give living credence to the assertion, 'I never did hear a cowboy with a real good voice. If he had one to start with, he always lost it bawling at cattle'.[15] Sometimes these hopefuls were lucky enough to support a big star at prestigious venues like Fort Worth's Panther Hall. Drawing the crowds would be names as familiar as a hitching post: Ernest Tubb, the Carter Family, Hank Snow, Eddy Arnold.

Mixing foot-stompin' hoedown, quaking sentiment and singalong evergreens, the unvarnished 'sincerity' of a lot of these artists, professional or otherwise, was as contrived in image as that of Liberace. Instead of that exquisite's candelabra and sequins were cartoon cowboy outfits: tengallon hats, furry chaparajos, rhinestones and loud embroidery.

Hank Williams' sole superfluous adornment when on stage was a plain white fedora. Yet in the early fifties, this gangling, besuited Alabaman's popularity guaranteed standing room only for virtually all his 200 one-nighters a year. He seemed to make a virtue of his whining down-home intonation, untutored phrasing and eccentric breath control. Although his accompanists, the Drifting Cowboys, utilized the expected Hawaiian guitar and mournful violin, Williams' plaintive vocal resolution was underpinned by unusual absorption with rhythm, hinged on his own guitar chopping. Without milking an audience as much as Tubb et al., he was inescapably more committed to the essence of his songs than previous country performers.

At the time, Roy Orbison 'didn't reckon him the genius I now perceive him to be'[4], but Hank created more C & W 'standards' than anyone else – from the 'big fun' of 'Jambalaya' to the wounded 'Your Cheatin' Heart'. He saw himself, however, more as an all-round folk singer like Leadbelly, who, defined as a blues shouter for convenience, actually

sang all kinds of material – from 'The Old Chisholm Trail'
via children's play rhymes to, yes, the blues. Williams' work
also spanned other idioms. The incorporation of blues into
his stylistic arsenal is best exemplified in titles like 'Moanin'
the Blues' and 'Howlin' at the Moon'. As his fame spread
beyond the south, his compositions were covered for the
pop market by the likes of Tony Bennett, Jo Stafford and
Rosemary Clooney. And, but for his early death in 1953,
Williams might have crossed over to the pop 'Hot Hundred'
in his own right.

Roy Orbison, however, found his music 'too "Tin Pan
Alleyish" for my tastes back then'.[4]

Hank Williams was bracketed as a C & W singer in spite
of all the efforts of his mentors, Fred Rose and Roy Acuff.
Before combining as the management-publishing concern of
Acuff-Rose, both had been known as C & W personalities
in their own right, Rose mainly as a songwriter, Acuff as
Grand Ole Opry compere and leading light of the Smoky
Mountain Boys, from whom Williams had derived certain
aspects of his style.

As well as looking after the business affairs of their clients,
the partners also had – to a diminishing extent – a creative
say in their output. Rose, for instance, co-wrote with
Williams such songs as the comic-sad 'Kaw-liga', complete
with its throbbing tom-toms. This blueprint would evoke
later Red Indian pastiches published by Acuff-Rose including John D. Loudermilk's 'Indian Reservation' of 1969 –
and, five years earlier, 'Indian Wedding' by one who had
reached the highest pinnacle of pop – as Hank Williams
should have done.

In the year before Williams' death, Roy Orbison of the
Wink Westerners was rewarded for past services by being
chosen musical representative for west Texas at the International Lions Conclave in Chicago – his first trip up north.
Moreover, the group itself had moved up a bit by now,
appearing regularly on local radio. Nevertheless, to pay for
equipment, Roy was still obliged to seek onerous holiday

jobs, some obtained through Orbie Lee, who was no longer a common roustabout but a drilling superintendent. However, after a Westerners bash in Kermit, a village a few miles north-east of Wink, the five were approached by a dance promoter who offered them 400 dollars to perform at one of his revels the following week. Courageously stretching out their limited repertoire for an entire evening, the band's first engagement as semi-professionals netted each member the same amount of money that Roy had earned shovelling tar for a fortnight the previous vacation. 'So then I really and truly knew I wanted to go into show business because I loved singing and you could make money at it too.'[11]

Notes

1   *Top Pop Stars* (Purnell, 1965)
2   *Punch*, 12 December 1988
3   *New Musical Express*, 20 December 1980
4   *The Face*, February 1989
5   *Evening News*, 3 June 1972
6   *Melody Maker*, 13 August 1966
7   *Rolling Stone*, 26 January 1989
8   Veronica (Dutch) Television
9   *On the beat* (Radio Merseyside)
10 *Rolling Stone*, 12 June 1969
11 *Tribute to the Big O*, Radio 2, 5 January 1989
12 *Woman's Choice*, 21 September 1974
13 *Record Mirror*, June 1970
14 *Melody Maker*, 11 October 1975
15 'Authentic cowboys and their western folksongs' (sleeve notes, R.C.A., RD 7776)

2

The Cause of it All

'To lead a Western Band is his after school wish and of course to marry a beautiful dish'[1] was the valediction printed beneath Roy Orbison's photograph in Wink High's yearbook when he graduated in 1954. This doggerel had come from the hand of a compiler who had latched onto artistic forces during an adolescence 'which at times was pretty frustrating'.[2] He'd never found school work arduous or been in terror over exams. However, who could pretend that a Euclid theorum or even the battle of Saratoga Springs could keep him from fantasizing about girls? Sucking at a Coke in the Wildcat Den Café on Hendricks Boulevard, he'd hang around the jukebox, trying not to notice Jack and Jill cooing over each other in the corner. They seemed so full of themselves, those condescending, hard-faced jerks – all 'oil and grease and sand and being a stud and being cool'[3] – with their tittering girlfriends on their arms.

Into the bargain, the so-called 'Western Band' had almost touched the ceiling of its fortunes, and the inevitable cracks had opened up. Richard West had got married, lucky boy. It had been farewell also to Charlie Evans, who, casting aside such childish follies as the Wink Westerners, now had to work to stay alive. With his own earnings from music hardly adequate, Roy too had reached a vocational cross-roads. Judged by his High School attainments, he had turned out to be the brainiest of the Orbisons, if no Einstein. In spite of his musical abilities however, an in-bred commitment to honest labour led him to seek proper qualifications – 'something to fall back on'.[4] A good all-rounder academically, he listened to the sound advice of Orbie Lee who, from first hand, 'knew there'd be a demand for geologists'.[4]

With every intention of majoring in this subject, Roy was accepted on a degree course at North Texas State University in Denton near Fort Worth. At last he'd be shot of Wink – he'd had quite enough of the oil fields. His spirit had nearly broken during a long, hot summer job working as a labourer for the Natural Gas Company in El Paso: 'cutting up steel and loading it onto trucks and chopping weeds and painting water towers. Our straw boss was Mr Rose, and he wouldn't cut me any slack. I worked in the blazing heat, hard, hard labour, and then I'd play at night, come home and, some nights, be too tired to eat or even to undress. I'd lay down, and I wouldn't even turn over. I'd wake up in the same spot and hit the oil patch again.'[3]

If he had to return to the family trade, his degree would at least put him a cut above the likes of Mr Rose. He wouldn't have to work his way up to a responsible position as his father had done. Waiting at the end of his four years of college would be a respectable profession, a mortgage – and maybe even wedding bells: 'I guess it was an attempt at being legitimate and not a free spirit.'[3]

From this conventional objective, however, he'd be corrupted from a distance. Hunched over his text books as he then was, Roy Orbison was on the verge of something he'd desire – had always desired – more than any tin-pot university grades.

Roy had already noticed that 'if you had a guitar and walked into a place, they'd say, "Hello, Elvis".'[5] With Presley as carrier, the disease of rock 'n' roll had started to spread right across the Land of the Free. During his penultimate term at school, Roy had been riveted by the sound of the Hillbilly Cat's first single, the 78 rpm 'That's All Right', on the radio – released by some Memphis record label with a chicken logo. Because it was a jumped-up treatment of a negro blues, some disc jockeys hadn't been keen on scheduling such a racially integrated disc. By August 1954, however, it had muscled in at No.3 in the C & W chart.

Adult redneck blood had run cold at Presley's noise, gibberish and loutish excesses. It was just like nigger music, wasn't it? And if you wanted a more objective opinion, why not ask the Limey bandleader who was there the night Nat 'King' Cole got what he deserved? 'I don't think "rock and roll" will come to Britain,' Ted Heath had confirmed. 'You see, it is primarily for the coloured population.'[6]

Many teenagers felt just as aghast as their parents – yet it was mixed with fascination. On 16 April 1954, before he'd even heard 'That's All Right', Roy Orbison had borrowed his father's car and set out for the Dallas Sportatorium – just over two hundred miles away – to catch this 'unspeakably untalented, vulgar young entertainer', as a television guide would describe him. Everyone was talking about Elvis.

At the venue – a C & W jamboree – Roy 'couldn't over-emphasize how shocking he looked and seemed to me that night'.[7] It was like nothing the bespectacled Wink Westerner had ever experienced before. Presley, sneering, didn't seem to care how badly he behaved up there – breaking guitar strings, spitting out his chewing gum, swivelling his hips in a rude way, doing the splits, knee-dropping and crawling to the very edge of the stage. He told jokes 'that weren't funny, and his diction was real coarse like a truck driver's'. With conflicting emotions, Roy observed the 'pandemonium in the audience because the girls took a shine to him and the guys were getting a little jealous'.[4] Nonetheless, while pulling out all the stops and unfettered by slickness, the lurid Presley's instinctive control kept the mob just short of open riot – though females continued to shriek and faint in defiance of their boyfriends' sporadic heckling. By the close, all had tuned into the situations's epic vulgarity. More than anyone, Elvis himself had given the impression that 'what comes out is not show. There are a lot of people who are good actors at singing so that they make you think they sound good but, with Elvis, he lives it altogether.'[8]

Even those who barracked still felt sick of the corny monotony they still had to endure at graduation balls, village hops and other occasions arranged and supervised by grown-ups to keep teenagers off the streets. With Elvis, 'it was everybody wanting to hear the feel of music; people really wanted to be involved with music, but at the time that generation had no music to be involved in'.[9] Beyond specific songs, all that really counted was the rhythmic kick. Let's dance – not hoe down or strict tempo – let's rock 'n' roll! In fact, let's get real, real gone for a change . . .

There was the contradiction of Presley carrying on like a pool-hall hood while garbed in the flashy clothes Roy associated with blacks and homosexuals: pink socks, hip-hugging slacks, black shirt, white tie, green jacket with upturned collar. Yet, set against these things, and his brilliantined but girly cockade and ducktail, the sideburns growing down to his earlobes showed he was a Man. Rearing up on that Dallas platform was all that Orbison's upbringing and character had taught him both to despise and fear.

Yet the quiet, cautious Roy had been entranced by the glorious trash he'd just heard. After all, it wasn't that far removed from the more up-tempo C & W the Westerners played. Other bands, so he understood, were already insert-ing Elvis numbers into their sets – among them Bonham's Fannin County Boys – who featured a lead guitarist called Joe Nelson – and a Nacogdoches combo led by a certain Bob Luman. Moreover, some R & B records had found their way onto Wink nickelodeons. Nowadays, Frankie Laine and Tennessee Ernie slid in and out alongside the shuffle of Fats Domino and the sly lyricism of Chuck Berry. When all was said and done, Berry's first hit, 'Maybellene' – which Elvis had sung in Dallas – owed almost as much to C & W, for all its springing from a blues environment. Roy was converted to the new craze. 'I really loved hearing it and couldn't wait for the next records to come out but, at the same time, I was kind of ready to go myself.'[10] To this end, the Wink Westerners had slipped a couple of sanitized 'rock 'n' roll' numbers into their act before their leader departed for Denton in October.

Settling into campus life, the impressionable Winkler County freshman was delighted that pop was encouraged there as much as 'serious' music – sometimes in preference to it. Every Saturday, there was a free concert in the Main Hall. Shortly before college went down that autumn, an evening's diet of orchestral favourites and western folk song was interrupted when onto the rostrum strutted two fellows from the year above Roy. One was holding a guitar. With the briefest of preambles, Dick Penner and Wade Moore launched into a number they'd made up themselves one lazy afternoon on a hostel roof. As a song, it was as nonsensical as its title 'Ooby Dooby', but they brazened it out and got a warm response. As for Roy, 'it knocked me flat. I was astounded because they made more music than the whole orchestra.'[4]

Though it had been conceived as a western-swing novelty, 'Ooby Dooby' had also reminded Roy of the Elvis Presley show – minus, of course, the unruly climate. Talking to Wade and Dick afterwards, Roy learned that 'Ooby Dooby' was 'rockabilly'. Apparently its precedents were traceable to particular records, such as Hank Williams' 'Move it on Over', 'Wild Side of Life' by Hank Thompson, and Tennessee Ernie's 'Shotgun Boogie'. Nevertheless, drawing from all points of the spectrum, from western swing to blues, rockabilly was the blanket term used to cover a strand of rock 'n' roll based on sparse instrumentation and natural rowdiness.

Anyone who'd mastered basic techniques could have a go. The core of its contagious backbeat was a slapped double bass and slashing acoustic guitar; drums didn't enter the fray until later. Over this rudimentary beat you could holler more or less any old how – as long as you got 'gone' enough with the hep-cat couplets about clothes, lust, violence and 'doin' the Ooby Dooby with all o' your might'. Two verses of this and an electric guitarist would take off from simple fills to full-blooded clangorous solo amid yells of encouragement – 'yep!', 'woo-hoo!' 'play that thing!' – until the vocal surged back in again.

Sometimes piano, violin, saxophone, harmonica, banjo or mandolin supplemented the guitars – or even replaced them. Though singers were usually male, Wanda Jackson and Janis Martin – the 'female Elvis' – were conspicuous among the exceptions. The idea was to find an individual vocal style – even with well-known material. You could embroider it with yelps, hiccups, low grumbling, high-pitched whining, insane falsettos – anything went.

Though you often had to be sharp to spot the differences, there were vague regional shades of rockabilly. West Virginia, for example, leaned towards an acoustic bias, whereas East Texas – as epitomised by the earthy 'Rockin' Daddy' of Houston floor-layer, Sonny Fisher – gave credence to one critic's summary of the form as 'the blues with acne'. In west Texas, rockabilly was tackled with a lighter touch – something like an extension of western swing with few overt rhythm-and-blues overtones. Though Roy Orbison had listened hard to black music throughout his first college term, it hadn't always been with much pleasure: 'I had heard groups like the Clovers and their hits like "One Mint Julep", all based on seventh chords, and I didn't really like them.'[6]

The Westerners added Moore and Penner's 'Ooby Dooby' to their repertoire, but it was a request made at a New Year's Eve party in 1954 that facilitated the group's complete switch over to rockabilly. Someone wanted 'Shake Rattle and Roll', a rousing number first recorded by blues belter Joe Turner. It had just been diluted for the white market by Bill Haley and the Comets, a northern dance band formerly known as Bill Haley's Saddlemen and, before that, the Four Aces of Western Swing. The Wink Westerners obligingly struck up 'Shake Rattle and Roll' on that festive night – 'but we had nearly ten minutes to go to the [midnight] hour so we kept playing the same song'. This rave-up was strung out with

call-and-response sequences to work up audience participation, and 'by the time we were finished, I was fully
converted'.[11]

By 'going rockabilly', the Westerners would effectively
bar themselves from the stuffy if lucrative adult functions
on which they'd depended for virtually all their bookings.
Doing their bit to cast out the pestilence, many town commit-
tees had banned rock 'n' roll, often illegally, as obscene and
subversive: 'It was strange because we played in movie
theatres; we played on a barge, a boat, we played anywhere
that we could draw a crowd. But there were places, certain
auditoriums, that we couldn't play because it was rock 'n'
roll. At certain times in the day, we couldn't play. Sometimes
we had to play in the afternoon and not play at night, and
it wasn't really, really bad but there were restrictions.'[10]

Out with all the 'Moonlight in Vermont' corn went the
old name. Not only was 'Wink Westerners' reminiscent of
school and the Lions Club but it was also rather too hoot-
nanny. What was needed was a punchier, more teen-orien-
tated image. Thanks in part to Elvis, the word 'teenager'
had been coined by the media to donate to all those 'twixt
twelve and twenty who were deciding whether or not they
wanted to grow up. Because of fuller employment and
increases in wages since the war, teenagers had become a
separate target for advertising. Rockabilly, for instance, had
caught on as teen music. Furthermore, no adult would be
seen dead in its outrageously coloured 'cat' clothes. Cashing
in on the Presley image, in came check-box jackets with
padded shoulders, loud cowboy or Hawaiian shirts, and
tapered peg trousers – plus the narcissistic greasy coiffure.

As this look wouldn't go down well with the more bigoted
heterosexual chauvinists in redneck counties like Winkler,
Roy's band weren't to squeeze into cat clothes immediately.
The next move was a different matter. Somebody had heard
about a new girl group from Chicago called the Teen Queens.
So – what about the Teen *Kings*?

When the Teen Kings began hawking their musical goods

in spring 1955, joining Ellis, Morrow and Orbison on stage was the burly Jack Kennelly who clutched the belly of his 'TK'-embossed bull fiddle between his thighs as he plucked that dissolute rockabilly throb. On a Spanish guitar with attached electronic pick-up was a short but effervescent youth, Johnny 'Peanuts' Wilson, who – for now – didn't mind thrashing a finger-lacerating rhythm while the older Roy hogged the lead guitar and vocal departments. Sharing the front man's instrumental solos, the gifted James Morrow would henceforth alternate between mandolin, tenor saxophone and – if handy – piano.

This motley crew of oil field apprentices, pen-pushers and a geology student rapidly attracted steady grassroots support. After winning a 'Battle of the Bands' tournament, judged on the volume of applause, the Teen Kings made their television debut on a light entertainment programme transmitted from Odessa to all the local Texan networks. Though he was now dying his hair jet-black as Elvis had done, the Teen Kings' singer was not a figure of such offensive magnetism. Indeed, because the quintet toed a subdued, amiable line before the cameras, they were re-booked for a whole series of fortnightly half-hour showcases sponsored by Pioneer, a Midland furniture conglomerate.

With this exposure, the next milestone loomed ahead: 'Television was new; we were new, and we were quite big in the area, so we decided to make a record.'[9] They had had a stab at recording a few numbers in a studio situated where Fort Worth dissolves into Dallas. In what now can be seen as the medieval period of sound recording, both demonstration and master tapes went down in single takes on heavy-duty equipment. There was no avenue for superimposition, overdubbing, or contrived atmospherics beyond reverberation and 'bathroom' echo.

The most logical choice for an A-side was the showstopping 'Ooby Dooby', the only repertory selection peculiar to the Teen Kings alone. No other song in their repertoire bore a stamp distinctive enough to set the Teen Kings apart from any other up-and-coming rockabilly outfit. Individually, Roy and – to a lesser extent – James and Johnny had yet to find their feet as composers. The group's principal asset, if it had one, was the assured, if overeloquent, lead vocal. Although it was short on the endearing imperfections of a Sonny Fisher or a Gene Vincent, Roy's own reaction to that first tape was 'that if I heard that voice again, I would know that I'd heard it before. I wasn't thinking, "Boy, that's great; that's beautiful", or that I sing wonderfully well . . . it was just that I said, "There might be something there."'[12]

There might well have been – but what had all this extra-mural messing about to do with geology? He'd applied himself diligently enough to his studies at the beginning, but gradually Roy's double life gave his tutors cause for concern. The cash flow from music had become such that even Orbie Lee was convinced that, if Roy kept at it, he might just make a reasonable living as a musician. However, owing to the prior claims of the Teen Kings, he began cutting lectures and handing in skimped essays. Finally, a run of late nights spent either performing or catching up with course work caused him to oversleep and thereby miss an important exam. There were, nevertheless, no hard feelings when, after discussing Orbison's academic future with his parents, the university authorities upheld a transfer closer to home. At the state teachers' college in Odessa, he'd try for an inferior qualification – an 'associate's degree' – in English and history with a view to becoming a secondary school teacher.

If he had not been so fully occupied with his music, Orbison's studious nature, excellent memory and methodical tenacity might well have earned him academic honours in geology. However, to other trainee teachers in Odessa, he couldn't be imagined swishing a cane or tormenting children with gerundives. His television reputation as a rockabilly rebel had preceded him but, for all that, Roy of the Teen Kings turned out to be a well-read, impassive sophomore.

When you got to know him, he revealed a dry wit and a deferential rural charm. Nevertheless, rumours about him had spread and magnified . . . Do you know that, on stage, he's demented like someone having a fit? He and his band are making a record. He knows Elvis.

To be strictly accurate, Orbison had *met* Presley by then. When Elvis appeared at Panther Hall in 1955, Roy, as a star of local TV, wormed his way backstage to invite him to guest on a Pioneer furniture broadcast. During the fleeting conversation in the bustling dressing room, Orbison was flattered when the very approachable idol readily agreed to a two-song intermission spot before the studio audience. On the day, however, the Teen Kings comprehended the folly of going on after the King of Western Bop: 'the crowd weren't too pleased when [we] came back for the second half. All of Elvis's contemporaries, even the household names, were in awe of his talent.'[13]

One such 'household name' who'd also made the mistake of following Elvis onto the boards – 'though it wasn't totally anti-climactic'[14] – was another Odessa student, Pat Boone, whom Roy had seen acting in a Greek tragedy. Boone was more adept than Orbison at reconciling college work with the stage: 'At the same time, he had a TV show in Dallas, a radio show, he was touring and he still got straight A's'.[15] Only two years older than Roy, Pat had led an eventful life. By the age of thirteen, he'd become something of a singing wunderkind on Nashville radio and at dinner-dances. During what he'd later write off as 'an age of confusion and doubt',[16] he eloped to Texas with his high school sweetheart, Shirley – daughter of C & W sweetcorn merchant, Red Foley. After the nuptials, Pat paid his own way through teachers' training college by performing with a country band. Brushing aside all opposition in a television talent competition in Gallantin, he was snapped up by Dot Records. To his bemusement, Dot had him covering black R & B rather than the hayseed slop with which both he and his father-in-law were most at ease. Nonetheless, this strategy paid dividends in 1955 when the undergraduate turned into a pop star with a polite version of Fats Domino's 'Ain't That a Shame'.

For the old and square, Pat Boone was a clean, well-mannered alternative to that ghastly Presley. Through the medium of teen magazine articles, this more palatable face of rock 'n' roll provided more thoughtful copy than the usual descriptions of a 'dream girl' and whether he ever dated fans. Revelling in his married state, Pat preached that your parents' word was law; that you should get your hair cut; and not talk dirty. These worthy ideals were later incorporated into *'Twixt Twelve and Twenty*, the Boone manual for wholesome boys and girls: 'We all have bad habits. Personally I'm not too good at getting up in the morning, and I happen to enjoy scrambled eggs for breakfast.'[16] When, like Elvis, he moved into films, he refused to kiss his leading ladies. Well, you never know what these things lead to . . .

Caught between the truculent in-concert sensuality of Presley – something he could never hope to emulate – and his own stolid conformity to middle-aged values, Roy found the Boone stance reassuring, a relief almost. There were already indications on record that the saintly Pat aimed to drop the raucous R & B that had been forced on him, and get on with the lush 'quality' stuff à la Como and Sinatra. This was on the premise that rock 'n' roll was just another fad that chanced to be going a bit stronger than the Jitterbug or the Creep. As late as 1959, Sinatra would still be voted 'Favourite Male Star' in a *Billboard* disc jockey poll.

As Boone was in his final year before embarking on a post-graduate course at Columbia, he and Roy had only a passing acquaintance 'but he was already into his career, and that's what impressed me – that he was going to school *and* singing'.[10]

Pat may have provided distant answers to Roy's artistic and moral dilemmas, but a less eminent collegian had made a more personal impression in the spring of 1956: at long last, Roy met his 'beautiful dish' – in the shape of an

attractive, vivacious brunette from Houston. Well-built for
her sixteen years, Claudette Hestand had never lacked male
attention back home. Self-confident, intelligent and with an
easy smile that showed off her fine teeth and mischievous
eyes, she was just the sort of girl that a Wink High football
palooka would feel proud to be seen with at the Wildcat
Den.

When Claudette and Roy began 'walking out' together,
common room gossips assumed that it was the attraction of
opposites. Jubilant as he was, Roy's courtship of his 'steady'
was conducted as if Pat Boone was chaperoning them. In
the days before the birth pill and the Swinging Sixties, pre-
marital sex was a much bigger issue. A man might brag of
his conquests to his friends – but everyone knew they were
either exaggerations or downright lies. He may have got to
'third base', but only a 'cheap' girl didn't 'save herself' for
her future husband. Her whole being might be screaming
for sex as much as the pimpled fumbler of her bra strap, but
a true daughter of the fifties would have none of it while still
unwed.

Roy and Claudette, however, were above undignified
gropings. Within weeks of their first date, she had accepted
his proposal. Before the wedding in Wink later that year,
Claudette even consented to spend a few days with her fiancé
in the sprawling industrial city of Memphis, Tennessee.
Nonetheless, according to Sam Phillips at whose house they
stayed, the lovebirds 'slept in separate rooms. I just found
him to be an almost grown kid, you know? He had so much
damn innocence about him – and he never really changed
from that.'

This Mr Phillips hadn't always been so accommodating.
His colleagues thought that the wild-eyed radio announcer
had finally flipped his lid when, lumbered with a wife and
two children, he dropped everything in 1950 to rent a tiny
recording studio next to a used-car lot at the junction of
Union and Marshall Avenues in Memphis, Tennessee. This
institution, he'd calculated, would become a Mecca for local

musicians. The untidy river port of Memphis was, after all, the 'home of the blues'.

For the first three years, the visionary Sam kept the wolf from the door with R & B masters. Many became hits when leased to Chess in Chicago and other northern record companies. However, in 1952, he declared his independence with the formation of his own 'Sun' label. Two years later, he hit the jackpot when Elvis Presley came by. Here was the money-making 'white man who could sing the blues' that he'd despaired of ever finding.

After Presley took the South by storm, there were howls of disbelief when Sun auctioned his contract to the mighty RCA in November 1955. What on earth was Sam playing at now? He reckoned that he could spawn another Elvis any time he liked. There were plenty to choose from. Not a day would go by without demo tapes thudding onto Sun's doormat and tongue-tied telephone callers begging for auditions from the great Sam Phillips. From all across the nation they came – even Alaska and Canada. Quite a few of them were worth a listen, too. With Elvis gone, Phillips had put his money on Carl Perkins, whose immediate Hot Hundred smash, 'Blue Suede Shoes', made RCA wonder if they'd signed the wrong man.

To give Perkins a clearer run in the rockabilly stakes Sam promoted another likely contender, Johnny Cash, as the label's C & W specialist. While an air force radio operator in Germany during the Cold War, Arkansas-born Cash had taught himself to pick country-style guitar – and developed a liking for alcohol. Discharged in 1954, he was drawn to Memphis where, whilst working as a door-to-door salesman, he met a pair of garage mechanics who twanged electric guitar and upright bass. With these new-found friends, Johnny landed a weekly show on local radio, singing not rockabilly but mainly straight C & W of a religious bent. He delivered these anthems in a heavily masculine growl. After two months of this, 'Johnny Cash and the Tennessee Two' approached Sun for a tryout. Disregarding their devotional songs, Sam Phillips asked if they'd anything teenagers might like. Cash responded with a string of secular numbers he'd composed in the Fatherland.

With his lowdown bass and facial scar, Johnny was too butch to be another Elvis but, after his first crop of Sun singles were all country hits, he became a virtual fixture on *Louisiana Hayride*. Moreover, his manager, Bob Neal, a Memphis record shop proprietor, was able to negotiate a strenuous round of engagements for Cash and the Two that would see them into next year and beyond. After the first round of poorly-paid bookings – some hundreds of miles apart – it dawned on them what a joyless grind now blighted their lives. The whole thing began to degenerate into a subsidized booze-up. Some nights they were scarcely able to totter on stage. As a result, the moody, introspective Johnny became an erratic performer, sometimes inspired, at others dazed and almost incapable of singing at all.

He was on form, however, for a regional television appearance in the autumn of 1955 – in which the Teen Kings had secured a guest spot. Watching Cash off-camera, Roy was struck by his vocal singularity: 'Very distinctive, yeah . . . if you hear John once, you hear him again, you know it's the same singer. So that works in your favour. It won't get you a hit record but it will help build if you have the rest of the goods.'[4] Cash felt much the same about Orbison. In a genial mood afterwards, he complimented Roy on 'Ooby Dooby'. He even made a suggestion. Why not give Sam Phillips a call? Here's the number. You can say Johnny Cash recommends you. Thus began an unlikely but lifelong amity between hard-drinkin' Johnny and virtuous Roy.

Cash hadn't been the only one to suggest Sun to the Teen Kings. For any aspiring rockabilly outfit, it made sense to start at the top. With Cash as the final incentive, the group's leader had screwed up enough courage by December to dial the number. Unfortunately, it might not have been the best time to ring as it wasn't all smiles then between the neurotic Sam and his infuriating C & W protégé. When the nervous

Orbison mentioned his referee, the Sun mogul erupted with rage. 'Johnny Cash doesn't own my record company!' he thundered before slamming down the telephone.

After a heated inquest, the Teen Kings hit on another idea: to fund their own record. They would put it out themselves. After all, people were already inquiring where they could buy 'Ooby Dooby'. They could sell it at bookings, and send it to major companies as a demo. Maybe Mercury, RCA or Columbia would accept it as a master . . . Roy was amongst the uneasy minority, but the motion was carried so that everybody could go to bed.

Charged by the hour, the harshly regulated session at the previous studio had had a dollar sign hanging over every fretful quaver. More inviting to an outfit of the Teen Kings' calibre was the rates policy and closer proximity of a newly completed studio in Clovis, a town on the New Mexico border. No clock-watcher, its proprietor, Norman Petty, was even amenable to working at a paper loss in exchange for first refusal on publishing rights of items recorded – and, if not rushed, a group might make a more marketable job of these for a lump sum. Mr Petty would record your song for however long it took. According to one client, Bob Montgomery – the 'Bob' in 'Buddy, Bob and Larry' – 'everything in Petty's studio was cut as a demo just about. People were coming in, recording there and then submitting their stuff to a label. If Norman liked them, he would go all out to interest a label in the demos.'[17]

Petty was well placed to do this as his own instrumental trio had recorded for Columbia and ABC; the proceeds from 'Mood Indigo', a modest hit of 1954, enabling the building of the studio. It had originally been intended for the sole use of the Norman Petty Trio, but one day organist Petty realized that he was the unwitting owner of the only such facility in the area. Confident in his own technical know-how as both engineer and producer, he went public in late 1955.

Among the first paying customers were the Teen Kings who, funded in part by Je-Wel, a local record company,

coughed up for an afternoon's taping of 'Ooby Dooby' and
a workmanlike if ponderous 'Tryin' to Get to You', featuring
the versatile Morrow on clarinet. The latter had originally
been released by the Eagles on Mercury but, more pertin-
ently, Elvis was doing it in concert and he hadn't yet put it
out himself.

Before they acted too hastily Petty mailed a copy of 'Ooby
Dooby' to Mitch Miller, his Columbia recording manager
in New York. Not letting his personal loathing of rock 'n'
roll stand in his way, Miller had made a bid for Presley in
November. He didn't like the Teen Kings much either but,
with Norman's foot in the door with 'Mood Indigo', he
thought it tactful to pass the song itself to Sid King and his
Five Strings, one of the C & W acts on Columbia's roster
that had been allowed to attempt rockabilly.

After some less fruitful letters of rejection, the Teen Kings
surrendered their 'Ooby Dooby' to Je-Wel, who supervised
its pressing and, from a car boot, its sale-or-return circulation
to whatever record shops would take a few.

From the two versions of their song going the rounds,
Wade Moore and Dick Penner sat back and waited for the
royalties. That they'd probably make more out of 'Ooby
Dooby' than the Teen Kings was not lost on Roy, who had
recently come up with two or three numbers of his own that
he felt were at least equal to some of the group's non-
originals. He was too shy to sing the one about his 'brand
new wife', but an earlier Orbison composition, the rocking
'Go! Go! Go!', was a bit like Bill Haley's 'Hot Dog Buddy
Buddy', and was absorbed into the Teen Kings' increasingly
wilder stage presentation. No longer merely rattling off a
fixed programme without fuss, Roy especially was now
anything but timid in his performances. 'I was very much
an extrovert, sensation-seeking fellow. I moved around more
than Elvis or anyone.'[7] Kay Vasquez, an eye-witness, confirmed that Orbison 'leaped all over the place in some sort
of leopard-skin get-up' on one occasion. Gyrating, snarling
and rolling about as if he had a hornet in his pants was,

however, not a pleasure but a duty – as it was for Bill Haley and the Comets. Haley, paunchy and kiss-curled, would apologize to the press for his band's on-stage frolics but, having struck lucky with 'Rock Around the Clock', they'd have been daft not to play up to it, wouldn't they? Anyway, one of the Comets had served under Benny Goodman.

Though Roy Orbison 'felt that for my style, it was a bit shallow', there had become such a keen differentiation between vocalist and backing group these days that, while the Teen Kings toiled behind him, Roy had to carry the visuals almost single-handed. His prominence was affirmed in the billing – 'Roy Orbison and the Teen Kings' – and by his wearing of stage gear that contrasted with the group's uniform of checked shirts and buff suits. The others might have been happy to go along with this new status quo, but Johnny Wilson – temperamentally a better qualified wildman – was casting covetous glances at Orbison's monopoly of the spotlight. Dishing out the same old chords while Roy put on the agony, 'Peanuts' harboured thoughts of chucking in the Teen Kings one day. He'd form another group with himself as Elvis. Besides, unless they pulled another stroke soon, the Teen Kings might fizzle out anyway, having reached the limit of their local impact.

Foreseeing this eventuality himself, Roy sought advice from a Mr Cecil Hollerfield, the fatherly manager of an Odessa record store. Though sympathetic, Hollerfield bemoaned the consigning of 'Ooby Dooby' to the fly-by-night Je-Wel who, he said, had an abysmal distribution set-up. However, as Roy was still a minor, he could wriggle out of whatever written pledges he'd made to them. When Sam Phillips was logging thousands of car miles peddling records in the early days of Sun, Hollerfield had befriended him – as he was now befriending Roy. He'd talk to Sam on the Teen Kings' behalf. He'd call right now and play Sam 'Ooby Dooby' over the wire.

Sure enough, Sam remembered 'Poppa' Hollerfield and trusted that he was in good health. Yes, the name 'Roy

Orbison' rang a loud bell. However, though Phillips showed a faint but unmistakable interest in what he could hear of 'Ooby Dooby', could Poppa send a copy to Union Avenue so that he could listen to it properly?

Sam was more eager than he'd sounded. 'My immediate reaction [was that it] resembled some of the cute, bouncy things that were big hits in the big band era, and there wasn't really much of a novelty thing going with rock 'n' roll at the time so I decided, if we could get the proper cut on it, we could probably get Roy Orbison and the Teen Kings before the public. I was very much impressed with Roy's inflection and the way he did "Ooby Dooby", and I think it impressed me more than it impressed Roy then.'[12]

Roy was indeed fed up with the gibbering 'Ooby Dooby'. He'd have dumped it altogether if it hadn't caught on so. It was a millstone round his neck – like 'Rock Around the Clock' to Bill Haley. He was already being introduced on stage by the 'Big O' nickname that some bright spark of a disc jockey had invented during one of its spasmodic radio airings. It wasn't as if the wretched record had a hope in hell of being a hit, was it?

Hollerfield, however, had some good news for Orbison and the Teen Kings. Could they be in Memphis for a re-make of 'Ooby Dooby' in three days' time? As the two-car convoy sped the 500 miles towards the ugly, twisting Mississippi, passers-by peered in curiously as the elated young Texans wound down their side windows and shouted insults at rednecks or thumped out a beat on the roofs of the vehicles. Though he had more to get thrilled about Roy didn't join in the skylarks so much. He had to mind his voice.

The merriment died down on the outskirts of Memphis. Slamming the car doors outside the fabled shrine of rock 'n' roll, 'in our enthusiasm, I don't guess we looked at how small the place was'.[10] About the size of the average hotel bedroom, the playing area in the one-storey building had no acoustic separation. As the equipment was unloaded and assembled, Roy braced himself to let rip over Billy's drumming. 'Fortunately, I'd been singing for so long that I could sing with a lot of power'.[4] Though the studio was a sophisticated two-track rather than a place where one would overdub the voice onto the accompaniment, the second track was used instead for Sun's trademark 'flutter' echo – or 'slapback' as it was jargonized.

Knowing that the rough edges and driving excitement of King Presley's output had been manufactured in these circumstances, the Teen Kings and Roy were putty in the hands of the hard-nosed Sam, although they soon gathered that Phillips 'was like quite a few people who are successful in this business who can't play an instrument, can't sing a lick, can't read a note, can't even whistle'.[12] Issuing commands from his glass-fronted booth of tape spools and switches, Sam 'wanted everything up, everything fast, everything with all the energy that was possible.'[12]

After they'd warmed up with a few run-throughs of 'Ooby Dooby', and the levels had been adjusted, Sam explained how he reckoned the number should sound. This he illustrated with crackling 78 rpm spins of the black R & B originals that he and Elvis had refashioned so sensationally. At this, Roy's hackles rose slightly, but he held his peace. Later, he'd articulate his suspicions that Phillips was 'an anachronism. He'd been recording black artists mostly, and when he included whites on his label, he'd try to get them to sing like Arthur Crudup. What he meant to say was "sing with feeling".'[9]

With an irresolute nod, Orbison returned to the skull-like chrome microphone and tried his best to forget to be himself. After 'Ooby Dooby' was down to Phillips' satisfaction, just the ticket for the other side was another up-tempo rocker. Roy, however, fancied a ballad for diversity. Dismissively, the man in charge said, 'No, you're going to sing what I want you to sing. You're doing fine. Elvis was wanting to sing like the Ink Spots or Bing Crosby, and I did the same thing for him – and for Carl Perkins.'[18]

Making amends for this little flare-up, Sam selected the disarmingly humble Roy's own 'Go! Go! Go!' from the B-side possibilities. Saturated with 'cat' slang, this shuffling two-minute odyssey in search of 'real gone love to drive a cool cat wild' was notable for Roy's rather ill-at-ease vocals, and Billy's quick-witted snare drums. Yet by the time the group retired to the restaurant next door, their job done, they had to admit that Sam Phillips had done his. You could hardly hear the piano, but that crude 'cardboard box' drum sound with Jack's bass and Johnny's unadorned thrumming had a danceable urgency that had been absent on the Je-Wel disc. As well as Roy's raw guitar soloing, what would sell 'Ooby Dooby' was the focused drive, the Elvis Presley 'feel'. You could take or leave the actual song.

In the cold light of the following day, Sam heard little in 'Ooby Dooby' to intimate that the Teen Kings were superior to countless other rockabilly outfits – except 'I knew Roy Orbison's voice was pure gold but I felt he'd be dead inside a month if people saw him'. Nevertheless, setting aside his misgivings, Phillips set an April release date for 'Ooby Dooby' and hoped for the best.

With the little-loved 'Ooby Dooby' given a new lease of life in the recording studio, Roy would now attack it with more venom than it warranted when the Teen Kings re-entered the familiar circuit of west Texan high school hops. Fired with the self-confidence of one who recorded for Sun Records, Orbison no longer behaved as though one day he might be spouting history to a class of wayward adolescents. He was past caring about his own education after the heart-stopping strains of 'Ooby Dooby' had poured unexpectedly from a drugstore jukebox as he'd been strolling by. On 16 July 1956, it cracked the pop Hot Hundred. There then followed some brisk to-ing and fro-ing of telephone messages as Bob Neal, in a quasi-managerial capacity, arranged the group's first tour – which would take in most of the South. The wages weren't brilliant – but it was sure to help sales of the record. While the others simply took their summer vacations early, Roy Orbison threw away his chances of becoming a teacher by quitting college a fortnight before his final exams: 'Had I seen any limitations, like "You're only as hot as your latest record" or "What are you going to do when you're thirty?" – had I listened to any of that, I would have cut the dream short.'[3]

For fifty dollars a day, Orbison and the Teen Kings would open for Sonny James, who was high in the C & W chart, Johnny Horton – the 'Singing Fisherman' – and bill-topping Johnny Cash who, Roy would discover, wasn't always the easiest person to rub along with, having graduated from spirits to amphetamines. During the tour, which began, ironically, in a schoolhouse in Charleston, North Carolina, Roy and his Teen Kings, as token hard-core rock 'n' rollers, 'danced and shaked and did everything we could to get applause because we had only one hit record'.[18] At a stop in Richmond, Virginia – one of Cash's 'off' nights – they even stole the show. As 'Ooby Dooby' edged to its high of No.59, the running order was altered in the newcomers' favour.

When the trip wound down in Memphis, perhaps an even greater accolade was the praise heaped upon them by a backstage visitor who'd sauntered across the stage for a short, half-time cameo. 'Marvellous show!' exclaimed Elvis Presley to a round-eyed Orbison, adding, 'Well, I'll tell you one thing: you're that good that I'll never appear on stage with you'.[18] This sweet lie came from one who'd 'got as much applause as we did just by being announced'.[19] Roy would guard as a relic forever the polaroid snapshot taken of himself and the King on that night of nights.

While in Memphis, the group seized the opportunity to sort out a follow-up to 'Ooby Dooby'. In the running was a risqué Johnny Cash creation, 'Little Willie Booger', which had much in common with the delicate 'Bugger Boy', a 1954 blues obscurity by Lightnin' Slim. Roy cleansed the Cash song with the more genteel title of 'You're My Baby'. After all, his mother might hear it.

The workshop ambience of Sun also permitted Roy to

tape numerous guitar-and-voice demos of the songs that
were now streaming from him: 'I'd write in the car. Even
when we'd take a break alongside the road, I'd jump on the
fender or the wing of the car and play the guitar and sing.'[4]
Not intended for public ears, these musical sketches – many
written with a friend from college, Terry McGill – were
punctuated with errors, hesitancies, microphone pops, impromptu busking and, on one, even an unscripted 'oh, crap!'

The very starkness of some of these items captured a
strange beauty, a freshness at odds with the more unre-
strained offerings of the day. In 'I Never Knew', 'Claudette'
and 'A True Love Goodbye', there were hints of what Roy
Orbison was to become. Not so cryptic was the unusual
atmosphere of 'The Clown'. The song seemed to have no
commercial precedent or reassuring reference point for Sam
Phillips and his assistant producer, Jack Clement. Devoid
of discernible 'hook' or chorus, this piece of haunting melan-
cholia was a decade ahead of its time – even in embryo. On
hearing it, Jack Clement declared, 'Roy, you'll never make
a ballad singer'.[12] Free of Sun's quality control himself, Elvis
Presley could appreciate Roy's bafflement at this judgement.

The affectionate draping of his royal arm around Orbison's
shoulder for the photograph had been the start of a friendship
that would endure until death. Roy spent many evenings
loafing about with his new pal. 'One night, we went by to
pick up Elvis's girlfriend in his purple Cadillac – I think he
was making twenty million a year at the time. When he
knocked on the door, the girl said, "I'm sorry. You're too
late", and walked back in. We all went on to his house and
had Pepsi Colas and potato chips. I couldn't believe that
some woman would turn down a date with Elvis Presley.'[5]

This incident did not belittle Elvis in Roy's eyes. Though
nobody's fool, Roy was enchanted to be in the King's court;
a confidant of the human being, only a year older than
himself, who'd become the voice of teenage escapism and
aspiration. Presley's fame and wealth had granted him a
splendid certainty in everything he did or said. America was

there solely for his pleasure. He was right – and that was all there was to it.

Roy soon discovered that you couldn't belong to the King's charmed circle, unless you owned a Cadillac and a diamond ring. Purchasing the former, a white model, with his first (and, allegedly, only) royalty cheque from Sun sent him into rapture for the youth who, for too long, had had his nose pressed against showroom windows. Orbison was, however, able to rein in his natural extravagance more easily than the feckless Elvis. 'I got a little bigger (turquoise) Cadillac and a little bigger diamond ring, and then I said, "That's foolish", and I stopped.'[3]

This economy was timely for 'Ooby Dooby' proved to be the only big seller of his four Sun singles. In its afterglow, a place was found for Roy on a second, bigger tour. While the Teen Kings crammed themselves and their instruments into a second-hand family saloon, the captain of the side shared a hired pink Cadillac with Johnny Cash, Carl Perkins and, a new Sun signing, Jerry Lee Lewis – a piano-pounding fireball from Louisiana. As Roy had done on the previous tour, Jerry Lee would make all the other acts seem tame with his electrifying stage act.

While 'the Killer', as Lewis styled himself, brought the house down, it became painfully obvious that all the fans wanted from the Big O was 'Ooby Dooby' as proved by the less fervent response to its successor, 'Rockhouse'. After a while, he didn't even bother with the new record. 'I'd go on stage, and I'd play everybody else's stuff – Chuck Berry's stuff, Little Richard's stuff – then I'd sing my one hit record and get off.'[3]

Roy had co-written 'Rockhouse' with another Sun artist, Harold Jenkins, whose backing group was called the Rock-housers. After each found out that the other was composing a piece of the same title, Orbison and Jenkins – who would shortly be calling himself 'Conway Twitty' – pooled their ideas rather than argue. The result was not dissimilar to Presley's fourth Sun single, 'Baby, Let's Play House', though its subject matter was closer to the fading Bill Haley's pre-occupations: 'Rock it in the morning/rock it in the daylight/rockin' through the evening', and so forth. Though a stronger record than 'Ooby Dooby', 'Rockhouse' was too predictable to reach far beyond loyal west Texas.

Thus, Roy was more often seen on his home turf during this time. As Claudette was still at college, the couple had moved into the apartment belonging to her recently-widowed mother in Odessa. Sometimes they'd enliven the town's glum streets by motorbiking together. Like the Cadillacs, this new pastime had sprung from Roy's Memphis playmate: 'It was Elvis who, without knowing it, made me a motorcycling fan. I saw a cycle outside Sun Records studio . . . somebody told me it belonged to Elvis Presley. I finally managed to get to take a cycle ride with the fellow who bought that machine from Elvis and that was the start of it.'[20] After Roy had taught her to ride and bought her a machine of her own for her birthday, Claudette's passion for the sport would last for as long as she lived.

Her spouse might be accosted now and then for autographs, but he wasn't enough of a pop star to be prevented from walking – rather than riding – to the local shop for newspapers and cigarettes. Nevertheless, for a while it seemed as though he was never off local television and radio. Outsiders could not be blamed for thinking he was simply flaunting his modest fame while he was still able. More pragmatically, however, Roy was consolidating his local media connections so that, if his rock 'n' roll Big Time was up, a place might be found for him as a presenter or a disc jockey. The oil fields would be such an anticlimax after all he'd achieved.

One November evening in 1956 even found him deputizing for an indisposed radio engineer at the station in Odessa until 5 a.m. Such tasks weren't exactly show business – but they would do while he waited for something else to turn up. Booked for a five-song live session that night were a vocal group called the Five Bops. They were agape to find none other than the Big O behind the instrument panel. During the small hours, Orbison also rendered first aid when the Five's lead tenor, Bill Dees, suffered a minor hand injury when the studio's coffee vendor malfunctioned.

This touching episode was one which had a more than incidental bearing upon the futures of both Roy and Bill. Doubling on piano and guitar, Dees was then studying music at West Texas State College. Formed on the campus, the Five Bops moulded themselves on the Diamonds, the Crew-cuts and other white harmony groups who plagiarized from black counterparts like the Gladiolas ('Little Darlin'') and the Chords ('Sh-boom'). The Five's first single, 'Jitterbug-ging', coupled with 'Unforgotten Love', a Dees composition, was released on a Dot subsidiary. It had sold well in New Mexico, even topping the regional chart in Amarillo.

With Dees as main advocate, the Five Bops updated their style – to be reborn as the Whirlwinds. In this form, they would be supporting Orbison one night in north Texas. Seconds before showtime, Bill's guitar strap snapped. Roy came immediately to the rescue with a replacement. Years later, Bill would remind him of this second kindness.

Another snippet from Dee's memory bank was that several months after the Teen Kings made their first tapes at Nor-man Petty's studio in Clovis, the Five Bops recorded there. Having hit it off more with the amiable Norman than Sam Phillips, Roy would continue to drive 'back and forth, on and off'[4] to the Clovis studio throughout his period with Sun. Often accompanied by Johnny Wilson, he would bring song ideas for the more experienced Petty to develop. The person who benefited most from these collaborations was Buddy Holly – of 'Buddy, Bob and Larry' – who first visited the studio in 1956. Holly, as lead singer, guitarist and founder of the Crickets, not only taped an unreleased version of 'Go! Go! Go!', but would also include two Orbison/Petty efforts on his first LP, *The Chirping Crickets*.

Of these, 'You've Got Love' – co-written with Wilson – was a medium-paced jollity whose title said it all. The slower

'An Empty Cup (and a Broken Date)', however, is more involved. Though flawed, this ballad betrays both period charm and, like 'The Clown', Orbison's growing interest in writing as the spurned suitor: 'my songs are all about the way I felt personally at one time or another.'[2]

Roy kept another Petty collaboration, 'A True Love Good-bye', for himself. Built around the fingerpicking two guitars, a master of this pleasant, ambling ballad was finished at Sun. Phillips didn't find it fiery enough for release, however. He made a similar judgement upon Roy's heavy-handed treatment of 'It's Too Late', fresh from the R & B chart as recorded by its composer, Chuck Willis. In a less doleful mood, 'It's Too Late' would also be revised on *The Chirping Crickets*.

Tidy-minded journalists later propagated a myth that Roy and Buddy had been bosom friends. There were, after all, similarities. They were both of the same age and social background; Holly's family had even lived in Vernon for a while. Another affinity was their domination of their respective groups. More to the point, both possessed creative talents that made up for other vulnerabilities, not least of which was a deficit of manifest sex appeal.

Nevertheless, the two were in each other's company on only a handful of occasions. The first of these was when the Crickets trooped backstage to pay their respects at the Lubbock stop during that first 'Ooby Dooby' tour. Although Orbison did likewise when Buddy's group – now renamed 'Buddy Holly *and* the Crickets' – played Odessa, there was a moment afterwards, and it stuck in Roy's memory, when the light-hearted banter suddenly turned into fierce rivalry. Yes, he liked Elvis too – who didn't? – but 'Blue Days and Black Nights', Holly's first single, 'sounded just like Elvis. Buddy followed Elvis and they were both tied up in my thinking.'[10] A year would pass and Orbison would struggle not to eat his heart out when Holly, blast him, became 'a big Number One star, and that was way out of my league. But I continued to record for Sun at the time'.[10]

As if to rub salt into the wound, Roy's third release for Phillips, 'Sweet and Easy to Love' was plummeting as the Crickets' 'That'll Be the Day' began its scramble to the top in May 1957. Sam had seemed to use Holly as a prototype on some of Orbison's recordings recently – most notably when taping 'The Cause of it All', with its hyperactive slapback bestowing the necessary adenoidal twang. In return, Norman Petty, on Buddy's behalf, had shanghaied the Roses, a family of singers that Roy had brought in from west Texas to assist on 'Sweet and Easy to Love', serving him as the Jordanaires did Elvis.

The disgruntled Teen Kings may have regarded the proposal of such augmentation as a slight on their abilities. Furthermore, as Orbison had been identified early on as the group's star, the Sun agreement covered only him. This left the other four in a ticklish position financially. Fuelled by Johnny Wilson's frustrated rancour, star and backing group had fragmented. Of the former Teen Kings, Johnny became the rockabilly showman he had so long wanted to be. Under Norman Petty's wing, one of his 45's in this capacity, 'Cast Iron Arm' (co-written with Orbison), became a collector's item. The more phlegmatic James Morrow, however, would be asked to lend a hand as his old chum's contract with Sun ran its ever more unsatisfactory course.

'Chicken-hearted', the last official Orbison single for Sun, was further gingered up by a jumpy two-note riff from Roy's new guitarist, Roland Janes, and Morrow's squawking saxophone. This song had been written by Bill Justis, a considerably better-known saxophonist from the realms of jazz, who had been appointed by the busy Phillips as Sun's musical director. After his own instrumental, 'Raunchy', became a huge hit in 1957, Justis was active in mellowing the label's still predominantly rockabilly sound for a public that was wanting more saccharine music.

This attempt at a clean sweep made Orbison all the more determined to slow things down a little. Nevertheless, his wishes continued to be thwarted by Phillips, who would insist to the end that 'contrary to the stories that you've heard, Roy was not displeased at the time with doing the things we did on Sun.'

Perhaps this was a misinterpretation of his artist's resigned compliance. Orbison knew that 'you did everything Sam's way or not at all.'[21] His acceptance of this condition made him 'one of the easiest guys to work with'[22] as he bottled up misgivings about the endless twelve-bar war horses he was made to sing. While it was 'hard to see what Sam saw in anyone',[10] Roy rocked as hard as he could – even coming on quite fiercely once in a while. By 1957, there were such remaindered gems in Sun's vaults as the aggressive, harmonica-led 'Mean Little Mama' with its adventurous guitar solo. More endearing – if rather ham-fisted – are 'Domino' and 'Problem Child', that weld Chuck Berry jangle to rockabilly. His final Sun B-side, 'I Like Love', had less going for it. It was composed by Jack Clement who, in mitigation, had put several of Roy's own songs before his principal production concerns, Johnny Cash and Jerry Lee Lewis.

The more highly-strung Killer remembered that Roy 'minded his own business, stayed in his place . . . he might come by just to say "hello" hug your neck real nice and get out of your hair. He was that kind of person. He was a pretty nice guy, wasn't he?'[3] Yes, he was – but he wasn't a rampaging giant of classic rock like Jerry Lee himself.

When Roy Orbison's time came, Phillips would recount how he gave him his first big break. Sam, incorrigible as ever, would then concede that 'Roy knew his limitations, and he knew all the time where his forte was – and that was in ballads.'[22] His lieutenant, Jack Clement, however, would never recant. Whenever their paths crossed down the years, he'd always ask Roy the same half-serious question: 'You still trying to sing those ballads, boy?'

Notes

1   'The Wildcat', 1954

2 *Record Mirror*, 9 June 1962
3 *Rolling Stone*, 26 January 1989
4 *New Musical Express*, 20 December 1980
5 *On the beat*, Radio Merseyside
6 *The History of Rock*, vol.1, no. 5 (Orbis)
7 *The Face*, February 1989
8 *The Guardian*, 8 December 1980
9 *Melody Maker*, 11 October 1975
10 Veronica Television (Dutch)
11 *The History of Rock*, vol.2, no. 21 (Orbis)
12 *Tribute to the Big O*, Radio 2, 5 January 1989
13 London News, 19 May 1987
14 Pat Boone to *Rolling Stone*, 22 September 1977
15 'For the lonely' (L.P.), Rhino RI 71493
16 ''Twixt twelve and twenty' by P. Boone
17 *Goldmine*, May 1981
18 *Illustrated History of Rock*, ed. J. Miller (Picador, 1981)
19 *Melody Maker*, 12 March 1966
20 *Melody Maker*, 13 August 1966
21 *Melody Maker*, September 1987
22 *Country Music Round-up*, February 1989

3

Sweet and Innocent

Colonel Tom Parker's billion-dollar manipulation of Elvis Presley was the tip of an iceberg that would make more fortunes than had ever been known in the history of recorded sound. All around, the hunt was up for more moneymaking Presleys; every region of the world seemed to throw up a contender. Off-the-cuff examples include France's Johnny Halliday and Mickie Most from South Africa. In England, it was Cliff Richard who took over from Tommy Steele as the poor man's Elvis. Needless to say, these sprouted thickest in the States where the likes of Troy Shondell, Fabian and Ral Donner mirrored the King's lopsided smirk, 'common' good looks and hot-potato-in-the-mouth singing.

Inevitably there were differences between them, but these were largely variations on a theme. Many thought that Jerry Lee Lewis was simply an Elvis who substituted piano for guitar. That was all they knew. The Capitol record company thought that it too had snared one in the rough-and-ready Gene Vincent from Virginia. When Vincent – 'The Screaming End' – came down to earth with a bump after his breakthrough with 'Be-Bop-a-Lula', Capitol realised that it was lumbered with the crippled runt of the litter. Yet despite finding Vincent and his music objectionable, Capitol was contractually obliged to cater for his hoodlum following, unreliable in the market place against the smoother certainties of the post-rockabilly Elvis sausage machine.

Acuff-Rose had more joy with a pair of quiffed brothers with delinquent-angel faces named Everly who could be visualized as two Elvises for the price of one. By 1956, the year they signed the Everly Brothers, the reins of power at Acuff-Rose had passed to Rose's son Wesley who, in his mid-thirties, was more aware than Fred had been that rock 'n' roll wasn't just another craze. Witness what had happened to former C & W star Marty Robbins, who had learned much from a tour of Texas with Presley in 1955. Testing the water with cover versions of 'That's All Right', 'Maybelline' and, like Pat Boone, 'Long Tall Sally', Robbins' conversion to the new style was vindicated financially when his 'Singin' the Blues', 'White Sport Coat', and other bland country-rock fusions charged up the mid-fifties' Hot Hundred. Acuff-Rose's own Don Gibson – albeit impossibly ancient in his late twenties, and with receding hair to boot – also took up the challenge by switching from a hillbilly-cum-honky-tonk style to a vague hybrid of classic rock and country ballad. Nevada-born C & W singer Sue Thompson's conquest of the pop charts with such novelties as 'Norman' and 'Paper Tiger' – often singing in duet with Gibson – was only just round the corner.

Many of her hits had come from the fertile pen of John D. Loudermilk – also on Wesley Rose's books – whose reputation as a songwriter was to exceed by far his modest achievements as a performer. Indeed, his migration from rural North Carolina to Nashville resulted from his composing the big-selling 'A Rose and a Baby Ruth', as sung by his pal George Hamilton IV, and produced by a third native of North Carolina, Fred Foster. John D's desire to 'tell the world how the guy in the filling station feels' was the thrust behind later hits by such diverse artists as the Chordettes, Bobby Vee, Frank Ifield and Jerry Lee Lewis. In the mid-sixties, the Nashville Teens would bear much the same mutually advantageous relationship to Loudermilk as

Manfred Mann to Bob Dylan. Loudermilk's golden year, however, was 1961 when he notched up a world-wide smash of his own with 'Language of Love', whose chorus, incidentally, centred on his burbling 'ooby dooby dooby doo' ad nauseam. Moreover, that was also the year when his song 'Ebony Eyes' shifted a million for the Everly Brothers.

This duo – christened Isaac Donald and Philip – had been born into the music business, and had been incorporated into their singing parents' Midwest radio shows almost as soon as they were weaned. In May 1956, nineteen-year-old Don and his younger brother auditioned for Wesley Rose. As the brothers' severe close harmony and clanging left-handed guitars filled his office with clues of what they were to become, Wesley affected nonchalance – as his father before him would have done. Inwardly, however, he knew that he had struck gold.

Cajoling label boss Archie Bleyer – who hadn't been immediately impressed – to chance Don and Phil on his Cadence outlet, their new manager grubbed through his filing cabinets for a commercial vehicle with which to present them to the public. At RCA Victor's Studio B in Nashville, the Everly Brothers would tape 'Bye Bye Love' by Felice and Bordleaux Bryant. Within an incredible month of its release in March 1958, it would be high in all three chart categories.

Next up was 'Wake Up Little Susie', whose banning by some radio stations for its 'suggestive' lyrics probably helped it on its way to the top of the Hot Hundred. This innocent opus of inadvertent flaunting of small-town values welded to a rock 'n' roll beat typified the forceful but romantic essence that would keep Phil and Don in hits for another decade.

Their own compositions didn't yet sound like hits, so there was a constant rummaging through demo tapes and manuscripts. This musical treasure hunt became especially urgent when the third single stuck at No.28 in the charts, signalling the fallibility of the Everly Brothers. By early

1958, another Bryant number, 'All I Have to Do is Dream,'
was earmarked as the next A-side. All that was needed now
was a strong coupling that might register in the charts on
separate sales as, say, the Coasters' 'Young Blood' had on
the back of 'Searchin'' the previous summer.

The search ended at the unlikely source of a warm-up act
at an Everly Brothers' bash in Indiana. Having been reduced
to borrowing money to get there, a weary Roy Orbison was
angry with himself for leaving behind the demo recordings
that he was hoping to press on the prize exhibits – if they
should speak to him. Not a natural hustler, he melted
into the background, smoking quietly on a window ledge.
Desultory backstage chatter amongst the Everlys and others
on the bill kept returning to that same aggravating question
– what to put on the B-side of 'All I Have to Do is Dream'.
Turning round, Phil Everly asked Roy if he had any tunes.
He wrote a bit, didn't he?

With all eyes on him then, the self-effacing Texan almost
shook his head to slough off the attention. Instead, he heard
his voice croaking, 'I've just got one'. Clearing his throat,
he stubbed out the cigarette. Then he lifted up his Gretsch
semi-acoustic and started chugging quavers. A deep breath
and he was straight into the line: 'I've got a brand-new baby
and I feel so good . . .' Soon he was in the throes of the one
that rhymed 'get', 'met' and 'pretty little pet' with its title.

Glistening with embarrassment while the words and three
simple chords hung in the air, he blinked at his feet as
'Claudette' died away. An exclaimed 'Yeah!' broke the
silence. Orbison glanced up at the nodding, smiling hubbub.
Because of past disappointments, he was bemused when,
before departing, the Everlys got him to write down the
lyrics and chords on the cardboard top of a shoe box before
they left. After all, they'd already turned up their noses at
demos that Buddy Holly had deigned to send them. Expecting nothing, Roy was astonished when 'the next thing I
know, Wesley Rose from Nashville's calling me in Memphis
at Sun Records, telling me to sign this contract for the song

'Claudette' that the Everly Brothers were going to record –
they actually already had recorded it'.[1]

Theoretically, Roy was still tied contractually to Sun,
though things were not going well. 'I'd sort of quit recording.
Sam had released a couple of songs that I didn't think he
should have, so I sort of retired.'[2] With Claudette now
pregnant, twenty-two seemed a good age for a one-hit wonder to settle down. Other than rare and unremunerative
expeditions like the one to Indiana, Roy had re-entered the
trivial round of parochial bookings at venues where
he'd always gone down well – though he could still play
support whenever a big name came to Texas. It was,
however, beginning to seem that 'Ooby Dooby' would be
his only hit. The white Cadillac he'd bought with the
proceeds was less shiny than it used to be. Maybe the El
Paso Natural Oil Company would give Roy his old job
back. He could still perform semi-professionally at
weekends . . . 'I lost all interest and quit, for seven months
I just ambled around. No, I didn't do a thing, except to
think.'[2]

This 'Claudette' windfall with the Everly Brothers would
allow him to 'amble around' for a while longer. On the
strength of it, there might be an avenue not so much for
expanding as consolidating his status as a rockabilly entertainer. The only barrier to proceeding with Rose's proposal
was the 'very likeable and affable'[1] Sam Phillips who claimed
a share of the proceeds. 'We had a three-way conversation,'
Roy said later about the incident. 'Wesley said, "Why do
you want Roy's money?" so Wesley sounded great and Sam
sounded like he was a . . . wanted a little too much, so I left
then. I left Sun.'[1]

Sooner than anyone could imagine, Phillips would be
repackaging every Sun track on which Orbison had ever
breathed – 'even just with me and my guitar, so it seemed
that after I did do really well in the business. They wanted
to cash in on it.' All the forgotten ooby-doobyings of his
flaming youth – including a crap try-out of 'Claudette' –

would surface as frequently as rocks in the stream over the next thirty years.

For all the shifty manoeuverings, the former protégé nonetheless found it in him to acknowledge his debt to Sam Phillips: 'I owe Sam so much'. And Phillips, incorrigible and self-glorifying, half-believed the prodigal would return. In 1961, a much wealthier Roy 'went back to Sun studios to pay my respects. Sam just looked at me, smiled and said, "You'll be back." His brother Judd was in the same room. He just looked at me, rolled his eyes and said, "The hell he will."'

During the haggling with Wesley Rose, the composer credits on the majority of Orbison's Sun recordings came to be attributed to Phillips. Leaving aside the question of financial rewards – 'he didn't even pay union rates!'[3] – and the uncertainties of copyright ownership, Sun 'had no publishing outlet, so all of us just had to leave.'[3] In this respect, Roy, for one, landed on his feet with Acuff-Rose, which had grown into a huge publishing concern. The drug-induced passing of its major source of revenue, Hank Williams, had been a body blow but, taking stock, the company and its affiliates would be occupying four addresses in Nashville alone by 1957. And its president, Wesley Rose, received enough supplications to be styled, even then, 'the uncrowned king of Nashville'.

Sure enough such fawning reverence also guaranteed, of course, that Rose was the unconscious victim of innumerable snide remarks in rival offices in 'Music City USA'. Nashville was – and still remains – the Hollywood of country music with, in the words of Buck Owens, 'songwriters under every rock.'[4] The centre of the music publishing business was tree-lined Sixteenth Avenue. Once a residential area, this Tin Pan Alley of Nashville had no high-rise glass towers in the late fifties, but in its environs were clotted music publishing firms by the score – most of them hand-in-glove with the record companies whose studios were within spitting distance.

Talent scouts would make nightly excursions downtown
to view the human goods displayed nightly on nicotine-
clouded stages in truckers' bars and honky-tonks – the true
heart of Nashville. More upmarket were joints like Tootsie's
and Merchant's Lounge along the city's Broadway, nicknamed 'Paradise Row'. There was always an outside chance
of a rags-to-riches leap onto the hallowed boards of the
weekly Grand Ole Opry – which was to the country entertainer as Everest is to a mountaineer. Once your name was
embossed on the garish billboard screaming across the brick
façade of Ryman Auditorium's world of cowboy suits and
rehearsed 'sincerity', the only other way was down.

That the Grand Ole Opry prohibited drummers from
defiling its sacred stage until well into the fifties illustrates
the rigid formality that both the commercial dictates of
Sixteenth Avenue and the conservatism of the Country
Music Association of America had imposed. It was as if
country music couldn't be recorded in any other way or with
any other musicians than that self-contained caste which, as
few of them could read music, improvised the orthodox
'Nashville sound' from a notation peculiar to city studios.
The 'Nashville sound' depended upon its originators' close
knowledge of each other's work through playing together as
sidemen at the Grand Ole Opry and in countless daily record
dates. Afterwards, they might unwind in late-night jam
sessions at Ronnie Prophet's exclusive Carousel Club.

Some of these craftsmen made records of their own.
Among the brightest stars in this firmament were Chet 'Mr
Guitar' Atkins, Floyd 'Mr Piano' Cramer and Boots 'Mr
Saxophone' Randolph. As well as scoring in the country
charts, these three had first refusal of virtually all Nashville
studio sessions until well into the sixties.

In a dramatised film biography of 1979, Buddy Holly
loses his temper during an ill-fated Nashville session in 1956.
As well as suffering the indignity of hearing 'That'll Be the
Day' syncopated with a corny swirl of fiddles and steel
guitars, Holly has been forbidden to play his own electric

Fender by a producer who treats him like an unseasoned hick. Rock 'n' roll, you see, was not considered a natural adjunct of country but a nigger-inspired heresy. No one was deliberately unfriendly, of course, but, unless he toed the line, there was no place in such a closed shop for a rockabilly rebel from west Texas.

A more amenable west Texan than the mercurial Buddy, Roy Orbison was quite open to careers advice from the troubleshooting Wesley Rose in 1958. Since its writer's extrication from Sun's clutches, 'Claudette' had netted over one million sales for the Everly Brothers. At No.30 on the *Billboard* charts, Orbison's song – with his name misspelt on the label – lagged way behind 'All I Have to Do is Dream', but the figure on his royalties cheque would be the same as the Bryants' for their chart-topping A-side.

As if all his birthdays were coming at once, another Orbison song backed Jerry Lee Lewis' 'Breathless', which stood at No.7. Unable to leave anything alone, the Killer had so warped the lyrical gist of 'Go! Go! Go!' that 'Down the Line' became forever the accepted title of what had once graced the flip of 'Ooby Dooby'. Even its composer would one day re-record it under this new name.

With these discreet achievements under his belt, Roy 'made enough money to move to Nashville and it set me up for about a year'. Orbison's gradual migration to the holy city 600 miles away was not, however, a decision taken lightly – or spontaneously. Brought to his knees as he had been by the music industry, Roy kept his options open by signing on as a house songwriter at Acuff-Rose. Although renting a pied-à-terre in Nashville, he still worked mainly from home in Odessa.

Within a few years, the Beatles and other self-created beat groups who wrote their own material would give the institutions of Tin Pan Alley a nasty turn. Prior to this semi-purge, however, the jobbing tunesmith was an indispensable part of the record business. In New York's Brill Building, there was even a songwriting 'factory' where such stars-in-embryo as Carole King and Neil Sedaka won their spurs churning out assembly-line pop for the masses.

Like any self-employed worker, Roy Orbison followed a strict routine. Generally around 8 a.m., he would 'sit down and say, "I'm going to write a song and I don't get up again until I've written it" – not hard when you know you can do it, but I didn't find it like that in the beginning.'[4] After tuning his guitar for the day's labours, 'the title is my starting point and you must have one that conveys the meaning. Ideas come from anywhere.' By early evening, he'd usually had enough.

When he'd accumulated sufficient product, he might submit demo tapes – of guitar and voice only, as with Sun – for consideration by Wesley Rose. Rose, who was now Roy's business manager, would then endeavour to place the items with suitable artists. If in Nashville himself, Orbison might even visit prospective customers and sing the number there and then. Nothing he wrote at that time was as saleable as 'Down the Line' or 'Claudette' had been, but he ticked over with country-pop songs for Sue Thompson, Kris Jensen and other singers on Acuff-Rose's roster. From the company's new London branch came Orbison-penned singles for Gene Thomas and the Allisons, future winners of the Eurovision Song Contest and one of Britain's 'answers' to Don and Phil. His confidence boosted by this distant syndication, Roy put offerings in the way of bigger fish like Burl Ives – international entertainer since the thirties – and Patsy Cline, country queen of the heartbreak ballad who, it was said, could 'cry on both sides of the microphone'.

One day Orbison was attempting to sell a song to Hank Cochran, former partner of, but not related to, Eddie Cochran, a multi-talented Oklahoman Elvis. After Roy had finished, Hank reciprocated by trying to interest the mildly surprised Texan in one of his own. The mistaken assumption that he was still a recording artist was one of several approaches that had given Orbison pause for thought in recent months. Every morning his shaving mirror would tell him that he'd never be Elvis Presley but, as he explained to Wesley Rose, 'Once the singing bug's got you, you always come back'.[2] He'd wistfully drink in travellers' tales from the Everly Brothers and Buddy Holly about touring countries that would always be an outlandish and unreachable prospect to a backroom songwriter, however content and prosperous. He was their age, but while they had climbed hit parades all over the world, Orbison singles hadn't even been released outside North America – though an extended-play record entitled *Hillbilly Rock*, containing four Sun tracks, had leaked to Britain in 1957 and thence to obscurity. With an inner ear cocked to the far-off roar of the crowd, Roy insinuated to his manager that it might do no harm to put out a belated follow-up to his Sun swansong, 'Chicken-hearted', which had been deleted for over a year. Loudermilk still made records, didn't he?

Orbison was no Mr Universe, but Rose conceded that, yes, he *could* sing – and in the pop universe that counted for something. The four Sun singles hadn't excited him tremendously but, not wishing to alienate this promising songwriter, the Uncrowned King of Nashville said he'd see what he could do. Starting at the top, Wesley sounded out Elvis Presley's label, RCA Victor. As he'd anticipated, the recording manager of its Nashville operation – who happened to be Chet Atkins – was glad to oblige such a prominent provider of chart fodder. This consideration loomed large when Atkins agreed to try out Wesley's boy on a couple of 45s . . .

'Mr Guitar' had pulled off some bold strokes recently. Promoted from backing guitarist to Elvis Presley's co-producer in 1958, Atkins had given Presley his head in the arrangements of 'One Night', 'A Fool Such As I' and other numbers from the once incompatible repertoires of country and R & B. Furthermore, he'd seen fit to foist on RCA Charlie Pride, a negro C & W artist which, in those less enlightened times, was tantamount to a contradiction in terms.

By his own admission, however, Mr Guitar was 'a little square, but it helps to be that way'.[5] Partly because he'd breathed the air around Elvis, Atkins was regarded as something of a wonder worker. If he took you on, you stood a fair chance of Making It as long as you 'kept your mouth shut and listened to the musicians. They know what it's all about. Of course, you've also got to know a good song from a bad one.' His involvement with dramas like 'Heartbreak Hotel' aside, thirty-five-year-old Chet as producer leaned towards lightweight tunes with jaunty rhythms – as road-tested in the charts by RCA's own Perry Como, Kay Starr and, more to the point, the harmless bounce of Jim Reeves' mid-fifties smash, 'Bimbo'. With 'Ooby Dooby' to go on, Atkins saw no reason for deviating from this rule when plotting this Orbison youngster's two sessions at the Victor studio on 17th Street and Hawkins.

In later years, Roy would confess to having been 'too much in awe'[5] of Atkins to splutter 'I'd rather not, sir' when presented with 'Seems to Me' (written by Bordleaux Bryant) and 'Sweet and Innocent' – songs as innocuous as their titles suggest – for his maiden RCA single. Bryant's initial impression of Roy was 'a timid, shy kid who seemed to be rather befuddled by the whole music scene. I remember the way he sang then – softly, prettily but almost bashfully, as if someone might be disturbed by his efforts and reprimand him.' Out of his depth in 1958, Orbison was indistinguishable from any other merely competent vocalist under the thumb of a big-shot producer. Even Bryant in retrospect called it 'the turkey of the season', but so lacking in conviction was Roy on 'Seems to Me' that Gordon Stoker of the celebrated Jordanaires – hired as four-part harmony backing – was instructed to sing along in unison behind the timid songbird's left ear.

After 'Seems to Me' bit the dust, Bryant's next effort for Orbison – the Frenchified 'Jolie' was demoted to B-side. Rejected even more emphatically were John Loudermilk's run-of-the-mill 'I'll Never Tell' and Roy's own 'Double

Date', which describes a buddy stealing Roy's girl. On a hunch, Atkins took a risk with another Orbison song. With its rapid-fire couplets, 'Almost Eighteen' was a great improvement on 'Seems to Me'. However, what might have been a fiery if derivative rocker was emasculated by its squeaky-clean and gutless instrumental precision, topped by the chinking of Mr Piano.

Questioning his producer's competence to channel his abilities towards the pop market, Orbison found an ally in Don Gibson, who likewise felt that Atkins' fixed ideas did him no favours. Kicking against these widely practised commercial methods, Gibson's more ponderous style would be summarized in the titles of his biggest hits – 'Sea of Heartbreak' and 'Lonesome Number One' – which, if doomladen and woebegone in content, were neither particularly sentimental nor marred by lip-trembling pathos. Big-eared, chubby and eight years Orbison's senior, Don Gibson played music that was so in keeping with Roy's own artistic frustrations that he would be turning regularly to the Gibson songbook in years to come.

Gibson's standing with RCA in early 1959 was a deal more assured than his young admirer's. During the firm's customary board meeting in New York, it was decided after a single hearing to waive the option on the third Orbison single. As if poor sales for 'Seems to Me' and 'Almost Eighteen' hadn't been enough, the best that Chet Atkins could conjure up next was a depressing little trudge to 'the blue side of town' entitled 'Paper Boy'. It might have helped if Chet could have got him to burst into tears on the tape as Johnny Ray had threatened to do . . .

At the post-mortem in Acuff-Rose, the artist listened quietly as his manager hit the roof. Wesley Rose railed against the shortsightedness of RCA's executive body, its mental sluggishness, and cloth-eared ignorance. Even if he had to dial his index finger to a stub on the phone, he'd set up a new contract for Roy right now. Before the afternoon was out, Rose would prove true to his word. Picking up the

receiver in the Washington office of the newly launched
Monument label was Fred Foster, a man whose will to
succeed was stronger than that of any RCA time-server.
This key protagonist in Roy Orbison's next and greatest
bout of success was the man who, Rose remembered, had
done wonders with Loudermilk's 'Baby Ruth' for George
Hamilton IV back in '56. Without mincing his words, Wesley
Rose wanted to know if Foster had 'ever heard of Roy
Orbison, and I said I'd heard "Ooby Dooby" and maybe
"Rockhouse".'[6] Later, Rose had complained, 'I don't want
Roy on RCA if they don't believe in him.' It was suggested
that Orbison might be an even better proposition on Monu-
ment where everyone (i.e. Foster) fired on all cylinders.

   Fred Foster did not come from a long line of musicians.
Nevertheless, his father's love of music was such that a whole
season's cotton crop from the family farm in the Appalachian
foothills was sold to buy an Edison wind-up phonograph for
his vast record collection. At the age of seventeen, Fred left
home and found a job as a curb manager in the Hot Shoppe,
a fast food drive-in in Washington DC. It was there that he
made the acquaintance of the shop's most flamboyant diner,
nightclub owner Billy Strickland. Through Strickland, Fred
came to put words to melodies from music publisher, Ben
Edelman. Their first effort, 'Picking Sweethearts', was
recorded in 1953 by the McGuire Sisters, a white vocal
group who specialized in watered-down covers of R & B hits
for the pop charts.

   Foster was given a greater incentive to chuck in his rotten
Hot Shoppe job when he was allowed to supervise a recording session for Jimmy Dean and the Texas Wildcats, a combo
then resident in the city's Covered Wagon bar. Although
he'd never produced a record before, it was thanks to Foster
that Dean and his Wildcats gouged a wound in the C & W
Top Ten.

   Fred's path became clear. Within months, he'd talked his
way into a record promotion post with Mercury. Scrambling
up the executive ladder, he transferred his allegiance to the

less confining ABC Paramount in 1955. Though officially a
regional promotion director, Foster would bring to the label
talent he'd discovered on his beat from the east coast to
Texas. Amongst these finds were George Hamilton IV and,
from New Orleans, Lloyd 'Mr Personality' Price, who would
beome one of the best-known R & B stars of the fifties.

Married with children who wanted him home more often
than his interstate journeyings would permit, Fred collected
his cards from ABC for a desk job heading the pop department of J & F Distributors in Baltimore. This settled period
ended in the spring of 1958 shortly after a confrontation with
Walt McGuire, the New York sales manager for London
Records. In the midst of McGuire's tirade about falling
profits in the Maryland territory, Foster patiently pointed
out that out-of-date London artists like warbling David
Whitfield and 'Forces Sweetheart' Vera Lynn had been
drowned in the rip-tide of rock 'n' roll. Stung by this stark
truth, the New Yorker flung down the gauntlet with a door-
slamming 'I'd like to see you do any better, Mr Foster.'

Buoyed by Foster's life savings, Monument opened for
business. In September 1958, the shoestring operation took
off with a reworking of the traditional 'Done Laid Around'
– retitled 'Gotta Travel On' – sung by former Texas Wildcat
guitarist, Billy Grammer. Rising to No.4 in the pop charts,
'Gotta Travel On' enabled Fred to set up another office in
the Nashville suburb of Andersonville. Two more releases
grazed the charts for Monument. Its owner was wondering
where the next hit would come from when Wesley Rose's
call came through. But Roy wondered later whether it may
all have been the result of a misunderstanding. 'I never
embarrassed Fred by bringing it up, but I got the feeling he
thought he was signing Warren Smith – Wesley told him
that I'd cut "Ooby Dooby", and Fred may have thought he
said "Rock and Roll Ruby". We all have genius after the
fact.'[7]

Fred Foster would have been the first to admit that he
wasn't a genius musician – he was just a self-taught producer

who could locate middle C on a piano. He knew what he
liked though. Unlike Chet Atkins and even Don Gibson, he
had little to unlearn in his quest for a new angle. He just
knew that there had to be some way of bringing country
and pop together in a manner acceptable to an audience
that might be biased against one or the other. The
answer was as likely to be found in Roy Orbison as anyone
else.

The responsibility for choosing Roy's debut on Monument, however, was not Foster's. Before signing any formal
agreement, Wesley Rose – still piqued about 'Paper Boy' –
had one stipulation: 'I want you to duplicate the session
Victor turned down because I think it's good. After that you
can do as you please.'[6] For this postscript to the RCA era,
it made sense to solicit the assistance of Chet Atkins – who'd
also played on 'Gotta Travel On' – and book a three-hour
session at the same studio.

With the cancelled master as a useful demo, Foster and
Atkins spiced up the paper boy's declamation that Roy and
his baby were through with a fat inter-verse trumpet section
and Chet's own echo-chambered arpeggios. For the B-side,
another go at 'Double Date' was unworkable so, for want of
anything better, 'Paper Boy' was partnered with some
country clowning exhumed from Orbison's days with the
Teen Kings, in which 'we had this imaginary bug we would
throw on each other – and when it hit you, you had to
shake'.[8]

Deadpan, he outlined 'With the Bug' to Atkins, Cramer
and the other 'Almost Eighteen' veterans, who found him
the same acquiescent shrinking violet. Roy's coyness this
time may have been aggravated by the fact that he'd arrived
late, due to a delayed flight from Texas, for his first meeting
with Fred Foster.

Rather than plant another back-up singer behind him, the
ever inventive Foster came up with a solution so simple that
Atkins wondered why nobody had thought of it before.
Referring to Roy as he would a piece of equipment, Fred

suggested that to enable this soft singer to be heard above
the instruments, why not place his microphone behind some
sort of barrier where it would pick up far less of the band?
After the engineer had found an acoustically compatible
corner, 'we put a coat rack in front of him and covered it
with coats and blankets, and I couldn't see him. Out of that
came the "isolation booth". They reckoned that that was the
first time it was done here in Nashville.'[6]

The taping of 'Paper Boy' might have altered studio
procedure forever – and, as a side effect, alleviated Roy's
painful self-consciousness. However, despite a favourable
review in *Billboard*, Wesley Rose wasn't yet able to thumb
his nose at RCA. Nonetheless 'Paper Boy' created enough
of a stir to jog a few disc jockeys' memories when Orbison's
next one came out.

While 'Paper Boy' bubbled under the Hot Hundred, way
above was 'Three Stars' by a certain Tommy Dee. This alias
for John D. Loudermilk had been assumed to preserve a
little self-respect because, lucrative as it was, 'Three Stars'
was one of those bilious 'tribute' discs that capitalize on a
celebrity's death.

Loudermilk/Dee's whimpering told of the Big Bopper's
elevation to 'new fame and fortune' in heaven but, though
its narrative extended to the also deceased pop star Ritchie
Valens, 'Three Stars' may not have inched to No.11 had not
Buddy Holly perished in the same four-seater plane crash
on 22 February 1959. Before they'd even wiped away the
tears, the moguls of his record company had been forced
into meeting the demand kindled by the tragedy. Rush-
released at the same time was Holly's 'I Guess It Doesn't
Matter Any More'. With a string section taking what had
once been the lead guitar part, it was an enormous hit,
resuscitating a flagging career.

Roy Orbison had hardly known Buddy Holly. All the
same, that fame had cost so dear was a sobering thought for
Roy in his obscurity. When he had first heard of Buddy's
accident – and, after hearing at a party a chilling account

of high altitude engine malfunctions from Elvis Presley –
Orbison had 'sworn that I would never use US charter flight
again unless it was to get a member of my family to hospital
in an emergency'.[9] More than this short-lived sacrifice, it
confirmed what was already a fundamental philosophical
tenet of Orbison's own. To rationalize triumphs and tragedies in his own life, he would 'take the edge off anything that
is supposedly super and, in the same way, with anything
that affects you adversely – have a sort of balance, an
in-between, as opposed to just stepping aside. You must
continue doing things that you normally do. Whatever it is,
continue and then everything comes out fine.'[10]

Mitigating the failure of his records, for example, was a
then happy marriage to Claudette, his muse and the doting
mother of that little rascal, Roy Duane named after guitarist
Duane Eddy. A by-product of the modest acclaim for 'Paper
Boy' was a more promising date schedule. The number of
bookings that once signified a month's work had become a
week's. This meant that Claudette wouldn't operate the
vacuum cleaner until the early afternoon when her husband
woke. Unfortunately the need to sleep off an accumulation of
late nights also necessitated the abandonment of his daytime
songwriting rota.

One major benefit of Roy's becoming a nightbird was that
apart from the occasional baby squalling now and then,
household distractions were reduced to a minimum. Conditions in the cramped apartment during the day had been
such that an irritated bard would sometimes be driven to 'go
outside and sit in the car and write, so that was a lonely
experience . . . I suppose it was a lonely area. There wasn't
much to do there.' As it always would, the cinema provided
solace whenever Roy hit a writer's block. It was while passing
an Odessa drive-in in the autumn of 1959 that Joe Melson
spotted the Orbison Cadillac.

Since the advent of Elvis Presley, there'd been no looking
back for twenty-four-year-old Joe. After leaving the Fannin
County Boys, his championing of rock 'n' roll soon became

audible to the whole district. Backed by the Cavaliers, the singing guitarist's cavortings before the microphone became a common sight in the clubs and high school hops of mid-Texas. The former Fannin County Boy's repertoire had been injected with an even bigger shot of R & B, much of it taken from the shooby-doo-wah school of black vocal groups. With guileless fervour, the likes of the Five Keys, the Pelicans and the Harptones would never shrink from stretching beyond their vocal compass. Joe Melson was also bold enough to insert a few of his own compositions into the set.

If a pop combo attempted anything unfamiliar at that time, dancers were inclined to sit it out, visit the bar or go to the toilet. Normally, the last thing anyone wanted to hear was a home-made song. However, one local impresario, Ray Rush, observed that some of Melson's originals were drawing more than passive attention from the clientele. Largely through Rush's machinations, Melson and the Cavaliers' 'Raindrops', their biggest crowd-pleaser, was released on a Texan label. The altruistic Ray was also the mutual friend who brought Joe Melson to Roy Orbison.

When the introduction was made in the Orbisons' living room, there was no instant rapport. The jovial, open-handed Joe was put off by his host's rather stand-offish manner. The Big O didn't look at you when you spoke to him. In the thick bifocals he'd never worn when stirring the nation with 'Ooby Dooby', Orbison sat dumpily with his wife, drinking nothing stronger than Cola. Far from the Sun wildman Melson had half-expected, the depths of depravity for Roy, it seemed, were twenty filter tips a day. Roy brightened up slightly when Melson complimented him on his singing, but the evening wore on with little more from Roy than polite platitudes, nodding agreement and a puffy smile when Claudette mentioned that she liked 'Raindrops'.

Four months later, Roy wound down his car window at Joe's tap. Over a coffee after the film, Joe then understood that the Big O's supposed aloofness was nothing other than diffidence. When you got him on his own, he was quite chatty. He even cracked jokes. Furthermore, it turned out that Roy liked 'Raindrops' too and 'he thought that if I could write a good song and he could write a good song, we might write a great one together.'[11]

No great one would be written immediately. There was no music-lyrics delineation between Melson and Orbison as there was between teams like Bacharach and David or Gilbert and Sullivan. More often than not, one or the other would have, say, a title, a riff, or maybe even an entire chorus from which a song could grow. They would then spend hours on their guitars, tinkering into the night. The sun would often rise on the two dozing over their instruments. When they became close friends, they developed a style of humour incomprehensible to anyone else – seemingly unfunny remarks would have Roy and Joe howling with hilarity on the carpet and waking the baby. Amongst their private criterions of quality were 'trying to get the mood of the song and the feel of it, the right lyrics. Then we'd play it in the daytime to see if it held up.'[8]

Now that 'Paper Boy' was over and done with, management and record company were drumming their fingers for the next Orbison single. In November 1959, Roy sang four possibilities to Fred Foster in Nashville. 'Pretty One', a mellow ballad from Roy alone was almost-but-not-quite – too much like Presley's 'I Was the One'. 'Blue Avenue'? Hmm, save it for an LP – if we ever make one . . . 'Raindrops'? Not bad. What else have you got?

The fourth choice it was. From Roy's title, 'Uptown', Joe had devised a blues-based strut in accordance with lyrics about a bell hop coveting some Mr Big's floozy. Pinioned by a swatting snare drum, 'Uptown' bore a resemblance to Eddie Cochran's 'Teenage Heaven', but it was nearer to the raucous urban blues contrived in the studios of Chicago – though Roy's restrained drawl added a generous dose of country.

In Nashville, if accompanying harmonies did not belong

to the Jordanaires, they were most likely emitted by choristers led by Anita Kerr, a less ubiquitous mainstay of the 'Nashville sound'. Enhancing the Anita Kerr Quartet's skittish doo-wopping on 'Uptown' was boogie continuo by Mr Saxophone and Mr Piano. An even more significant innovation was the addition of a string section.

The worm hadn't turned completely, but Roy's more convincing singing on the 'Uptown' session betokened his greater say in the running of the operation. Prodded by Joe Melson, he'd 'wanted to use violins, and since I'd had such a rough time at Sun trying to get what I wanted, I was really ready to fight for violins, and Fred Foster said "OK. No problem." Then I think maybe it was all the flavouring and the special musical things that happen on my records came out of my hunger. I'd wanted to do that for a long time and wasn't able to.'

To this unprecedented and determined glint in his artist's eye, Fred Foster had metaphorically touched his cap and scuttled off to confer with the gifted Anita Kerr, who was equally at ease writing string arrangements for the Nashville Symphony or department store musak. The scoring for 'Uptown' would be simple enough, 'but she didn't know if we'd be able to find too many string players in Nashville. It just wasn't being done then.'[6] Anita Kerr rounded up four violinists who could sight-read and were available – two from the city orchestra and a couple of music students.

Bill Porter and Tony Strong, the engineers at Victor's two-track studio, did what they could with double-tracking and reverberation to fatten this sparse endowment. It wasn't anything as dense an accompaniment as that pioneered above the Mason-Dixon line earlier in the year by the Skyliners, the Drifters and, while in New York, Buddy Holly. Strings were now gnawing at songs as much as saxophones and guitars did.

More conventionally, the Nashville violinists fairy-dusted 'Pretty One' – a more reliable sketch of Roy's future direction than its A-side. Taking a leaf from steady Don Gibson's book, he would never stoop to simulating sobs of despair, as Johnny Ray almost had. Needing only to digress into a hitherto unrealized falsetto, Roy Orbison could concoct the same sense of submissive devotion to his 'lovely, unfaithful pretty one' without sounding pathetic.

Notes

1   Veronica Television (Dutch)
2   *New Musical Express*, 20 February 1965
3   *The Face*, February 1989
4   *New Musical Express*, 20 March 1965
5   Chet Atkins
6   Fred Foster
7   Quoted in sleeve notes to 'Roy Orbison: For The Lonely' (Rhino PL2 20574)
8   *Rolling Stone*, 26 January 1989
9   *New Musical Express*, 14 June 1963
10 'On the beat' (Radio Merseyside)
11 Joe Melson

4

The Crowd

'Uptown' reached No.72 on *Billboard*'s pop chart – high enough to keep on hoping. Though this was twenty places behind 'Ooby Dooby' of four years before, Roy Orbison was no longer either a one-hit wonder or a backroom songwriter, assumed at twenty-four to be past it. Indeed, he was looking forward to maturing into 'a middling singer, you know – comfortably off.'[1] With a few more modest hits like 'Uptown' behind him, he'd be in a favourable position to negotiate lucrative and respectable nightclub work – residencies maybe – rather than the thankless slog of one-nighters in back-of-beyond dance halls, gyrating and rolling on his back as the Ooby Dooby man.

With more application than ever, the Orbison organization – star, co-writer, manager and record producer – scrutinized the Hot Hundred because 'if a lot of people have put the records in the charts, there must be something about them. So I always listen carefully and then find out why it's popular. It's no good getting bitter and saying so-and-so's record shouldn't be there.'[2]

In the spring of 1960 pop was at its most harmless and ephemeral; it was doggerel to be hummed, whistled or sung imperfectly by the milkman, while the powers prepared another ditty by reworking the same precept from a slightly different angle.

Following a hit single with records that sounded similar

was especially common in the early to mid-sixties in America. That was why former chicken-plucker Chubby Checker twisted like a man possessed for two years. Soon after Len Barry's breakthrough with '1-2-3' in 1965 came 'Like a Baby', which regurgitated all the salient points of its lightweight predecessor. It was happening in Britain even as late as 1974 when martial arts were all the rage. Carl Douglas zipped into the charts with 'Dance the Kung Fu', three months after 'Kung Fu Fighting' had topped the charts.

Dance-craze records making the charts usually means stagnation in pop. This was certainly the case in Britain at the dawn of the punk era; but much worse was the period from 1960 to 1962 with its endless variations on the Twist, and other maddeningly catchy but entirely inconsequential, assembly-line drivel. The year 1960 alone threw up Brian Hyland's 'Itsy-bitsy Teeny-weeny Yellow Polkadot Bikini', a song which he'd never live down, as well as Perry Como's 'Delaware', which tortuously name-checked every state in the Union: why did Cally 'phone ya?

Most of the fiercest practitioners of fifties' classic rock were by then dead (Buddy Holly, Eddie Cochran), gaoled (Chuck Berry), disgraced (Jerry Lee Lewis), in holy orders (Little Richard), or otherwise obsolete. The Everly Brothers were a year away from enlisting as marines when Elvis Presley was labelled a sergeant and 'all-round entertainer'; his taming was epitomized by Italianesque ballads and infrequent, self-mocking rockers – as if he was almost obliged to humour his old following while at the same time smirking in the direction of the Frank Sinatra 'Rat Pack' who'd guested on his home-coming television spectacular from Miami. With the King of Western Bop's capitulation to show business proper, the grubbing record industry seemed to demand the isolation of what it regarded as his more palatable, all-American aspects.

The hit parades of North America – and, by extension, everywhere else – became choked up with insipidly handsome boys-next-door, all doe-eyes, hair spray and bashful half-smiles. Their forenames and piddle-de-pat records matched – 'Swingin' School' from Bobby Rydell and Johnny Tillotson's 'Jimmy's Girl'. If they faltered after a couple of Hot Hundred entries, queueing round the block would be any number of substitute Bobbies, Jimmies and Johnnies – like stock Hollywood chorus girls hoping to be thrust into a starring role.

There were few sparkles during these years. Bobby Darin scored with a finger-snapping translation of Brecht and Weill's 'Mack the Knife', while the Everlys' lovelorn blue-grass polyphony was still making an impact with 'Let It Be Me' and 'Cathy's Clown'. Tamla Motown, a promising black record label from Detroit, manoeuvred its first fistful of signings into the charts in 1960, while Ray Charles and Fats Domino, without compromising their R & B determination, were still very much Billboard contenders. These, together with throat-tearing assaults on old piledrivers like 'Way Down Yonder in New Orleans' and Kid Ory's 'Muskrat Ramble' by the aptly-named Freddie Cannon, seemed to validate Roy Orbison's argument that 'whatever is the dominating factor of the day, its opposite extreme is never completely submerged, and is always represented to some extent'.[3]

One turn-of-the-decade musical seam noted by Orbison was mined profitably by Jim Vienneau, a young producer based in Nashville. Later taken on board the Orbison ship of state, Vienneau's speciality was overblown melodramas of disaster and torment. Exploiting the public's morbid fascination with death were the likes of Jody Reynolds' 'Endless Sleep' (though the girl is saved), 'Teen Angel' by Mark Dinning – which spent a fortnight at No.1 in March 1960 – and Ray Peterson's car-crash epic, 'Tell Laura I Love Her'. Like dance crazes, a proliferation of 'death discs' exposed periods of pop's creative bankruptcy.

'Tell Laura I Love Her' even prompted the desperate reply, 'Tell Tommy I Miss Him', from Marilyn Michaels. Another 'answer' record was Jeanne Black's 'He'll Have to

Stay' to Jim Reeves' 'He'll Have to Go', in which the Bimbo
Boy dials a girlfriend when she and his rival are entwined
on the sofa. High in the pop charts as these were, their C &
W undercurrent of guilt, infidelity and loss had much in
common with the death discs, and had been anticipated
already in pop. Apart from specific songs like the unhappy
'Danny' (a 'King Creole' out-take) and the Drifters' 'There
Goes My Baby', the 'beat-ballad' (or 'rockaballad' as it was
sometimes known) was pioneered by, and became central
to, the work of certain artists. Amongst these were Conway
Twitty (whose 'It's Only Make Believe' was prototypical),
Don Gibson – and Roy Orbison himself, some of whose
recordings with Sun can now be seen as dry runs for the
sixties. The contrition of 'I Never Knew', for example, was
resurrected in 1963's 'Falling'.

In the Wink Westerners' repertoire had been the fanciful
'Dream' from a Fred Astaire musical, composed in 1944 by
Johnny Mercer. A more distinguished antecedent was the
work of French poet, Gérard de Nerval, whose suicide in
1855 may have been related to confusion arising from his
investigation of the dream as a bridge between reality and
the supernatural. Not quite so earnestly highbrow or self-
immolatory were those who used the dream motif to sell
records in the middle of the twentieth century. Released by
RCA in 1959 were 'Afraid to Sleep' and 'Sweet Dreams' by,
respectively, Chet Atkins and Don Gibson – both artists
who were esteemed by Roy Orbison. That same year saw
Bobby Darin chart-riding with 'Dream Lover', while Johnny
Burnette cracked it in 1960 with just plain 'Dreamin''. On
his third album, Roy would pay respects to the other side
of the disc that established him as a songwriter with his own
version of 'All I Have to Do is Dream'.

From the elements present at the time and from his own
and Joe Melson's hard-won artistic dossier came Orbison's
pedantic rise to pop stardom. An astrologer might have
deduced that he was a typical Taurean in his astute expansion
of another's idea – for it was Melson who devised the 'dum-

dum-dum-dummy-doo-wah' vocal counterpoint from which emerged 'Come Back to Me, My Love' – addressed to a girl who had died on her sixteenth birthday.

This song was among many presented to Fred Foster in Nashville during a short-listing for the next single – which took the best part of a fortnight in the autumn of 1959. Fred thought that 'Come Back to Me, My Love' was too much like the up-and-coming 'Teen Angel', but he liked Joe's dummy-doo-wah bit, which reminded him not so much of the extraordinary background chanting of black vocal groups as the gentle, close harmony of the white boy/girl Fleetwoods he'd seen in Washington. They'd just wended their way to No.1 with 'Come Softly to Me', which had begun with a 'dum-dum-dummy-doo-dummy-doo-bee-doo'.

Another offering from the Melson/Orbison catalogue was one that had already exhausted three provisional (and un-original) titles – 'Cry', 'Why' and 'Young Loves'. The song's verse boasted a lengthy rubato melody, with the phrase 'only the lonely know the way I feel' coming at the beginning of its short chorus. After some discussion, 'I suggested we drop the verse, take the vocal figure out of "Come Back to Me, My Love" and insert it between the lines of "Only the Lonely".' Adhering to this executive brief back in Odessa, Melson proposed that a falsetto should end the final eight-bar crescendo. 'Joe wrote a good bit [of "Only the Lonely"] and he had some of it when we started even. I remember [rehearsing] one day and it was sort of heading up and I just went with it . . . for a baritone to sing as high as I do is ridiculous. It only comes from the fact that I didn't know what I was doing.'[4]

The composers were as unsure of the outcome as the other participants when the 'Only the Lonely' session shifted into gear on 15 April 1960. Potentially the bitty song – or medley – was as trite as any Bobby/Jimmy piffle, given the tinkling piano triplets, the bright string clichés and the rhyming-dictionary lyrics which covered the old ground of romantic bust-up and consequent heartache. There was even a lift from 'There Goes My Baby'. None of this necessarily mattered though. These days you could get a hit with any sort of crap.

To this unappetizing brew was added a transforming ingredient: Roy had found his voice at last. No longer the Sun hillbilly cat or RCA goo merchant, he unfurled a rich, supple purity that, without plumminess, grafted a *bel canto* eloquence onto 'Only the Lonely', investing it with a hitherto unrealized maturity of gesture. By the same instinct that governs street-corner clusters of youths singing for their own amusement, operatic pitch and breath control were Roy's without years of carping tutorials or tedious exercise. He'd stumbled upon a sound reserve that came not from his throat but deeper within. Like a fisherman's tall tale, media hyperbole would extend Orbison's tonal range to an impossible six octaves. Though his vocal daredevilry grew with succeeding records, 'my octave range isn't extremely wide but what I do have is solid and useful'. Even when his untrained diction verged on slovenliness, it only reinforced endearing idiosyncrasies whereby, in the opinion of no less than Duane Eddy, if others attempted to 'sing the songs that he sang, they didn't have the same raw power and the same sound that he created . . . when you thought he'd sung as high as he possibly could, he would effortlessly go higher and finish up with a big finish and it was wonderful.'[5]

More subliminal than the way Roy told it was the augmenting of the Anita Kerr quartet's dum-dumming with the edgy sibilance of Joe Melson, who thought, however, that, although a silk purse had been made out of 'Only the Lonely', it might be more profitable all round if, rather than risk it with Roy's name on the label, a major artist could be persuaded to record it. Five months of peddling, however, had come to nothing. Elvis, for instance, couldn't be bothered to rise from slumber when Roy, tape in hand, had called at Gracelands, albeit at six o'clock in the morning. The Everly Brothers, having found their own feet as composers, passed it up more courteously when Roy had played it to them in the Lubb Studio at Acuff-Rose.

'I don't know . . . What do *you* think?' was the spirit that pervaded Monument's unleashing of 'Only the Lonely' on the crowded wavelengths of North America in June of 1960. And there it nestled uneasily among the likes of 'Robot Man' by Connie Francis and the novelty 'Alley Oop' from the Hollywood Argyles. On the air too were more comparable challenges in 'Lonely Winds' by the Drifters and Don and Phil's 'When Will I Be Loved'.

Little by little, 'Only the Lonely' sneaked into the Hot Hundred's low seventies – where 'Uptown' had peaked – and seemed poised to equal 'Ooby Dooby'. Then an avid chart-watcher, imagine Orbison's exhilaration next week when it shot up thirty places: 'So I knew what was to follow.'[6]

Roy Orbison arrived at No.2, threatening Connie Francis' chart domination. Unlike callow Gene Vincent, whose gladness had come too fast, 'I was fortunate that I had been playing and singing for thirteen years when success came. It touched me deeply but it didn't make me crazy.'[7] Concurrent with its four-month harrying of the US Top Twenty, 'Only the Lonely' also splintered hit parades worldwide, actually climbing to the top in both Australasia and – after a sluggish start – Great Britain, where only the latest from Elvis could drag it down.

He couldn't retire on it, but suddenly there were more dates offered than Orbison could ever keep. Summoned from the ballrooms, Roy made his national television debut on 'American Bandstand', broadcast from Philadelphia, whose purpose – according to its clean-cut presenter, Dick Clark – was 'to reflect what's going on early enough to make a profit on it'. As the new sensation didn't bear even a passing resemblance to Presley, and was, therefore, more perishable than any Bobby, it was prudent to cash in quick by shunting Orbison onto a punishing schedule of coast-to-coast appearances that would drag on for up to three months – Friday

was some kitsch palais on the Bronx; Saturday, the local boy
would make good at the Texas State Fair. Because of the
vast distances and the uncertainties of flight connections,
later he acquired a tour bus with fitted bedroom, TV and
telephone to hurtle more comfortably across the continent.

Those who knew noticed that the on-stage Orbison had
cast aside the awkward, hip-shakin' shufflings of the fifties.
Although rock 'n' roll wildmen were now outmoded, neither
did he go in for the scripted grins or inoffensive playfulness
of the Bobby-type. His future stage act did not take hold
with the same jolt as the new voice, but even on 'American
Bandstand', he gave 'Only the Lonely' no help whatsoever
beyond just singing and strumming its four chords. He let
it fend for itself, 'rather than by selling it with a lot of gesture
and body movement. I'm not a super personality – on stage
or off. I mean, you could put workers like Chubby Checker
or Bobby Rydell in second-rate shows and they'd still shine
through, but not me. I'd have to be prepared. People come
to hear my music, my songs. That's what I have to give
them.'[8] Never again would his self-respect be damaged by
garish 'Ooby Dooby' capering – not when he might yet
fulfil an unspoken ambition to 'do a show of just my own
material.'[5] So far he could rely on the three Monument A-
sides, plus 'Claudette' – and soon the new single, 'Blue
Angel'.

As would be the case with Len Barry and Carl Douglas,
a law of diminishing returns applied to Orbison, whose 'Blue
Angel' and, more markedly, the one after that, 'I'm Hurtin'',
both fell far short of the 'Only the Lonely' precedent
which had gained a platinum disc. 'Blue Angel' was actually
a more substantial song than 'Only the Lonely', but it was
so similar in arrangement that it paid only the most fleeting
visit to *Billboard*'s Top Ten. With a title taken from a Don
Gibson number, 'I'm Hurtin'' battled to an unobtrusive
No.27, while barely registering anywhere outside America.
'Let's not start changing immediately' had been Fred Foster's
counsel, and so the falsetto was transposed and the

melodramatic circumstances shifted. 'Blue Angel', for instance, had suitor Roy comforting a girl who was still carrying a torch for her previous lover – a scenario later re-enacted
by the Beatles in 'Baby's in Black'. Like snatches of kindergarten babble, 'dumdumdumdummydoowah' mutated to
'shalaladoobywahdumdumdumyepyep' then 'dumbydum-
bydumoooyayyay.'

Rather than sticking with the devil they knew, maybe
the alternatives should have merited more consideration.
Perhaps because none were Orbison/Melson concoctions,
their use as A-sides was regarded as a regression. 'I'm
Hurtin'' was coupled with a routine, but not unattractive,
re-run of Don Gibson's 'I Can't Stop Loving You', but a
greater departure from format was the 'Blue Angel' coupling,
'Today's Teardrops', whose composer, a Connecticut teenager named Gene Pitney, was surprised to hear Roy do
it: 'I don't know if I could imagine anyone who would
do "Today's Teardrops" but there were some I couldn't
imagine doing it.' Sticking strictly to the multi-tracked
demo, Orbison's voice was even speeded up mechanically
to resemble more closely Pitney's dentist's drill whinge.
It was a piece that owed much to Buddy Holly's frenetic
'Rave On'.

The paths of Gene Pitney and Roy Orbison crossed only
twice in twenty-five years. According to Pitney, on the
second encounter – at Nashville airport in the seventies –
'we said "hello" and laughed about it because promoters
would never have us out at the same time as it would be
cutting into the same audience.'[9] Stereotyped – as Orbison
would be – as a purveyor of woe, Pitney likewise put in a
generation's hard graft on the road, staggering his sixties
winning streak in foreign sales territories, thus postponing
an undignified demise at home. Another victim of the same
passion and vintage was Del Shannon, a square-jawed hunk
from Michigan whose trademark was an abrupt falsetto.
Stating his intent with 'Runaway' in 1961, Shannon continued his best-selling exploration of small-town soul torture

with the likes of 'Hats Off to Larry', 'Little Town Flirt' and 'Two Silhouettes'.

All three had their professional ups and downs, but when their individual moments came, each one had acquired enough experience of the music industry to outlast the prettiest Bobby without jumping too heavily on passing bandwagons – there was never a twisting Orbison, a psyched-elic Shannon or a punk Pitney. All three had big voices, an understated image and cautious business acumen. Although each made unwise decisions over the years, they alone accepted responsibility for them. While advised by managers and other payroll courtiers, Shannon, Orbison and Pitney were never corporation marionettes. Indeed, they maintained an intense and often unwelcome interest in every link of the chain from studio, to pressing plant, to marketplace.

In 1961, Roy was anxious about his sixth Monument single. Having lost his grip on the Hot Hundred, he was clear-headed enough to realize that 'most of the time, an artist is the last person to know what is best for him. It doesn't follow that a composer should sing his own songs.'[10] This was why in the running for the next A-side was 'Love Hurts' (a title that speaks for itself) from the pen of Bordleaux Bryant. Though they recorded it later for an LP, 'Love Hurts' was another likely smash given the thumbs down by Phil and Don Everly since they'd discovered composing royalties. Roy's became the definitive treatment of this mournful pop standard, which might have been wasted had it B-sided a lesser song than 'Running Scared'.

Once more, born loser Orbison found himself the other man in an eternal triangle. He'd win this one, but his victory might have been only Pyrrhic on account of the quivering hopelessness in Roy's most impressive performance on record so far. More demanding and higher-pitched than any he'd ever tried was the ending of 'Running Scared'. Despite a pep talk from Foster, Orbison puffed several fretful cigarettes in the studio while the musicians tuned up. During the now customary fortnight's preparation for each single, 'it came down to a simple matter of finding the right beat,' recalled Foster. 'I asked him if he knew Ravel's *Bolero* and he said he did not.' With this foreboding rhythm as the pulse, the allotted hour of recording time got under way with Bob Moore's band call. Gaining confidence behind the coat stands, Roy managed what he thought to be a passable take within twenty minutes. He'd swerved into falsetto for that nerve-jangling *coup de grâce* but, since sound technology wasn't yet advanced enough, the engineer had been unable to catch it on the console. Roy would have to belt it out louder. Either that or the orchestra had to play a touch quieter – which clearly wasn't on. Another try and Fred seemed pleased, even if Roy clearly wasn't. 'We've got a good one,' reasoned the producer, 'but I guess we could re-do it. Just go for broke, Roy.' Two minutes after the tape rolled again, even the most grizzled session player was stunned when, from his hiding place, the singer reached that apocalyptic G sharp with his natural voice. A re-take was out of the question.

As well as a cut that everyone agreed was more promising than 'I'm Hurtin'' had been, a blueprint had been established to which the team would revert to most of Orbison's best-loved songs over the next four years. Whether he was playing the part of rejected lover or romantic martyr, Roy's ominous narrative, stripped of all that superfluous dum-shooby-wah nonsense, would build up from apprehensive muttering to ultimately overpowering anguish, each instrumental section being introduced gradually as the lament gained in tension. 'He used such intricate, beautiful melodies,' enthused the catalytic Foster, 'He brought a kind of baroque, classical style to pop music.'[11]

In the spring of 1961, however, all Fred knew was that with 'Love Hurts' and 'Running Scared' he had a record that – if there was any justice on the airwaves – would restore his reputation – as well as Orbison's. With acetates in attaché case, he flew to Chicago to conduct market research around this key territory's radio stations. At WIND, the last port of

call, Howard Miller – then the Midwest's king disc jockey –
said that if Foster left the white-labelled waxings, he'd spin
both of them and take calls from listeners to gauge their
preferences. During a fifteen-minute ride to the air terminal,
Fred learned the result from the taxi radio: hands down, it
was 'Running Scared'. They'd never heard anything like it.

The Windy City's verdict proved correct as the rush-
released 'Running Scared', into the Billboard charts like a
bullet on 10 April, shot to the top of the Hot Hundred before
the month was out, ensuring that its singer's twenty-fifth
birthday was unusually auspicious. As with 'Only the
Lonely', this feat was repeated in varying degrees throughout
the world.

Monument could then afford to declare its independence
of ABC Paramount and, with no middlemen taking a cut,
press and distribute its own product. Furthermore, to para-
phrase 'The Ballad of Jed Clampett', the next thing you
know old Roy's a millionaire – but, as he had long understood, show business was a fickle mistress, ready to fling
him back to 'Ooby Dooby' oblivion at the drop of a seventy-
eight. With this worrying psychological undertow, Orbison
had started investing, wisely but unadventurously, in
middle-range real estate. In this modest bracket had been
the Orbisons' unpretentious first home in Nashville, without
either the obligatory swimming pool or a trophy room for
the breadwinner's disc awards. 'You may not believe this,'
gasped his fan club secretary, 'but Roy likes the simple
life. He gets all the exeitement he wants just shopping for
groceries with his wife.'[12]

Prosperity did not completely alter this uncomplicated
ritual. Roy might not have been too upset if he'd been
condemned to return to the safe anonymity of straightsville
– or worse: 'If I had to go to prison or was shipwrecked,
and I had a guitar, I would go on singing.'[2] Travel refined
him, but part of Roy Orbison would always be the pipe-and-
slippers watcher of American football on TV. Though he
acquired a taste for spicy Indian food, he always preferred

steak and mushrooms. As his fame necessitated longer and longer spells away, he grew to value more than ever 'just being home with my wife and boys. I have a lot of fun with them. And, frankly, I just enjoy getting on some loose rough-and-tumble lounging clothes and relaxing.'[13]

Often the anti-social hours of his profession would turn night into day – he would take breakfast in the late afternoon so that he would be fuelled for composing into the small hours. Another problem was that inspiration would manifest itself when it was least desired. The idea for 'Running Scared' had come from a newspaper headline glimpsed on a flight to New York. Song fragments would materialize in hotel lounges, backstage passages, or when sinking into sleep: 'I wrote a couple of songs in my dreams but I thought they were someone else's.'[14] He kept a notepad and biro beside the bed just in case.

Wherever it came from, the raw song – just voice and guitar – would be transferred onto a domestic tape recorder for elaboration when demos were tried at either Acuff-Rose or, now he could afford it, Orbison's own studio: 'I generally write the bare bones of the song then leave it for two to three months. And if they still hold up, have some value . . . then we think we have something and rework it finally.'[1] Sometimes he would write at the speed of a train, while at others he would sit 'brooding for hours – and absolutely nothing comes'.[15] There were no advance drafts or weeks spent agonizing over a lyric or a chord sequence. 'All my best songs took only half an hour to write,'[6] he once admitted. They were a potpourri of virtually every idiom Orbison and his collaborators had ever absorbed – Mexican, rockabilly, light classical, Zydeco, western swing, the Drifters, Don Gibson – you name it. Untroubled by the do's and don'ts that traditionally inhibit creative flow, there were only habits ingrained since the Fort Worth Defence Plant singalongs to fall back on, although 'I'm sure we had to study composition or something like that at school, and they'd say "This is the way you do it," and that's the way I would have done it, so being blessed again with not knowing what was wrong or what was right, I went on my own way . . . So the structure sometimes has the chorus at the end of the song, and sometimes there is no chorus, it just goes . . . But that's always after the fact – as I'm writing, it all sounds natural and in sequence to me.'[4]

As with 'Cry Guy' Johnny Ray and the surfing Beach Boys, Orbison's initial handful of early hits branded him forever as a specialist in one particular style. Over a quarter of a century later when he volunteered to sing a section of a George Harrison B-side, the ex-Beatle felt he had to 'bung in a sad bit for Roy'.[16] Just as Chubby Checker would always be twisting, so Roy's rut would be grief-stricken ballads – even if on closer examination there was a happy conclusion to the emotional traumas – or, at least, the hope of one. Like Bob Hope, Roy sometimes got the girl. When he didn't, he usually faced desolation with dignity and plaintive sadness rather than self-pity: 'Like "Cryin'" – I didn't mean that song to be taken as neurotic. I wanted to show that the act of crying for a man – and that record came out in a real "macho" era when any act of sensitivity was really frowned on – was a good thing and not some weak . . . defect almost.'[6]

By 1961, Orbison and Melson were ceasing to write to order. Generally, their compositions were registered with Acuff-Rose, who weren't canvassing these days so much as distributing material the pair felt was unsuitable for Roy to eager supplicants. While they never produced any massive money-spinners like 'Yesterday', 'Moon River' or even 'Claudette', there were over one hundred of these rejected compositions recorded by other artists, including one by the longest serving Bobby of them all, Bobby Vee.

Perhaps the last commissioned work, 'Cryin'', developed from 'Once Again', which had been earmarked for Don Gibson. From a casually crooned phrase by Joe, the title became 'I Am Crying'. That very instant, a mental image of an old flame, willowy and heartless, reared up before Roy.

Though it had taken its cue from Gibson's – and, once upon a time, Orbison's own – C & W style, the result that emerged could not be divorced from pop. Even if it would be fifth in an unbroken line of melodious morosities, it was far enough removed – slower and more fragmented – from 'Running Scared' to warrant inclusion on the next single.

In case the masses couldn't tolerate a lachrymose Roy, 'Cryin'' – the 'I Am' was later docked for being 'too country' – was coupled with the infectious R & B bounce of 'Candy Man', which betrayed a carnal side of Orbison hitherto unsuspected by most of the self-doubting adolescents who'd adopted 'Only the Lonely' as an anthem of sorts. Now their blue angel unveiled a laconic snarl on 'Candy Man' in which a crunching rhythm was overlaid with interaction between belligerent electric guitar and slashing mouth organ. This song was the brainchild of two oddly-matched New Yorkers, Beverly Ross and Fred Neil. Ross's breakthrough as a song-writer came with 'Lollipop', a vacuous 1958 chartbuster for the Chordettes, while Neil, a frustrated pop singer, was to surface as a Greenwich Village cult celebrity, best known as the writer of 'Everybody's Talkin'', the theme tune of the Oscar-winning film, *Midnight Cowboy*.

'Candy Man' prowled the US Top Forty for two months, but disappeared long before its vinyl companion which, proving that moonlight and love songs are never out of date, cried all the way to No.2. 'They're therapeutic,' explained the artist of this and his other *cris de cœur*. 'When people hear my songs, they realize they're not in such bad shape after all.'[17]

'Cryin'' had been the only Orbison composition passed by Fred Foster without prescribed alteration. In the studio, weeping violins, wobbling xylophones and menacing tom-toms evoked the picture of one who, after short-lived relief, fought to keep his misery in check when breathing the air round its still tantalizing source. Enhancing 'Cryin'' further were some of many minor tracking and miking experiments that Foster imposed on all Orbison's Monument output.

In later years, Roy would acknowledge that the musically unlettered Fred had been 'the perfect patron for a young artist because his attitude was "Here's the canvas. Here are the paints. Get on with it."'[14] Foster – like George Martin with the Beatles – functioned as Orbison's sounding board, editor and fixer, head-to-head in the control booth with 'the greatest talent I ever worked with',[11] while the session crew awaited instructions.

By 1961, the favoured accompanists on Orbison records – nicknamed the 'A' team by Foster – were drummer Murray 'Buddy' Harman, Floyd Cramer and, depending on the needs peculiar to each piece, a pool of three lead guitarists, Jerry Kennedy, Hank Garland and Gray Martin, anchored by the subordinate rhythm fretting of Ray Edenton. Whatever the line-up, the general supervisor was always Bob Moore, whose double-bass throb was often supplemented by Harold Bradley's new-fangled Framus electric. With the audio synthesizer still a twinkle in Doctor Moog's eye, human additions to this instrumental bedrock required musical scores which, as Roy could barely sight-read, had to be notated – often laboriously – by Moore or Bill Justis as the composer dah-dah-dahed. 'I always felt each instrumental and vocal inflection had to be special . . .' explained Roy. 'I'd spend almost as much time on those as I'd spend on the song itself. Looking back on it now, I feel I was blessed much like the masters, I guess – the guys who wrote the concertos. I'd just have it all in my head.'[14] With finance now less of a restriction, the sparse quartet of violinists roped in for 'Uptown' could be expanded into an orchestral string section of up to twenty players. Roy's 'good luck charm', Boots Randolph ('I'd pay him even if he didn't play'[13]) would head the brass and woodwind section, if one were needed.

Because acoustic separation in the early sixties hinged on primitive, ad hoc measures such as coat racks, the danger of leakage – not to say voice/fretboard co-ordination – precluded Roy's playing guitar on his own recordings. Besides, he could never claim to be an instrumental genius. 'Sufficient,

I suppose,' estimated a later member of his backing group, on 'rhythm – and a bit of lead. Technically, he wasn't very proficient – though his guitar was superb.'[18]

Of the twelve guitars he would own, the six-string most associated with Orbison was his black, semi-acoustic Gibson – but this had been preceded by an expensive, red Gretsch Tennessean. What happened to that one? 'It wasn't much of a guitar, so I took a rubber hammer and knocked the neck off. I was going to put on another one, but it got to be a real job, so I had some professional help and they found another neck for me. Then they put steel guitar pick-ups in and we sprayed it black – it was a new creation, a great guitar. The Japanese wanted to make copies of it. So I let them have it and never got it back: no royalties, no guitar, no nothing.'[19]

That he could shrug off such misplaced trust was an accurate barometer of Roy's grip on the unreal world of the pop star suddenly rich. In common with Elvis, money was no object if the Orbison entourage wanted to watch a cinema film in the middle of the night. The building's proprietor simply had to state a price for re-opening at 2 a.m. for a private viewing. If he was merely peckish in the sort of diner where you were expected to order a full meal, Orbison would satiate his appetite with the soup before telling the waitress not to bother with the other courses – just bring the bill. Biting back his annoyance with one particularly intransigent New York restaurateur, Roy stalked out, only to return within the hour – he'd bought the place for the sheer pleasure of sacking his aggressor. If such free spending was ever mentioned in the gossip columns, it used to be accepted – even lapped up – by the fans as the prerogative of glamour.

There was much apologetic bowing and scraping in one London showroom when a careless salesman's scornful re-mark about pop singers having too much money led the offended Orbison to re-consider the purchase of a Rolls-Royce limousine. Roy's obsession with automobiles became such that 'if he saw a vintage car he liked on the road, he'd chase it and make the owner an offer he couldn't refuse.'[18]

A Lord Montagu in microcosm, by 1966 he'd accumulated enough antique vehicles to consider founding a museum in Houston: 'Maybe my old car mania will end up like my diamond rings. Those rings just get bigger and bigger so I couldn't carry them round on my little finger any more.' Housed either outside on asphalt or in one of his three-car garages, the Orbison collection ranged from a rickety 1916 Ford to the tarnished splendour of von Ribbentrop's staff Mercedes.

The acquisition of the executed Nazi ambassador's property gave some piquancy to the self-improving Texan's continued study of contemporary military history in the pages of such standard works as William Shirer's *The Rise and Fall of the Third Reich* and the four volumes of Churchill's *Memoirs*. These and many other books would fill the library of the opulent, ranch-style family home to be built on a tree-shrouded 11,000-acre plot overlooking Old Hickory Lake in the postal district of Hendersonville. Although habitable by 1961, its planned extensions and structural idiosyncrasies – including a cavernous music room, the waterfall for the entrance hall, the living-room swimming pool, the hydraulic lift to the beach where Roy would go angling or piloting his speed boat – would take years to complete.

At the touch of a button, their father would amuse Roy Duane and Tony by winging his radio-controlled model Spitfire high over the lake. This toy was the *pièce de résistance* of a squadron of miniature aircraft worth a small fortune. Of his and Claudette's more adult pastime of motor-biking, he enthused, 'It's a thrill, a pure joy – and a health factor.'[20]

To cater for the more immediate needs of stomach and household, Mr and Mrs Orbison would journey more serenely by Volkswagen to shops in Hendersonville, a township whose municipal pride reflected that of Nashville, the 'Music City,' twenty miles south-west. As well as its public holiday in honour of Jim Reeves, once its most renowned addressee, Hendersonville had also been the birthplace in 1918 of Eddy Arnold, another of RCA's paladins of sweet-corn.

On either side of the Orbisons lived Johnny Cash – who was gradually assuming Hank Williams' crown as both enter-tainer and drug abuser – and Bob Luman, an older acquaint-ance from Texas who had crossed over to the pop charts in 1960. Despite a continuing tendency not to plug C & W on pop radio, Johnny Horton, Skeeter Davis and Jimmy Dean would also notch up entries in the Hot Hundred. Yet living and recording in the environs of Nashville was not an auto-matic guarantee that a pop record would find its way onto the C & W stations' playlists – as the eventual exclusion of the Everly Brothers, Brenda Lee and Conway Twitty demonstrated. They – like Jerry Lee Lewis and Elvis – were thought to have somehow reneged on their roots by their unremittent wooing of pop consumers.

Apart from a one-shot duet with Emmy Lou Harris in 1980, not once did Roy Orbison ever make the country charts. However, though his had been the city's first major pop record success, the Nashville élite were not as derisive of Orbison as might be imagined. After all, he had served under the revered Chet Atkins, chosen his pickers from the 'Nashville sound' hard core, and had always said of his songs that 'they are derived from and influenced by true country music'.[10] To an amused cheer, he even got away with perfor-ming on a Nashville stage in a mickey-taking cowboy outfit. Indeed, it didn't seem at all strange to Hank Snow, Skeeter Davis and Bob Luman when Roy joined them on a tour of Canadian music fairs.

At the Winnipeg stop, nineteen-year-old Neil Young, the son of a local journalist, was in the audience and was enormously inspired by what he heard. In fact, he would carry the contradiction of enjoyable depression to absurd lengths with the coming of the 'Woodstock Generation' in the later sixties.

Perhaps it was through his father's connections that Young

got to see the show at all. Most of the Canadian venues were semi-private functions in which music was incidental to the wheeling and dealing of the promenading entrepreneurs. Consequently, the entertainers' approach to their tasks was less intense. At one or two of the venues, the onlookers were neither seated nor silent and, to make matters worse, the bands played virtually in the round, bereft of curtains or light show of any kind. Competing against the stadium's other attractions, it was necessary for singers to address the passing crowd. Disquieted by this, Orbison picked the brains of his musicians for some ad lib one-liners. 'We got together some really corny one liners like "I've just flown in from England and my arms are tired" – that kind of hick joke.' Prior to Orbison's entrance, his group cranked out fifteen minutes of instrumentals 'and the drummer did all the gags. Then Roy came out and did exactly the same lines. We were falling about and he's looking round and wondering what's happening.'[18]

Chuckling along with such pranks against himself, Orbison proved an amiable, considerate employer – one who'd stand a round from the crew, smiling quietly at dirty jokes and monotonous accounts of the previous night's carnal antics. He usually confined himself to the role of the tolerant observer of human folly, though one calamitous evening in a Las Vegas casino resulted in Orbison's renunciation of roulette – just as he had denied himself spirits after that first and only youthful slug of whiskey.

As the principal asset of what was now grandly titled 'The Roy Orbison Show', he was above petty jealousies, and could lend warm and generous encouragement to his backing musicians. Enlisted in January 1962 to strum chords alongside John Rainey Atkins' lead guitar was Bobby Goldsboro, a Floridan just turned twenty-one, in whom Roy saw much of his former self.

The onset of puberty had found Goldsboro looking for an opening in pop; but as an Auburn University undergraduate he'd been heedful enough both to keep up with his studies and to freelance on guitar with the various combos that worked the clubs in and around the campus. His exhausting but exciting three-year apprenticeship with the Orbison band was to have a long-term beneficial effect. Backstage and in hotel rooms, Goldsboro would tinker with tunes and lyrics, often seeking the guidance of the easy-going Orbison, who was impressed enough to co-write material with him. Two Goldsboro/Orbison numbers, 'Stand By Love' and 'Baby's Gone' were even recorded by Gene Thomas.

That such a liaison could come into being was indicative of Joe Melson's growing disenchantment with his role in the wayfaring Roy Orbison Show and its negligible rewards. When his brief spot was announced, he'd bound into the spotlight to rattle off 'All Shook Up' or something similar, plus his own latest single, be it Phil Everly's 'What's the Use' or his own 'No One Really Cares'. Both titles too aptly summarized Joe's diminishing hopes of a hit record and, inevitably, the parting of ways with Roy Orbison. One development that had particularly embittered him was that the economics of many future ventures – especially tours outside North America – were to exclude all the stalwarts of the Roy Orbison Show – barring the star himself, of course. He'd use a pick-up band and be supported by local heroes.

Orbison first set foot on foreign soil in the spring of 1962 during a whistle-stop tour of Australia. Concerts in Melbourne, Sydney and Brisbane – playing alongside rough diamond Johnny O'Keefe, Down Under's answer to Presley – culminated in a slot on the national TV broadcast, 'Bandstand', amongst whose regulars was a trio of brilliantined brothers called the Bee Gees.

Visits to Australasia invariably added inches to the Orbison waistline. No longer the college pudding he'd been in the fifties, he was, nevertheless, too self-conscious of his figure to wear jeans. However much his weight dropped, the most flattering of camera angles could rarely hide the penumbra of the double chin, the puffy jowls and the doughy complexion. Like gawky Buddy Holly before him, Roy's soft-focused features *sans* spectacles would adorn the early record sleeves. Even when encircled by encroaching shadow on one EP cover, no photographic miracle could make Roy's face his fortune.

The advice Jerry Allison of the Crickets once gave to Buddy Holly was then practised by Orbison: 'If you're going to wear glasses, then really make it obvious you're wearing glasses.'[21] Thus, offsetting Roy's amorphous pallor would be a huge pair of black hornrims. Mothballed forever were the seedy, flash rockabilly duds of yore. Instead, Orbison garbed himself in sombrely tailored suit, plain shirt and slim-jim tie. Never coy about his marriage and children or a liar about his age, he would always retain, as one French correspondent put it, 'all the characteristics of an office worker'.[22] As if corroborating this observation, Roy had once commented, 'I'll probably be on the administrative end of the business in about three years. I'll have plenty to do.' This level-headed forecast would forever be held in check by the unexpected longevity of the unprepossessing Orbison's performing career.

On Elvis Presley's recommendation, Cockney pop singer Tommy Steele had caught Orbison's act well before it was seen in Britain. After the instrumental opening, the pro-claimed 'Mister Roy Orbison' strolled centre-stage to begin a tentative 'Only the Lonely'. Appearing to Steele 'like a mechanical mole, I sat and hoped that he wouldn't be great – he *couldn't* be, not looking like that . . . But he *was*! Once into the lyric, he had me – the rhythm and the tune all added to the magic of the moment.'[23] Belying the off-stage Orbison, stoic deliberation evoked by the hits accentuated the intro-spection of one so bound up in tragedy that every hypnotic utterance seemed to have been wrenched from his very soul. So 'gone' was he when in performance that even a fire in the theatre's stalls was no distraction on one occasion: 'It wasn't gallantry or anything but I could concentrate on my perform-ance and forget the smoke.'[23]

Thrown together on an aeroplane flight, Roy and Georgia

soul-shouter Otis Redding had once mulled over the feasibility of cutting an album together, even bestowing upon it the provisional title of 'Big O – Black and White Soul'. That a project like this could be contemplated seriously was because Orbison was also a soul singer. The scarcity of instrumental breaks might have obliged him to remain close to the microphone; but Roy's stationary stage persona was as contrived as Redding's hammy exhibitionism. Yet, beneath these trappings, both artists did much more than just put on the agony for the audience. Even after years with his name in lights, Roy would never assume that he would be acclaimed automatically. Never delivering less than his utmost, 'I'd always wait until I reached "Only the Lonely" before I stopped being a bundle of nerves.'[24]

It was symptomatic of Orbison's diffidence – as well as his dowdiness and meagre teen appeal – that the picture on the front of his second LP showed not a portrait of the artist but a theatrical mask in keeping with its title track, 'Cryin''. Most pop stars were geared for the singles market until the close of the decade. Albums containing a best-selling single could still do well – in the States especially – even if they were short on needle time and padded with previously released B-sides, forgotten flops, hackneyed showbiz standards, stylized 'originals' and sometimes even time-consuming instrumentals. Some were driven to copying their rivals' current smash hits – as did Johnny Tillotson with 'Only the Lonely' and Bobby Vinton with 'Cryin''. Roy attacked three Everly Brothers' hits with more assurance, even re-arranging 'Bye Bye Love' for a fuller production which incorporated pizzicato violin arpeggios – translated across the Atlantic as 'Stringbeat' by Adam Faith who tore up the British charts with this conceit.

Albums circa 1962 were often haphazard programmes rather than rounded entities in some logical order. They served as singles' chasers, displaying nothing more than an artist's 'versatility', and of no real musical value. Good looks and vibrant personality could render the fans uncritical enough to digest what was, frankly, substandard produce. This may explain why, in an age when some record companies would schedule as little as six weeks between an artist's albums, Roy Orbison's steady output of one album per year from 1961 to 1963 testified more to quality than commercial pragmatism. Nonetheless, it was not until 1966 that a compilation of his greatest hits would earn him a gold disc in this field.

Like everyone else, Roy looked to his Hot Hundred entries as the chief selling point for the albums. Though they may have been stuffed with old chestnuts like 'Cry', 'My Prayer' and 'Beautiful Dreamer', his versions of these numbers had been honed and perfected in hick dance halls over the years, stretching back to the days of the Wink Westerners.

Rather than merely regurgitate old material, however, Orbison leaned more on his and Melson's efforts, as well as on those of other professional songwriters such as Gene Pitney ('Twenty-two Days') and Lee Pockriss, whose made-to-measure 'House Without Windows' was a distinct improvement upon his 'Itsy-bitsy Teeny-weeny Yellow Polkadot Bikini'. Wesley Rose contributed 'No One Will Ever Know', which fused the story line of 'Cryin'' with a familiar bolero beat, while Joe and Roy re-wrote the atrophied 'Come Back to Me, My Love'. There were other re-cycles of this kind together with such image-boosting titles as 'Blue Avenue', 'Loneliness' and Kitty Wells' 'Lonely Wine', in which Roy's tipsy musings can be seen as a sequel to 'Wedding Day', the saga of a jilted bridegroom and the nearest that Roy as a recording artist would ever come to lip-trembling pathos. By contrast, 'Sunset' and its companion piece, 'Nightlife' – which lived in its stalking horn riff – have Roy rubbing his hands in anticipation of a tryst beneath the stars. Probably too *risqué* (and under-produced) for a single was his captivation by the wanton 'Gigolette', in which Roy makes the transition from forewarned pleasure-seeker to beguiled victim, insinuated by seductive fiddle and a swirling latinate melody.

Returning to the more mundane realities of the Hot Hundred on which his income would always depend, it was not with his own song that Orbison first dabbled in the symbolism of dreams. Cindy Walker's upbeat 'Dream Baby' equalled 'Cryin'' in the number of records sold. It also broke the pattern of plodding vinyl misery that had hounded Roy since 'Only the Lonely'. Mooning over his dream baby, his eventual happiness is by no means guaranteed, but he's egged on by a skittish girlie chorus and packing-case snare drum in an instrumental accompaniment more subtle than in the ballads. The rasping saxophone, for example, intrudes only at the end which, for once, fades rather than climaxes. Nancy Sinatra's smash of 1966, 'These Boots are Made for Walking,' noticeably echoed the introductory double bass and jogalong acoustic guitar of 'Dream Baby'.

However successful it may have been in the charts, the use of a non-original as an A-side seemed to emphasize further the deterioration in the professional relationship of Roy and Joe. Prompted by family commitments and unabated disgust at the shabbier depths of the music business, Melson gradually withdrew from the Orbison cabal, though they remained friends. This impasse took place at a time when Roy's second career peak was beginning its downward spiral with 'The Crowd', which could only manage the lower reaches of the Top Thirty. With its martial tempo, stop-start arrangement and hackneyed grandiloquence, it was a deterioration in quality, let alone sales, and a reminder of how great 'Running Scared' had been in comparison.

This breath of stale air set Orbison off in a desperate search for creative stimulation. Without Melson at his side, it would be thirteen months before he struck gold again. Bound to four singles a year both by contract and the needs of the time, his coterie decided to take a shot in the dark over Christmas, 1962 with two sides penned solely by Roy – 'Working For the Man', which harked back to Sam Cooke's back-breaking 'Chain Gang' of 1960, and 'Leah', a stand-by death disc. After much um-ing and ah-ing, two finished

masters from the Melson era had been put in cold storage –
a rather languid item entitled 'Blue Bayou', and the anach-
ronistic 'Lana' which, like 'The Monster Mash' of that same
year, substituted euphonium for bass guitar.

A few months earlier, a John D. Loudermilk B-side,
'Darling Jane', had concerned a honeymoon drowning.
Laughable though it may have been with its convoluted
rhyming and offhand angst, it is likely that this number,
also published by Acuff-Rose, may have sparked off the
abundantly superior 'Leah'. 'Working For the Man' was
technically the A-side, but the tear-jerking 'Leah', deserv-
edly, rose higher in the charts. The floating marimbas and
pattering tenor drums, together with a ghostly choir and
Hawaiian guitar, captured to perfection the underwater
world, the ambivalence of a pearl diver's nightmare, and his
sweetheart's unspecified but watery doom. In the death, it
is Orbison's vocal outpouring in the keening, one-word
chorus that intimates the singer's yearning for the lost Leah
is too deep for satisfactory verbal articulation. 'Leah' would
be in Roy's set at the last concert.

'Working For the Man', however, wouldn't be. 'Rather
mediocre' was the verdict of one reviewer: 'pounding beat
and little else'.[24] In retrospect, this seems harsh since this
jumping, modernized cottonfield holler – enhanced by appo-
site grunts and moans – is still quite danceable and succeeds,
in less than 2½ minutes, in condensing a plot with the
complexities of a soap opera: a labourer's homicidal hatred
of his tyrannical paymaster is tempered by the love-struck
attentions of the latter's daughter, which the overworked
hand intends to exploit in an intended takeover bid . . .

This diversionary tactic of a single spread itself thinly
enough to eventually shift a million copies, without ever
actually breaching America's Top Twenty – though, of all
his records, it was the one that first struck oil for Roy in
France. Yet for all that, the less than spectacular showing
of these last two 45s signified that, unless Roy Orbison

received another 'Running Scared' godsend, a career as 'a middling singer' might be beckoning still.

Notes

1 *New Musical Express*, 20 February 1966
2 *Melody Maker*, 24 October 1964
3 *New Musical Express*, 30 April 1964
4 Veronica Television (Dutch)
5 *Tribute to the Big O*, Radio 2, 5 January 1989
6 *New Musical Express*, 20 December 1980
7 *Q*, February 1989
8 *Hit Parade*, July 1963
9 *Record Collector*, April 1988
10 *New Musical Express*, 22 March 1963
11 *Country Music Round-up*, January 1989
12 *New Musical Express*, 12 April 1963
13 *New Musical Express*, 12 March 1966
14 *The Face*, February 1989
15 *New Musical Express*, 30 April 1964
16 *Kaleidoscope*, Radio 4, 30 November 1988
17 *Evening Post*, 7 December 1988
18 Barry Booth
19 To *Spencer Leigh*, Radio Merseyside
20 *Daily Express*, 2 May 1966
21 *Buddy Holly*, J. Goldrosen (Granada, 1979)
22 *Special Pop* (ORFT, 1968)
23 *Daily Mail*, 8 December 1988
24 *Melody Maker*, 6 September 1988

5

Distant Drums

If Roy couldn't come home, then a home of sorts came to him. More often than not, he'd be arm-in-arm with Claudette when he stepped off a plane. After 1963, flash bulbs would frequently catch Roy Duane too, clasping Mummy's hand and looking proud of Daddy's celebrity. Shielding the lad from the nicotine clouds, rude words and late nights on the road, Claudette preferred to commute occasionally to her husband's places of work from some central location. For his second British tour, for example, the Orbisons decided on a Victoria Embankment apartment within spitting distance of all the sights of London – St Paul's, Big Ben, Westminster Bridge and the wonderful British bobby. Roy even engineered a few uninterrupted free days before the first show on 28 September 1963, so that he could soak up a little of the history of London and she could browse around the West End stores.

During his first round-Britain trek only three months earlier, Roy's exhilaration when a Spitfire zoomed above the tour bus had bemused John Lennon, a singing guitarist with one of the other acts. Boredom may have set in had Lennon accompanied Roy to the Imperial War Museum, where the American wandered for hours, lost in wonder at this Lancaster bomber nose section and that Volksturmmann rifle mechanism. He splashed out on the inevitable vintage car to be shipped back to Hendersonville, but time restrictions and wishful thinking forced several disappointments: 'I would have loved to see Sir Laurence Olivier in a play; I intended to visit the Tower of London; I wanted to visit a big car factory . . . But most of all, I would have liked to meet Sir Winston Churchill – just for the pleasure of shaking that great man by the hand.'[1]

This endearing naïvety was indicative of Orbison's captivation with Britain. His love affair with these islands overruled even the financial realities of touring. 'I can earn three times the money I make in England by just carrying on working at home . . . by the time all the expenses are paid and I've paid the band, it's not worth all that much to me.'[2] There was also the cold and the rain; the overpriced lard and chips in fly-blown wayside cafés with no public toilets; the toytown currency; the unfinished motorways; only two television channels; and, except in the poshest lounge bars, no ice in your Coca-Cola. What Yank couldn't help but adore the place? Female traffic wardens called you 'love'; cigarettes could be purchased in ten-packs; and pubs were more than just places where guys got drunk. From the bluster of the States, Roy would always look forward to Britain's more sedate pace of life.

Sometimes, he'd cross Britain up to three times a year – as he did in the twelve months from May 1963. However, unlike such dissimilar Anglophiles as the outrageous P. J. Proby, blues pianist champion Jack Dupree and actress/singer Marsha Hunt, it was not in the less financially vulnerable Orbison's long-term interest to make Britain his home. Besides, with the architect putting the finishing touches to their dream home in Tennessee, Claudette's appetite for travel was evaporating.

Roy Orbison had given his first public performance in the United Kingdom, unannounced and free of charge in the reception area of Mayfair's Westbury Hotel. On an unseasonably cool June afternoon in 1962, he and a pick-up group had run through ten numbers – including, naturally, his new single and his most recent hit – before a few score fan club members and the handful of journalists who were still around after the press reception in the Americanized establishment's Mount Vernon room. Along with attending a Decca Records awards ceremony for easy-listening maestro Henry Mancini later that week, Orbison's 'impromptu' concert was part of a public relations strategy to be employed on other occasions during his European business trip with manager and producer to view market conditions and meet major distributors: 'It's one of my ambitions within the next two or three months to really consolidate the world market for my records.'[3]

Prior to his regular appearances in England, Roy's 45s did less well in the British charts than at home – with the notable exceptions of 'Only the Lonely' and 'Dream Baby'. 'I'm Hurtin'' missed the charts completely, while 'Workin' For the Man' died after only one week in the Top Fifty. However, it was in this minor sales territory and jumping-off point for more lucrative continental killings that Roy found an audience who would support him unswervingly through a decade of hits and into the resulting nether world of cabaret. Barring the remote Elvis, Orbison came to command the most devoted British following of any American pop star and he would be the only one to top the UK charts during the fifteen months after Presley's 'Return to Sender' was dislodged by Cliff Richard, his principal English rival. Both Elvis and Cliff would be shovelling out a greater proportion of potboiling ballads and banal musical films of cheery unreality than Roy Orbison when confronted with the rearing monster of Beatlemania and its aftermath.

Rather than beat a calculated retreat from the pop mainstream – or adjust his style towards ersatz Merseybeat – Roy 'did very much what I like to call "my truth" or my real thing and not follow or get thrown by whatever comes along. I thought maybe in '64 I could have been swamped by the Beatles and people, but it turned out the other way round and I was voted number one male vocalist in '65 [in a British music press popularity poll].'[9] In March 1964 – that month of the first ever all-British Top Ten – Associated Television contracted Orbison to headline two 'Sunday Night at the London Palladium' spectaculars and, for a record-breaking fee, his own forty-five-minute 'Roy Orbison Show' in the autumn.

Pop is an erratic business. The most arbitrary isolation can change the whole course of an artist's career – a sore throat at an important audition; Brian Epstein turning up when you're valiantly overrunning because the main attraction hasn't sobered up yet; a top disc jockey flipping his lid over the B-side of your record and spinning it into the charts. In 1965, Dave Berry, a vocalist from Sheffield, Yorkshire, suddenly found himself the Presley of the Flatlands after a comparative flop at home became Holland's biggest selling disc ever. In that same year, P. J. Proby's fall from grace was precipitated by his too-tight trousers splitting from knee to crotch during a second house at the Luton Ritz.

Variables as bizarre as these intruded upon Roy Orbison's professional life too, but his profound success in Britain cannot be explained away so tidily. Leaving aside the relatively small hard core of fans who'd buy before listening, whether Roy's records sold or not depended almost entirely on their commercial suitability, though he sustained and often increased interest in his output by constant touring and scrupulously plugging each current release on television and radio. In an age when he and his peers were only as big as their latest single, it was binding on Roy to balance cash amassed in the hit parade with his self-image as a creative artist. Later and less well-loved singer/songwriters would be able to convince their fans that 'Top of the Pops' excursions were of marginal importance when compared with their main body of work on albums. At least Roy was no such snob; in the mid-sixties, he couldn't afford to be. Plugging 'Borne on the Wind' on the BBC Light Programme's 'Saturday Club' was all part of a day's work.

The acceptance of Orbison as an honorary participant in the British beat boom was partly because, as Alvin Stardust

– then 'Shane Fenton' – admitted, 'None of us could sing,
but some got the breaks and some didn't.'[4] One of the few
exceptions was Ray Phillips of the Nashville Teens who,
during the group's season at Hamburg's Star Club, won
frauleins' hearts with his note-for-note copies of 'Cryin''
and 'In Dreams'. He and others such as the elegant Colin
Blunstone of the Zombies and Cliff Bennett, leader of the
Rebel Rousers, were all deprived of the acclaim they deserved because they belonged to bands that lacked 'image'.
One whose backing combo faded away the moment he
scented success was Welshman Tom Jones – a favourite
singer of Orbison's. Like Roy, he was blessed with a most
professional projection, flexible vocal command and a certain
steady consistency – 'squareness', some would say – that
wasn't effeminate or subversive like some of those bloody
long-haired guitar groups. Moreover, the likes of the Beatles
and Rolling Stones 'couldn't sing'; not 'real singing' like Roy
Orbison.

Though this intimates that Orbison was idolized only by
older pop consumers who had been disenfranchised by the
Big Beat, the fact that he was also a songwriter who scorned
on-stage ostentation merited the respect of both ducktailed
Rocker and backcombed Mod.

Predictable as he became – and, to many, irritating in his
later refusal to give encores – no one could complain about
the quality of the performances. It was like expecting a
racing bike for your birthday and getting one. 'He didn't
have to introduce any songs', reminisced one of his British
musicians, 'because he'd be confidently aware that they
would know, and the reaction was always the same – an
initial burst of applause that would then subside. Then he'd
say no more than "thank you so much" or "mercy!" And if
he did introduce the next song, it'd be no more than "here's
a song . . ." Lack of verbal contact seemed to add to the
nature of the performance.'[5]

A crucial supplement of the introspective Orbison persona
were the striking Ray Ban Wayfarer sunshades he was

obliged to wear on stage for the first time on the opening
date of that first British tour: 'I found myself getting photographed, and when the pictures went around the world,
everyone commented on my [sun] glasses. From that day,
I decided to stick to glasses. When I don't want to be
recognized, I take the dark glasses off.'[6] With a gimmick as
distinctive as the Beatle fringe, Manfred Mann's beard and
Johnny Kidd's eyepatch, further UK visits brought gradual
refinements of this image. Out went the bank clerk threads;
in came five-inch Spanish heels, high-waisted trousers and
puffed-sleeve jerkins. Apart from intermittent medallions
and his gold wedding ring, every sartorial detail – socks,
watchstrap, buttons – had to be bible-black. Sometimes he'd
sport biker gear – though leather made him sweat. Of course,
it is incumbent upon any entertainer to take heed of his
public image. However unintentionally, Roy – who leaned
towards green garments off-duty – had stumbled on one that
worked and 'once you become successful, you don't want to
change anything too drastically, so I sort of stuck with all
that, but it wasn't anything I designed.'[7]

In its full flowering, Roy's mid-sixties' stage act was as
preordained as James Brown's cloak-laden Grand Exit or
Screaming Lord Sutch's cartoon horror. After the master of
ceremonies build-up, you'd hear a lone guitar strumming the
'Running Scared' bolero as the curtains parted in dream-like
slow motion. On a stage lit only by tiny amplifier bulbs, a
pencil spot would fade in round the central microphone. A
murmur would arise, swelling into unacknowledged hero
acclamation. This wasn't television or an LP sleeve mug
shot: veiled in flesh but impenetrable, The Big O was
actually there. Embarking on the first verse, and accompanied only by the strumming of his own guitar, this
weird cynosure of all eyes would seize possession of the
audience as the boards filled with light and the orchestra
struck up behind him.

Clustering towards the front might be fascinated Quant-
cropped dollybirds to whose bolt-upright boyfriends Roy

Orbison did not represent a threat. A good few of them would also rush up the aisles to gape at one who was as erotic as a favourite uncle.

Because he was neither sexy nor sinister, you didn't mind your girlfriend signing letters 'Orbisonly yours'. His was the sombre side of Freddie Garrity's coin. For all the smash hits they clocked up, both were four-eyed and unglamorous. Although 'Dream Baby' had once been in the Beatles' repertoire, Freddie's was one of the few acts at Liverpool's famed Cavern Club to include Orbison numbers. Nevertheless, although Freddie Garrity was just as 'professional' and mindful of the paying customer as Roy, the trouser-dropping chief show-off of Freddie and the Dreamers was never as dignified in the teeth of the hooliganism that was ever present on the package tours. Orbison even kept his cool when 'someone leapt on stage at Newcastle and whipped his specs off. He was at a bit of a loss. It's a severe loss of part of the image, isn't it? So he went and got another pair. He made no comment on it. He just took it as part of the index of possibilities of what might happen.'[4]

While deploring the Geordie souvenir hunter's conduct, this travesty of legitimate admiration may be seen as an attempt to penetrate the mystique that Orbison generated for the ordinary British fan. What's he like? Is he blind? Albino? Does he never talk to anyone? What's with the black outfit? What is he *really* like?

Building on Roy's monochrome precedent, later 'men in black' such as Lou Reed (who pioneered black male lipstick), the sleazy Stranglers and ghoulish Dave Vanian of the Damned tended to affect a sullen, moody intensity off stage too. The more conservative fan was delighted to discover that Orbison did not live the part; the brooding aura vanished as soon as he ambled into the wings after the final bow. Smiling indulgently, he let a giggling Marianne Faithfull remove the famous sunglasses in one backstage corridor encounter because she'd 'always wanted to see what he really looked like'.[7] He didn't mind a bit when a snap of this 'unveiling' –

as Marianne called it – was splashed across *Melody Maker* in February 1965.

Back in 1962, however, Roy Orbison had been the one thought least likely to garner such coverage in six months – let alone three years' – time. When his maiden British tour was under discussion, promoters Danny Betesh and Peter Walsh – who was to name his Surrey home 'In Dreams' – were so dismayed by their subject's homely looks and staid demeanour that they questioned whether a television slot beforehand wouldn't damage the ticket and record sales. Echoing this argument, impresario Tito Burns would 'never forget my feelings on seeing Roy's photo after agreeing to present him here in Britain. After all, this was the era of the good-looking boys like Cliff, and here was, let's face it, an older person wearing tinted spectacles, singing slow, sad songs who, I understood, didn't move a muscle on stage.'[8]

Even when posing for camera shots without his glasses at the Westbury Hotel press shenanigans, there was indeed no escaping it: the boy looked a square. It wasn't just the Jodrell Bank ears, weak chin and slicked back hair – he'd compounded these further by owning up to being married with children. Furthermore, he acted neither sullenly nor brashly in his dark business suit: no jive talk, no prima donna tantrums, no good copy. He seemed more like a manager than a heart-throb pop sensation: 'I had a contract to sign . . . and decided that I might as well sign it in London, fix up a few details and take a look 'round the British market.'

'I shall cut a record especially for the British market,' he promised. 'It will be very near the C & W style, but will be tempered to your taste.'[3] Words are cheap. Orbison had noticed that, as in North America, Ray Charles was in vogue again, having shelved his jazz-gospel fusions to chance an arm with the first of his 'Modern Sounds in Country and Western' albums, which ran a stylistic gauntlet from Ted Daffan via Hank Williams to the Everly Brothers. While Roy was in London, its promotional single – a revamp of 'I

Can't Stop Loving You' – was racing to the top of the British charts where, after a fortnight, it would be unseated by home-grown Frank Ifield's seven-week reign with a C & W arrangement of 'I Remember You' – complete with yodel selling point.

For want of a better description, Orbison had been branded an exponent of C & W by British reporters and, in the light of current trends, it seemed prudent not to deny that. 'The guitars of C & W could mean a lot here,' he conjectured. 'You don't seem to have the kind of rhythm groups that we have in the States – and I'm sure that is what the kids want: strong, beaty rhythms that make them jump.'[3]

Nobody in the plush Mount Vernon room on that summer's day could foresee that native British 'rhythm groups' would shortly be jumping up the hit parade in unimagined abundance. However, with 'Please Please Me' almost a year away, solo stars, American or taking their cue from America, still dominated the charts. In some cases, the late fifties' 'Somebody and the Somebodies' formula still held good, differentiating between the 'featured singer' and faceless backing combo. This was the case with Brian Poole and the Tremeloes, who earned a footnote in history as the ones Decca chose instead of the Beatles on New Year's Day, 1962.

One consolation for Decca's high command after their Scouse supplicants were grabbed by EMI would be the continued licensing arrangement with key US record companies through its London–American subsidiary, whose roster embraced the cream of top-selling US pop. This included Roy Orbison, who thought the deal with Decca so satisfactory that, even when he eventually switched labels in the States, a special clause would be inserted in the new agreement whereby he would remain on London–American in the UK. During that exploratory visit in 1962, for example, there had been no raised eyebrows when Fred Foster, attracted by a new British system of recording strings, suggested a session with Roy at Decca's west

Hampstead studio – maybe during the forthcoming British tour, whenever that would be.

Whilst in London, Foster had also engaged a new assistant to handle British affairs from Monument's Nashville office. Amongst former EMI secretary Janet Martin's qualifications for the post had been her co-founding of Roy's British fan club. Her new duties included apologizing to the press for her idol's recent poor showing in the UK Top Fifty: 'He was very disappointed about "The Crowd" and "Workin' For the Man" not making it, which ended his big run of chart success in Britain. He has some theories about why this was so. "The Crowd" he thought too fussy while in "Workin' For the Man" he reasoned that the lyric was too complicated.'[9]

Popular with the Orbison children and a frequent guest at the unfinished Hendersonville mansion, Janet noted with patriotic pride that, in one room there, a corner was set aside for memorabilia and keepsakes from British well-wishers. Roy also subscribed to the London music press, which he normally studied as a stockbroker would a shares index. Still procrastinating about returning to tour, he 'inadvertently picked up this [British] magazine. It said "highlight of the evening was Del Shannon's version of Roy Orbison's 'Cryin'' or 'Running Scared'. Or both." So I got to thinking that if he did that well with my songs, I might do as well if I came over.'[10]

Three weeks' worth of dates were pencilled in for October 1962, but no such undertaking proved feasible – especially with 'The Crowd' peaking at a humble No. 40 in the summer. He was not considered powerful enough at the box office to headline alone. No available British performer was judged to be an adequate co-star and, after negotiations for soul crooner Sam Cooke and then Carl Perkins petered out, Orbison and his investors, crestfallen, elected to wait a while longer.

Transferred back to England in early 1963 to reorganize the fan club, Janet Martin was thrilled to report that Roy was 'mighty relieved about the success of his current release, "In Dreams",' which actually crept fractionally higher in Britain than the States, its five-month chart run matching that of 'Only the Lonely' long ago in 1960.

Suddenly he was back on form again having shaken the curse of either looking to other writers for hits or having his own composing efforts being consigned to British bargain bins after indifferent sales. 'In Dreams' had been conceived 'half asleep and my thoughts were still racing when that whole introduction just came to me. I thought, Boy, that's good. I need to finish that. Too bad these things don't happen in my dreams. I woke up the next morning. Twenty minutes later, I had the whole song written.'[11] On vinyl, it eases in like an off-the-cuff strummed lullaby perhaps to his second son, Tony, born in 1962. However, breaking into an agitated moderato, 'In Dreams' was to be no soothing children's favourite like the Chordettes' 'Mr Sandman' from 1954. After a 'magic night' of unconscious reverie, dawn brings only the agonizing reality of the departed lover, conveyed so well by Roy's despairing falsetto coda.

'In Dreams' had relegated Cindy Walker's exotic 'Shahda-roba', with its snake-charmer ostinato, to the B-side. On the rebound, a heartened Orbison – again, without Joe Melson – penned a follow-up, 'Falling', which was likewise coupled with a Walker flip. As much of a holding operation as 'Blue Angel' had been after 'Only the Lonely', the remorseful 'Falling' likewise wasn't as big a hit as its predecessor, but it was a hit all the same. In retrospect, the blood-and-thunder B-side, 'Distant Drums', may have been a wiser choice (Jim Reeves had a posthumous No.1 with it three years later).

'Falling' hit the charts shortly after Roy had embarked on that long-awaited British tour. Fresh from the Top Ten, he no longer needed a Cooke or a Perkins to guarantee profit. It had been arranged for Orbison – replacing his indisposed friend, Duane Eddy – and his supporting programme to open at Slough's Adelphi theatre on Saturday 18 May. Second on the bill, so Janet Martin informed him by transcontinental telephone, were the Beatles. 'I had never heard of the Beatles,' reflected Roy, 'and it seemed to me at first like it was just a rehash of rock 'n' roll that I'd been involved with for a long time, but what it turned out to be was these four guys, their particular spirit . . . putting out rock 'n' roll as they saw it and it turned out to be very fresh and full of energy and . . . vitality. So I recognized it at the time.'[12]

Once upon a time the Beatles *had* been 'just a rehash of rock 'n' roll', and they would always remain in artistic debt to the trailblazing sounds created in the studios of Norman Petty, Sam Phillips and, more recently, Fred Foster. Of 'Please Please Me', John Lennon recalled that, in its down-beat lyric and slowish tempo, 'it was my attempt at writing a Roy Orbison song.'[13] The faster version that was the making of the Beatles also suggested Orbison in its flights of falsetto.

Aspects of the Orbison dialectic were also felt in such post-Beatle British hits as Dave Berry's 'The Crying Game' and the equally tearful 'Juliet' from the Four Pennies. One of the best songs that the Moody Blues ever recorded, 'From the Bottom of My Heart', took the musical mountain climbing of 'Running Scared' and 'In Dreams' half a step further by swelling over three minutes from a murmured *sotto voce* to a wailing horror-movie crescendo. The influence of 'Borne on the Wind' is apparent in John D. Loudermilk's 'This Little Bird', a 1965 high-flyer for both the Nashville Teens and Marianne Faithfull.

Even when furthest from their British grammar school interpretation of American pop, traces of Orbison lingered among the sitars, electronic collages and drug-dazzled vision of the Beatles' later work – as exemplified by the melancholy melody of 'She's Leaving Home' and the nothingness-to-eternity structures of 'A Day in the Life' and 'Happiness is a Warm Gun'.

Back in 1963, however, the Moptops had surfaced as self-assured but unpretentious Liverpool lads, still slightly bewildered by their sudden fame. On that first Orbison

expedition too were Gerry and the Pacemakers, who were
on terms of fluctuating parity with their fellow Cavern
dwellers. Introduced by mahogany-toned interlocutor Tony
Marsh, the all-styles-served-here fare was completed by
stand-up comedian Erkey Grant, balladeer David Macbeth,
and baby-voiced Louise Cordet. During their allotted ten
minutes each, these small fry were accompanied by the
Terry Young Six, who kicked off the proceedings fronted
by hip-swivelling vocalist Young.

The remainder of the Six – which included Barry Booth
on keyboards and future Shadow John Rostill on bass –
were also responsible for backing Roy Orbison who, they
had heard, expected his musicians to follow precisely the
scores notated for his records by arranger Bill Justis.
Rumours about the competence of English backing groups
from other Americans prompted Orbison's wish to 'arrive
about a week early and rehearse with my backing group until
I'm satisfied.'[9]

Roy's schedule was such that this became impractical.
The best he could manage was a swift run-through in the
late afternoon, using the Slough Adelphi's own sound system
amid a clutter of cables, guitar cases and Ringo Starr's
unassembled drum kit. In the dusty half-light beyond foot-
lights that were still being tested, the newly arrived John
Lennon and the odd road manager looked on as the star
tuned his Gretsch Tennessean to Barry Booth's purring
electric organ. A feedback squeak from a nervous amplifier
launched them into a pleasantly unproblematic rehearsal.
Items that Roy had inserted into the set recently were picked
up with minimum instruction by the Terry Young Six.
Instead of an imperious martinet who'd bust your ass if you
played a bum note, the Six five found their new employer
'very easy-going – I don't know why we should have felt in
awe of him. But his material was solid and interesting to
work. He had the quality that I don't think in those days
was that common. He just turned up with these songs –
some of which we'd made ourselves acquainted with prior

to his arrival – and just dived into the rehearsal situation.'⁵ Roy was especially impressed with academy-trained Booth for whom, in retrospect, the occasion became one of those Momentous Encounters.

Afterwards, as the Six cleared a space for the Beatles' more pristine equipment, another Momentous Encounter could no longer be postponed. In his dressing room, the jet-lagged American had barely sat down when Lennon – now joined by his manager, Brian Epstein – asked if he had a minute. According to Orbison, he said: '"How should we bill this? Who should close the show? Look, you're getting all the money, so why don't we [the Beatles] close the show?" I didn't know whether that was true or not, whether I was getting that much more than they were. It wasn't that much – and the tour had sold out in one afternoon.'¹⁴

No one could pretend that Roy was the foremost cause of this quick profit. The Fab Four's third single, 'From Me to You' would be a No.1 fixture for the duration of the tour. At one stop they were even presented with a silver disc backstage by Gerry Marsden, with whom they would be slugging it out in the UK charts for the rest of 1963. John, Paul, George and Ringo were still a few months short of becoming a national treasure via the Royal Variety Show, but it nevertheless made sense for the last scream-rent chord of 'Twist and Shout', their signature tune, to signal the final curtain – and their escape to the limousine that would be waiting in the back alley, engine running. It was goodbye to the insipid Bobbies and Jimmies of post-Presley America forever. Within a year, local-boy-made-good Frank Ifield would also be in supper-club obsolescence.

Aware of the chasm into which even he might plunge, Roy, in the murk behind the plush curtains of the Slough Adelphi, steeled himself to face the facts in front of someone else's audience. Into the bargain, he felt vaguely uncomfortable in the prescription sunglasses. They were all he had to shield his eyes since mislaying his clear spectacles on the aeroplane to London from sunny Alabama where he'd played

the previous night. Over there, they would have just finished
lunch by now . . .

Opening with what else but 'Only the Lonely', it was a
walkover. While the Terry Young boys basically sight-read
behind him, all he had to do was stand his ground with his
black guitar and sing. Apart from a tapping heel, a few chord
changes and rare directive nods for the band, his only other
gesture was when he whipped out a harmonica for 'Candy
Man'. Another up-tempo concession to the prevalent mood
of the evening was trading 'heys' and 'yeahs' with the audience in a 'What'd I Say', which he took down easy, working
the tension up again to a state of raving panic. This was
quelled with a plaintive 'Cryin''. Of his bigger rockaballads,
he was required to reprise 'Running Scared' mid-set; while
the sustained cheering – rather than screaming – that followed 'In Dreams', the closing number, was such that a
relieved Tito Burns at the back of the hall bore witness to
the fact that 'after thirty minutes – he was booked to do
fifteen – we still couldn't get the Beatles on. This was the
first time I'd seen a standing ovation in Slough.'9

The pattern was set not only for the three weeks that he
had to precede the Beatles, but also for subsequent nation-
wide jaunts during the golden age of British beat. 'He'd
slay them and they'd scream for more,' sighed Ringo. 'In
Glasgow, we were all backstage listening to the tremendous
applause he was getting. He was just standing there, not
moving or anything.'15 At one venue, 600 autograph books
were left for Orbison to sign. Even when his record sales
began to decline in late 1965, he could still work that old
magic without obvious effort – enough to disconcert any
beat group, chart-riding and frantic, on the same bill.

'The nice thing with Roy,' recounted Gerry Marsden,
'was that when they got American stars over, they used to
do a big thing of supplying them with a car. Roy, God bless
him, said, "No, I don't want a car: I want to travel with the
boys." We'd have singsongs on the coach – it was good fun.
Roy had this very, very extraordinary ability for doing three

to five octaves with his voice which we all tried to do and it
made us speak strange for days after singing his songs – but
they were nice songs to do.'[8]

Though perhaps slightly exaggerated, this anecdote typi-
fies the underlying good nature of British pop's most optimistic period. Roy's initiation into its spirit began in Slough
when he remembered 'Paul and John grabbing me by the
arms and not letting me go back on to take my curtain call.
They [the audience] were yelling "We want Roy! We want
Roy!" and there I was, held captive by the Beatles saying,
"Yankee, go home." So we had a great time.'[4]

Roy enjoyed chatting about music with his new-found
touring friends from Liverpool – and he was flattered to
learn that one musician's favourite pub was called the Blue
Angel. The 'Nashville of the North' held more C & W bands
than anywhere in Britain and naturally the Pacemakers and
Beatles were lay experts on the genre's obscurer trackways.
Among numbers common to many Merseybeat groups were
'Beautiful Dreamer', 'Money', 'What'd I Say', and 'Sea of
Heartbreak', which had all passed through the Orbison
repertoire. New song ideas were tossed around, but the
laugh-a-minute ambience of tour bus and artists' bar pro-
scribed serious composition – though Roy, as always, continued to revise and develop flashes of inspiration in the
seclusion of his hotel suite. Persistent jet lag aggravated his
inclination to oversleep – a trait he shared with the Beatles'
lead guitarist, a ponderous youth called Harrison: 'George
and I missed the bus a lot. They left without us. We slept
in.'[16]

Roy considered George's group pretty rough-and-ready,
'but they had the magic there', and, as for Gerry, 'I think
that monster smile would sell him before they even heard
his voice.'[17] Marsden's progress in America would be surpris-
ingly sluggish but, within a matter of months, the Beatles
would spearhead what has passed into myth as the 'British
Invasion' of the States by beat groups, an eventuality pre-
dicted by Orbison after he touched down for some California

dates that June, with English screams still ringing in his ears.

As the US music industry had long regarded British pop as merely the furbisher of nine-day wonders like the Tornadoes or Acker Bilk, few believed him. Two who did were Del Shannon and Gene Pitney, both of whom had also had first-hand experience of the hysteria surrounding the Beatles. Like Orbison, these two had not been found wanting by Britain's beat-crazy teenagers either. Del and Roy had first met that previous tumultuous month in England. A break in Shannon's UK itinerary had allowed him to book a London studio for a crafty cover version of 'From Me to You', thereby hoping to steal a march on the Beatles before they hit America. Through breathing the air around the Rolling Stones, Pitney would shortly be entering the British Top Ten with a ballad written by Mick Jagger and Keith Richards.

Roy's fascination with British pop would never be as practical. Nonetheless, if his new-found friends were criticized, he would always be ready to charge to their defence. His rejoinder to some sour remarks made by that mainstay of 'American Bandstand', Len Barry, was, 'I hear he said some things about the Beatles and the Stones. If he's really that all-knowing, he should be able to tell us if there's life on Mars and when and if there's another world war coming. I just don't think he's qualified to say things like that.'[18] This outburst could be justified by Roy's better-informed overview. Not only was he enchanted by worldwide smashes such as the Searchers' 'Needles and Pins', but he was also startlingly in the know about relatively obscure numbers like 'Why Did You Bring Him to the Dance' by a Coventry quintet called Peter's Faces, though 'I don't know who Peter is – or his Faces – but they sure sound good to me.'[19]

The emotive vocabulary of both this disc and 'Needles and Pins' had much in common with the lyrics of Orbison. His second British tour of 1963 coincided with the release of 'Blue Bayou', a song which barely rippled *Billboard*'s Top

The Teen Kings (left to right) Billy Par Ellis, Roy, James Morrow, Johnny Wilson and Jack Kennelly. 1956. *(Martin Hawkins)*

A year before leaving Sun Records in 1958, Roy posed for this winsome publicity shot. *(Martin Hawkins)*

A pensive moment shortly after signing with Monument in 1959. *(Martin Hawkins)*

ONLY THE LONELY

Only the lonely
Here comes that song again
Blue angel
Today's teardrops

Roy Orbison

Like Buddy Hol
before him, Roy
focused features
(minus the dark
glasses) would a
early record slee
(London Record

'Oh Pretty Woman': Claudette and Roy in 1963. *(Central Press Photos Ltd)*

'Go! Go! Go!' Roy stands his ground in concert, 1966. *(Associated Television Ltd)*

Roy and Barry Booth (left) relax with agreeable company in Marylebone's Diwan-I-Am restaurant. *(Barry Booth)*

'I've always wanted to know what he really looked like,' said 18-year-old Marianne Faithfull after divesting Roy of his famous sunglasses during the 1965 UK Tour. *(Daily Mirror)*

Lost in wonder outside the House of Parliament Roy commences the 1966 London to Brighton Historic Commercial Vehicle Run. *(Rex Features Ltd)*

British fan Molly Weston enjoys removing her idol's Chelsea boot after a performance. *(Thompson Newspapers Ltd)*

'Truly Truly True': Roy with Wesley and Barbara, the new Mrs Orbison, at the Westbury Hotel, 1970. *(London Photo Agency)*

Roy cuts into a guitar-shaped cake at Soho's La Dolce Vita on his 30th birthday, 1966. Guests included the Walker Brothers and Scotland's Lulu, all of whom were touring with Orbison. *(United Press International Ltd)*

On the boards at the Coconut Grove: (left to right) Roy, Bruce Springsteen, Elvis Costello, T-Bone Burnett, 1987. *(Melody Maker)*

Posing for a Travelling Wilburys publicity shot: (left to right) Bob Dylan, Jeff Lynne, Tom Petty, Roy and George Harrison, 1987. *(London Features International)*

Laminar Flow publicity shot with Roy's operational chest scars airbrushed out. *(Elektra-Asylum Records)*

On stage at the Mean Fiddler, Roy's final show in Britain, 1987. *(Bernard Futter)*

'Goodnight': Roy's last concert in Akron, Ohio, 4 December 1988, two days before his death
(Rex Features Ltd)

Forty, but rose to No.3 in the British charts. Stimulated by Joe Melson's drive through Arkansas in 1961, 'Blue Bayou' had no precedent in the Orbison canon. Considered too risky for a single then, it was too intriguing to bury on a long-player. Largely as a result of Roy's lengthy absences in foreign parts and on understandable indolence whenever he could snatch a few days at home, his partnership with Melson had all but fizzled out by the late summer of 1963. Fresh out of new material, he blew the dust off 'Blue Bayou'. For insurance, it was coupled with a straightforward rockin' re-run of 'Mean Woman Blues', a Jerry Lee Lewis B-side from 1957. In America at least, this caution could be excused by the rise of 'Mean Woman Blues' into the Top Five, but it is 'Blue Bayou' that more piquantly activated memory banks. Not another Himalayan ascent like its two chart forebears, the low-dynamic, jogalong verse/chorus format is undercut by a lazy harmonica and wordless female vocal harmonies. In counterpoint to this we have Roy's close-miked homesickness for a sleepy pastoral haven where there's always nothing doing.

'Blue Bayou' is all the more poignant in the context of Orbison's increasing travelling life in the Swinging Sixties. Zigzagging round the world in the torpid warmth of jet, limousine, train and luxury coach to strange towns, strange venues and strange beds, even his days off were often filled with photo calls and interviews. Caught off guard by an abrupt rise in sales in France, he'd have to drop everything in the middle of a tour of the Philippines to wearily mime the track that had done the trick on television in Paris before dashing back to the interrupted campaign in the Far East.

In a trunk call to Hendersonville, he'd enthused that, of all the places he'd been so far, he'd got the softest spot for Britain, adding – so he informed one reporter – 'Believe me, I say in all sincerity that I cannot wait to get back [to Britain] in September with my good friend, Bob Luman.'[19] Not doubting her husband for a second, Claudette was there when the Sons of the Piltdown Men – a renamed Terry

Young Six – piled into the instrumental prelude on that first night in September – once more at Slough's Adelphi. For subsequent Beatles tours, the Six had been supplanted by Sounds Incorporated. The group backing Orbison was a five-piece amalgam of ex-Young veterans, bass guitarist Danny Thompson (later of Pentangle), and Roy's American drummer, Paul Garrison, all pulled together by Barry Booth who, as Orbison was discovering, was worth his weight in gold. Another familiar British face at that Saturday afternoon soundcheck was Tony Marsh, who would be officiating for the supporting cast, featuring the Searchers, Freddie and the Dreamers, and Brian Poole and the Tremeloes. In a land where nearly every town and shire was now supposed to have a 'sound', these acts represented Liverpool, Manchester and Essex respectively. Originally, Roy was to have head-lined an all-Merseybeat rival troupe, already under way, with Billy J. Kramer, the Fourmost and Tommy Quickly. Like the Beatles, these were all Epstein clients, so Roy's choice of even a Terry Young Six without Terry Young might have been among the factors causing the change of plan. Moreover, the substitution of the doubtful Tommy Roe for Roy Orbison would be less intimidating for Epstein's second division chartbusters.

The Fourmost's counterparts on the Orbison tour were Freddie and the Dreamers, whose act also depended on getting laughs. A comedy element was also present in the recorded works of Poole and his group. Therefore, it was to be expected that the camaraderie on the road would be even more uproarious than last time. A poker-faced Tony Marsh assured the American contingent that passports had to be produced by aliens wishing to enter Scotland. With all such documents safe with Claudette in the London flat, a tense Roy, Bob and Paul fidgeted as the coach hurtled from the previous night's stop in Blackburn to the Glasgow Apollo. At a border pub, the landlord, going along with Tony's jape demanded passports from any foreigners among the drinkers. 'Gee, Roy, what're we gonna do?' moaned Luman.

A Glaswegian policeman on traffic duty outside the Apollo fell victim to some high jinks springing from Orbison's hobby of collecting uniform cap badges – a pastime he shared with Elvis Presley. With a communal kitty as prize, points were awarded according to the various degrees of success in gaining possession of a stranger's headgear. These would include: first accosting the wearer; initiating a conversation about the hat; removing it; and, for the maximum allocation, bringing the hat back to the other players, who would then explode with laughter. A turbaned Sikh had been the hardest nut to crack; but Barry Booth did well to lure the Scottish constable into Roy's dressing room to surrender his badge in exchange for an autograph.

A less elaborate remedy for relieving the tedium of the road was recalled by Freddie Garrity. Freddie had blown most of his first big royalty cheque on an E-type Jaguar three times the price of his humble abode in a Manchester suburb. With time to kill before the performance at the city's Odeon, he invited Orbison round for a meal, 'so he came to this two up and two down like on Coronation Street . . . and he owns a ranch with all these acres of land and I served him salad. He had these lovely songs and a great voice, and I just liked the guy.'[15]

After much persuasion, another Orbison admirer consented to close the show for the last six nights. On 10 October Brian Poole's rendering of the Contours' 'Do You Love Me' had toppled the Beatles' 'She Loves You' from the No.1 spot, having fought off a rival version by the Dave Clark Five. With 'Blue Bayou' about to slip, the relinquishing of his bill-topping supremacy for the second time in five months made sense to Roy – so long as he still got paid as per contract. Overwhelmed, Brian – shy and over-modest off stage – wasn't happy about lording it over one whom he, Freddie and the Searchers revered as a Grand Old Man. Roy hadn't yet turned twenty-eight.

Dragged into Brian and the Tremeloes' vexing back-seat discussion about a suitable successor to their chart-topper, the venerable Orbison suggested, and then played, 'Candy Man'. As a two-year-old B-side, it would be unknown to those consumers unacquainted with pop before 'Please Please Me'. In a backstage alcove the next day, Poole asked to hear 'Candy Man' again. Taped immediately after the tour finished, Brian and his band's cloning of the Orbison arrangement was, to their frustration, put on ice by Decca in favour of the lacklustre 'I Can Dance'. When this stopped short of the Top Thirty, out came 'Candy Man', which restored Poole and the Tremeloes to the higher reaches of the charts. As bringer of their good fortune, Roy also lent moral support when the group – about to record 'Someone, Someone' (their last Top-twenty entry) – sought the practical help of Roy's old colleague, Norman Petty, who had supervised the original version by the Crickets.

Roy's current producer was also in London, keen to try out a new method of recording strings. Rather than trust a solitary, omni-directional microphone slung above the heads of a section numbering up to twenty, each individual string player would wear 'a neck mike, which made a tremendous recording sound – and this was the thing Fred Foster wanted for Roy Orbison.'[8] So said Ivor Raymonde, musical director of the session that yielded 'Pretty Paper', Orbison's only single with a Yuletide theme, and the sole Willie Nelson composition to breach the British Top Ten. Roy's approval of this chiming sob story in waltz tempo, after a demonstration in a hotel room, gave Nelson's bank balance a vital shot in the arm after the destruction of his Nashville house by fire had forced his move back to Austin. Possibilities of a Nelson/Orbison songwriting team were, therefore, precluded by geography – though the pair cobbled together 'Summersong', which boasted an arresting instrumental preamble reminiscent of Stravinsky.

In 'Pretty Paper', Roy observes Christmas shoppers ignoring a roofless beggar – of the sort who would gravitate at dusk toward the shelter of the Embankment, not far from the Orbisons' spacious *pied à terre* which had been chosen because of its indoor swimming pool. Though the rush-release of 'Pretty Paper' caught the pre-Christmas market in the States, 'the tapes got fouled-up on their way over here, so it couldn't be issued in Britain. We had to have something, so we decided on "Borne on the Wind" – though I didn't expect it to do very well.'[20]

Backed by a workmanlike 'What'd I Say,' this stopgap effort was the first fruit of Roy's collaboration with Bill Dees, a partnership that was to prove more productive than any either had known before. Since the sundering of the Whirlwinds, Dees had retreated from the limelight to try his luck as a full-time songwriter in Nashville. With Joe Melson unwilling to face another moonlit mile, Bill gladly took his place in Orbison's growing nomadic retinue – which, by 1964, catered for two trios of violinists and backing singers.

After one show, Dees trailed along to a party to which his co-writer had been invited. Made to feel that he had somehow gate-crashed, he slipped back to the hotel where grief for a drowned friend flooded his thoughts. The skeleton of 'Borne on the Wind' was tangible on Roy's return.

With its juxtaposition of other worldliness and pulsating Spanish-Mexican canter, it is a refinement upon those windswept 'Johnny Remember Me' console inventions pioneered by the formidable English producer, Joe Meek. Underrated by its composers and the public, this careering drama flitted briefly into Britain's Top Twenty in February 1964, and was not even deemed worthy of release in the States.

Notes

1   *Disc*, 23 May 1964
2   *Melody Maker*, 11 March 1967
3   Press conference transcript, 2 June 1962
4   *To Spencer Leigh*, Radio Merseyside
5   Barry Booth
6   *Daily Mirror*, 8 October 1988
7   Rejected photo caption – *Melody Maker* archives
8   *Tribute to the Big O*, Radio 2, 5 January 1989

 9 *New Musical Express*, 12 April 1983
10 *New Musical Express*, 20 December 1963
11 *The Face*, February 1989
12 Veronica Television (Dutch)
13 *The Playboy Interviews* (Playboy Press, 1981)
14 *To Spencer Leigh*, Radio Merseyside
15 *The Beatles*, by H. Davies (Heinemann, 1968)
16 *Melody Maker*, 26 March 1977
17 *New Musical Express*, 24 May 1963
18 *Melody Maker*, 24 October 1964
19 *New Musical Express*, 14 June 1963
20 *New Musical Express*, 30 April 1964

6

It's Over

When Roy Orbison confided to a journalist in 1963 that he had 'such a tight schedule that if I take a vacation, I can feel the work going by,'[1] was he bragging or complaining? He was certainly leading what the economist would call a 'full life'. Within the space of two years from 1963, his globetrotting encompassed extensive touring of Australasia, the Far East and Europe. There was also a trip to South Africa, whose apartheid policy was reminiscent of Texas in the mid-forties. When it had been used as the film location for the Jim Reeves' vehicle, 'Kimberley Jim', hardly a liberal eyebrow had been raised.

Immortalized in song by her husband, Claudette Orbison was warranted a second-hand celebrity. Gripping Roy's arm proprietorially, she wandered an earth that seemed less and less eye-widening. Brussels resembled a cold Fort Worth – the same comparison holding between the British Midlands and Tennessee. A luxury hotel in Canberra was just like one in Johannesburg: the Coke tasted exactly the same. At each capital city, the couple would split up like amoebas, he to go through his paces in a monotonous round of concerts, she left to her own devices with a cheque book and room service.

How then could Claudette possibly be bored? She couldn't be homesick either, with at least one of the children and, more often than not, her father-in-law along for the ride. Softening her drawl at reception desks, she'd still be stung by the muffled titters of those to whom wealth was second nature. With the switchboard relaying greetings, complimentary tickets and invitations from the loud-mouthed show-business periphery, how could she possibly be lonely? At parties where she'd pass a dozen famous names on a single staircase, she felt more irked than out of her depth. In the powder room, some Quant-cropped girl with sooty eyes and wasp waist would start up an inane conversation, congratulating her on hooking such a well-heeled pop star of a man as Roy Orbison. Just as travel had brought Claudette souvenirs without wisdom and fatigue without stimulation, so Roy's fame elicited flattery without friendship.

An additional incentive for her stepping off this facile roundabout was that, with only a few months to go by April 1965, the new house on Old Hickory was no longer an unserviceable no-man's-land of rubble. After being a stranger in his own home for most of his life, their son Tony could now look forward to leaving his grandparents' care in Texas. The only impediment to this restoration of family stability was his father's job. It was one thing after another: ten days in New Zealand; a month in Canada; six days of television in the Netherlands; a weekend in Cyprus . . . 'This means I don't get much time with my family,' said Roy in 1964, 'and they are looking forward to me spending three or four weeks at home from the end of October.'[2] The sound of his engine dying on the gravel outside would signal one more deliverance from the treadmill of the road as a weary Roy, as if from another time zone, would drop his cases in the hall, hand out the presents and tramp upstairs for some shuteye, dumping his travel-stained clothes on the bedroom carpet.

Admitting that he was 'not very good at just sitting around',[3] he would be shut away for hours in the music room, making sense of and collating the song fragments born during his travels. If household noise distracted him, he'd repair, guitar on back seat, to Nashville and his office at Acuff-Rose. With these out of the way, he might listen to how Roy Duane was progressing on guitar and, more recently, piano. When he'd had time, Roy used examples from his own repertoire to show his son enough fret-board chords for the eight-year-old to stun his father with a soprano rendering of 'Cryin'', as well as some precocious original compositions.

Freeze-framed in a backstage photograph with his parents and the Beatles, starstruck Roy Duane's ambition to follow in his father's footsteps had been quickened by the Beatlemania sweeping America. The four guys who'd patted his head in Slough were now omnipresent on TV. At the height of their success – a large-scale re-run of Britain's beat delirium – they had five records in the US Top Ten – and Roy Duane's dad was their friend. 'I talked with them on the phone and invited them to my home where they would be guaranteed no publicity but, in their own humorous way, they replied that they weren't interested if there was no publicity. Anyway, I hope to catch up with them when I'm next in England.'[3] He did indeed – when they arrived at his twenty-ninth birthday party in the basement of the Quo Vadis restaurant in London's Soho, having been forced – as their host had been – to enter by the fire door thereby sidestepping the fan bedlam that had hailed every limousine drawing up at the front entrance.

But Dad could raise riots of his own without the help of the Beatles. The showbands who dominated the Irish music scene took their inspiration from the pop end of C & W. This ranged from the sentiment of Jim Reeves to Frankie Laine's cowboy dramas, punctuated with rockabilly and singalong evergreens by the likes of Ned Miller and Guy Mitchell. It was small wonder then that Roy Orbison, who was himself a product of the same musical background, caused a sensation when he played six Irish ballroom dates in October 1963 – immediately after the attentive silences and considered ovations on the Brian Poole tour. Girls screamed frantically, totally deaf to warnings about rushing the stage. The shows were stopped three times as PA columns toppled and an astounded Orbison was mauled. Here, at least, he was the kind of pop star you *did* mind your colleen liking.

For static Roy – a four-eyed throwback from the fifties – to whip up such a storm hammered home to Claudette that the time hanging heavy between one concert and the next wasn't only killed with hat contests and museum visits. Generally speaking, singers on tour kept a vow of silence about illicit sex. But no one was in any doubt that a strong motive for any red-blooded lad to become a pop singer was that, no matter what you looked like, you could still be popular with young ladies. Look at spindly Freddie Garrity, for example, or Ringo with his nose. Look at Roy Orbison.

Occasionally, fan letters less demure than the 'Orbisonly yours' sort would fail to amuse Claudette – as they sometimes did her husband. Fêted wherever he went, he may have had requests to meet girls in the romantic seclusion of a backstage props cupboard, but there is scant evidence to suggest that Roy was ever unfaithful to his wife. After figuring out what hour it would be in Tennessee, he would telephone her every day without fail from whatever region of the globe his work had taken him.

Of hard drugs, Orbison remained uninformed. 'I was invited to an LSD party recently . . . I wasn't even tempted,'[4] he said in 1966. Among his few indulgences on tour were the old ones. During a two-day British stopover in 1964, he sat through two showings of the Hollywood epic, *The Fall of the Roman Empire* – just a couple of hours after a vast sum had changed hands for a 1939 Mercedes-Benz 300 with a mahogany dashboard to be shipped back to Hendersonville.

For all his exemplary behaviour, Roy was no universal aunt. As long as his backing musicians were punctual and efficient on stage, he was tolerant – even sympathetic – towards their vices. He even got drawn into the ensuing ribald mirth about his drummer's frustrated tilting for the downfall of Marianne Faithfull's knickers throughout an entire three-week tour.

If any of his boys were below par through no fault of their own, Orbison proved a considerate boss. Having plucked Barry Booth from the Sons of the Piltdown Men, Roy's concern about a throat infection contracted by the twenty-five-year-old Yorkshireman en route to a show in Dawson City on the Yukon was such that 'he plonked me into a hospital in British Columbia. They did a date and I got some massive jabs and stayed overnight and they came back and picked me up.'

The most hair-raising part of Booth's initiation into Orbison's service was caused by the non-arrival of a work permit. 'My first entering of the States was illegal. I had to secrete myself in a car boot – albeit a generous one – under a blanket.' For the next three years, Barry would function as Roy's keyboard player, musical director and confidant on the road.

He also introduced Orbison to the gastronomic delights of Marylebone's Diwan I Am, an Indian diner haunted by Booth when a student at the Royal Academy of Music. A photograph of Barry and his distinguished guest would later adorn the restaurant's menu card. An Indian dinner lasting for hours was amongst the newer diversions favoured by Roy at a time when most square meals served in Britain after 10.30 p.m. were foreign. He was also sighted eating on more than one occasion at the Italian trattoria in Soho which had replaced the fabled 21's coffee bar where the likes of Tommy Steele and Cliff Richard had been discovered. Picking at a Huddersfield snack bar dish without enthusiasm, he mused, 'These boys in their early twenties, their digestion can take it. I'm conscious that I'm getting too much fried food.'[5]

During that same interview in March 1965, he mentioned that he'd been home only for two months of the previous twelve, and that 'this business takes years off your life, and I know, even though I keep myself fit, that I'm going to have to slow down in the next year. I doubt whether I'll ever take a tour like this again.'

A man so busy is apt to be an inattentive spouse. True enough, he'd undertaken this most recent and seemingly endless slog round the world to pay for the palatial spread amidst the pines of Old Hickory. Absent when Claudette's third labour began, he lamented, 'Nashville is full of people like me. They don't often see home. When they do, they like to stay in it. There isn't much social life, except among the wives.'[5] Appreciating what an ordeal of conviviality his job could be, Claudette was tolerant when her overworked man didn't want to go out much. Nevertheless, she hoped he might unwind a little, talk to her and enjoy their brief leisure with the new baby they'd christened Wesley.

Instead, he kept to his odd hours, even insisting that he was 'compelled' to compose as he disappeared to the music room or Acuff-Rose. Before midnight recording sessions, he liked to see 'at least six hours of films . . . It freshens my mind. If there is nothing good on at the local cinemas, then I watch them on television. We have full-length colour films on Fridays, Saturdays and Sundays, so I always try not to get booked on those nights.'[6] To his tired wife, he didn't seem to be trying all that hard any more. At times, he even acted as if she was there only to provide refreshments, and hand him packs of duty-free Gauloises while he frowned over contracts or scrawls of chords and words.

One of the house's interior designers had become Claudette's most frequent companions as she grew accustomed to life without Roy. Good-looking and amusing, this young bachelor would accompany her to the ski club, coffee mornings and stuffed-shirt suppers. So far, she had resisted being alone with him – but he quickly grew impatient of always meeting her in public.

Hunched over guitar and tape recorder – with or without Bill Dees – or surrounded by papers and cigarette smoke, it scarcely occurred to Roy that there was a limit to wifely loyalty and affection. He'd provided her with everything she could possibly want, hadn't he? Neither of them were lusty young teenagers in Odessa any more but he still loved her in small fondnesses and in the respect granted to the mother of his boys. Twenty-four-year-old Claudette's frank nature would not allow her to remain silent about her increasing disinclination to play Joan to Roy's Darby – but all too soon would come his hand-squeezing departure for Nashville airport and another distant stage.

He'd been at home on 25 June the previous summer when an English journalist had rung with the news that 'It's Over', the follow-up to 'Borne on the Wind' had knocked a song by former Cavern cloakroom attendant Cilla Black off the top of the charts. 'At a time when British artists are all-powerful in their own country,' began the measured reply, 'I regard the attainment of No.1 position in Britain as the high spot of my career.'[2]

The premonitory 'It's Over' was perhaps a hint that Roy was not unprepared for a confessional outburst from Claudette. Disarmingly described as 'a ballad with a lush arrangement,'[7] a strummed C major chord serves as the briefest of preambles to the bald utterance, 'your baby doesn't love you any . . . more,' and the snare drum rataplan which ignites an artistic statement that is the embodiment of Roy's oft-quoted remark about packing as much poetry and philosophy into a two-minute single as possible. Though 'It's Over' is almost bombastic in metaphor, Orbison, always in control, advances on its falling stars, weeping rainbows and lonely sunsets with the grace of a fencing master, amid flurries of cinematic strings, murky horns and a wailing choral headwind. A suicide note set to music, the cheated lover's anguish reached boiling point as trees claw the moon. He then slumps into a forlorn void before the next and final explosion. The bleak apotheosis of the 'Running Scared' tension-building blueprint, 'It's Over', like its subject, stood alone.

The musical climate of its B-side, 'Indian Wedding', which dates from the apocryphal period between Melson and Dees, had many precedents. Evoking images of tomahawk-

wielding redskins dancing around a campfire in the approved
fashion, its pulsating tom-tom beat had figured previously
in Hank Williams' 'Kaw-liga' – later recorded by Orbison
– and, both from 1960, Johnny Preston's 'Running Bear'
(composed by the Big Bopper) and Larry Verne's comical
'Mr Custer' (covered in Britain by Charlie Drake). In 'Indian
Wedding', however, the matter-of-fact account of how the
newly-wed Yellow Hand and White Sand are united in death
is a backward glance at the drowned 'Leah', who is also
remembered in the high-pitched construction of Yellow
Hand's 'wedding song'.

For this section, rather than dual-track the harmony, Roy
was joined at the microphone by Bill Dees. So interchange-
able were their voices that the co-writer actually took the
lead in the chorus of 'Yo te amo Maria', a gaucho love refrain
which rode on the back of 'Oh! Pretty Woman'. Released
four months after 'It's Over', this was the only Orbison
record to top the charts in Britain and at home.

'It's Over' had been predominantly Roy's baby, but it was
with 'Oh! Pretty Woman' that Bill Dees came into his own:
'We'd just begun about six in the evening. What you do is
play anything that comes to mind, and my wife wanted to
go to town to get something. I said, "Do you have any
money?" And Bill Dees said, "Pretty woman never needs
any money." Then he said, "Would that make a great song
title?" I said, "No, but 'Pretty woman' would." So I started
playing the guitar and he was slapping the table for drums.
That was the conception, and by the time she got back –
which was about forty minutes – we had the song.'[8]

When subjected to Fred Foster's quality control, the
pay-off line – 'she's gone and walked away from me/but
there's other fish in the sea' – was thought 'too negative'.
Revised, the shameless vision of loveliness parading past
lonesome ol' Roy not only proffers him a second glance but
also slinks seductively in his direction. Maybe disillusion-
ment will result – she's his long-lost sister or a transvestite
– but, for one incredible moment, our wishful hero is ahead

when the number ends. He's actually picking up a girl with no strings attached.

There were twinges of desperation in the doleful 'middle eight' section – Bill's idea – and the teasing coda, but the re-entry of Jerry Kennedy's swaggering eight-note guitar riff revived Roy's confidence. It improved his bank balance too by outselling all his other records. The unseating of 'Oh! Pretty Woman' from the top, however, precipitated a restless farewell from the charts. As 'Only the Lonely' had bid him welcome in 1960, 'Penny Arcade', with almost mathematical symmetry, would wave him out of sight in the dying weeks of 1969.

Only teetering on the edge of the Top Thirty in Britain, and doing even worse in America, 'Penny Arcade' would see Roy off with a chart-topping bang in Australia. That most of his singles in the later sixties scaled the Australasian Top Twenties with ease while struggling elsewhere may be ascribed to the lasting impact of his tour of the continent in January 1965. He'd been given second billing to the Rolling Stones, of whom one Illinois newspaper had just written, 'You walk out of the Amphitheatre after watching the Rolling Stones perform, and suddenly the Chicago stockyards smell good and clean by comparison.' Derided so by adults as much as Presley had been, they were, naturally enough, just as rabidly worshipped by the young.

In the teeth of his toughest test to date, Orbison recreated much the same tumult as he had going on before the Beatles in 1963. Mick Jagger, outrageous and frantic, was still able to whip up the screeching rabble, but the reaction would sometimes be more subdued than he had come to expect. As the last night approached in New Zealand, a half-serious Jagger proposed to Roy 'that I sing the worst record that I'd ever made, and I said that I'd be happy to if he did the worst record he'd ever made. So I went on and I figured that "Ooby Dooby" was the worst . . . so I sang it. Then they went on and I watched the performance but they didn't do their worst record . . . There was a little gathering afterwards and, in lieu of their not doing their worst record, they gave me a silver cigarette case. "From the Rolling Stones to Ooby Dooby," it's inscribed.'[8] In Los Angeles that May, the Stones recorded the epoch-making '(I Can't Get No) Satisfaction' which combines the same percussive unison and eight-note riff as 'Oh! Pretty Woman'.

Via the Far East, Orbison plunged next into a headlining British tour, having supplemented his six-piece band with a native flautist and a female vocal trio, the Three Quarters. Deliberately untroubled by usurpers of the Beatles/Brian Poole persuasion, there were, nonetheless, some very competent vocalists in the support bands. Cliff Bennett, for one, could tackle updated versions of American R & B without departing from its over-riding passion. Like him, the next band on, Birmingham's Rockin' Berries, were bathing in the afterglow of a solitary hit. Though sugared with conscious comedy, the Berries closed their act with their own cover version of the Tokens' 'He's in Town'. This throbbing sob story in the 'Running Scared' mould was sung almost entirely in pleading Orbisonesque falsetto by rhythm guitarist, Geoff Turton.

Unperturbed by pretenders, Roy as usual gave them nothing that hadn't made the charts for him, including the latest entry, 'Goodnight', and the postponed 'Pretty Paper', which had restored him to the British Top Ten in December 1964. Because he was the undisputed star this time around, screaming mayhem broke out as each smash hit cadenced – and when he let out the lecherous gurgling growl that, previewed in 'Mean Woman Blues', had been resurrected for 'Oh! Pretty Woman'. This was to become as familiar a vocal gimmick as Frank Ifield's burdensome yodel.

More of a household name than the others, Orbison would be recognized across a wayside eaterie's formica table whenever the tour's fifty-seven seater took a break. Pestered for autographs, he'd sign and smile at the most interruptive fan. Back on the coach, Cliff Bennett noticed that 'Roy played poker at every opportunity'. Stakes of up to a fiver curbed the participation of all but the most expert gamblers in days when a ten-bob note (50p) was thought an adequate consolation prize in a television quiz.

Though they, too, joined in the fun, everybody close to Roy Orbison knew that an uneasy press wouldn't keep quiet. During a break between the final date of the tour and facing the TV cameras on 7 March for his three-song part in 'Sunday Night at the London Palladium', Roy confirmed that he and his wife, once considered ideally matched, had parted: 'Very few people were in on it. Divorce is something you don't rush out and shout to everyone,'[9] he said.

He had been granted a decree nisi in Tennessee on the all-embracing grounds of 'cruelty'. Undeniably, it had hurt when a 'friend' spilt the beans about her and the interior designer – before Claudette could tell him herself. What had at first been a light-hearted flirtation on Mrs Orbison's side had taken a dangerous turn. Roy was incredulous, but he didn't erupt with anger. He gently implored his wife to help him grasp what it all meant. Thinking aloud, with the same questions coming up again and again, he seemed to be groping for some reason that might explain and excuse her conduct. He was still searching when he drove off, pride smarting, to another faraway soundcheck, leaving Claudette wondering whether divorce would mean her losing the house.

A less personal estrangement would take place later that turbulent year as the expiry date for the Monument contract loomed ever nearer. After meeting with representatives from every major record label and rubbing his chin over their bids for Orbison – hot property then – Wesley Rose coolly informed Fred Foster that even to qualify to re-sign Roy, 'I would have to guarantee him a million dollars – which had never been done for an American pop artist at the time; that I'd have to guarantee a minimum of twenty prime time TV appearances, and also offer him a movie contract. I told him I didn't have a movie studio and that, as far as television appearances were concerned, after all these hits, Wesley would have no problems getting them himself. None of this went down too well.'

Rose was more unhappy about the whisperings concerning Monument's financial difficulties – though the company would survive into the seventies. Next there was the dubious criticism that Foster wasn't recording enough Acuff-Rose material. To add injury to insult, Wesley Rose was now occupying the central chair behind the console relaying instructions to the playing area. As he'd done when the Everly Brothers reached their optimum moment in the charts, Rose took over as *de facto* producer when 'It's Over', on the way down from the top, collided with 'Oh! Pretty Woman' on its way up. After Rose had directed operations on '(Say) You're My Girl' – Orbison's first serious flop since 1962 – Fred Foster bit his tongue and left quietly.

The more tidy-minded would attribute Roy's fall from the charts to this *coup d'état* but, although world sales for 'Goodnight' had been respectable enough, it was a real comedown in comparison with 'Pretty Paper', let alone 'Oh! Pretty Woman', Orbison's last million-selling single. Against the maelstrom of 'It's Over', 'Goodnight' seemed pallid – despite its plangent finale. However, its singer's longing for his unfaithful woman can only be heard today as a snatch of autobiography – and to a lesser extent the flip side, 'Only With You'. It also lends credence to a remark about 'hopes for a reconciliation' that Roy addressed to his father minutes before he left the London Palladium's star dressing room to sing 'Goodnight', 'Cryin'' and 'In Dreams'.

There seemed little hope of kissing and making up in the remaining months of 1965. Claudette, taking the children with her and yet insisting that 'I never really wanted to leave him',[10] went home to mother, now in Houston. Meanwhile, her ex-husband resumed his interrupted sales campaign with renewed urgency as the slight '(Say) You're My Girl' was given a rough ride in the summer charts.

Perhaps the new deal with Metro-Goldwyn-Mayer would bring an improvement. Not only was it worth a reputed

£800,000, but the most attractive fringe benefit was the promise to make Roy a film star as Paramount had Elvis. In 1964, Orbison had expressed interest in composing sound-tracks and – perhaps, as a far-fetched afterthought – direct-ing. After all, he was quite a film buff. During the Beatles' tour, he'd spoken with quiet pride of 'going to three different cinemas in a day and [seeing] more than a dozen films since I came to England. I think *Fifty-five Days in Peking* impressed me most.'[6] His liking for this allegorical retelling of the Boxer Rebellion showed an intelligent – rather than an intellectual – passion for the cinema that did not extend to its avant-garde extremes.

On the lookout for an acting opportunity in 1965, he was offered 'only singing spots in movies but, through going along, building contacts and getting to know people in the business, I got what I wanted in the end.'[11] A script for a moralistic Western in which the male lead plays a spy for the South in the Civil War was found; shooting was to commence as soon as a large enough gap could be found in Orbison's taxing schedule. What about September 1966?

For a start, films were incidental to his main purpose. What is more, MGM had him down for forty songs per year, and he'd have to unload some of them on a new album before 1965 was out. Theoretically, the new company allowed him greater artistic freedom and bigger promotional budgets, and that would result, hopefully, in a rapid improvement in sales. Trade figures already signified that, though 45s were still going strong, there was a burgeoning market for albums these days – and ones that didn't give short weight either, as had the throwaway *Orbisongs*, a Monument patchwork of A-sides, B-sides and tracks arbitrarily extracted from earlier LPs. Issued to squeeze revenue from 'Oh! Pretty Woman', this kind of record had become an anachronism now that the Beatles with their *Help!* soundtrack, Bob Dylan's *Bringing It All Back Home* and even *Session with the Dave Clark Five* – all without time-consuming fillers – were showing that the age of long-players created around a hit single were numbered.

In this respect, 1965's album, *There Is Only One Roy Orbison* was his first true album as a worthy product in its own right. Approaching thirty and in no position to take hits for granted, this new horizon seemed, superficially at least, to be part of a contingency plan for Roy to make headway as a 'quality' entertainer. Excuses offered for flop singles by the likes of Tony Bennett, Al Martino and their syrupy sort was that they were 'too good for the charts'. This plea was conveniently forgotten in 1966 when Frank Sinatra suddenly found himself at No.1 with the schmaltzy 'Strangers in the Night'.

Despite the lilting cocktail piano, a noticeable shying away from falsettos and growls, and the selection of Bob Montgomery's semi-standard *Big As I Can Dream*, *There Is Only One Roy Orbison* was no *Songs for Swinging Lovers*. Nevertheless with the exception of the jarring 'Sugar and Honey', it was a 'bedsit' rather than a dancing album. More cohesive than *Lonely and Blue* or *Orbisongs*, it also had a crisper sound – thanks to MGM's more advanced studio facilities. Roy sang on a separate track which meant that the accompaniment could now, if required, feature the Orbison guitar.

The hero of the hour, however, was Bill Dees who, either alone or with Roy, composed the five new songs from a programme of twelve. There'd been much delving into the Orbison/Melson file for items given originally to other artists – 'I'm in a Blue, Blue Mood', which had been recorded by Bob Luman, for example – as well as a recourse to non-originals like Chet Atkins' 'Afraid to Sleep'. Such back-sliding tended to occur when Orbison was unhappy or discontented: 'I couldn't eat, I couldn't sleep, I couldn't communicate, and I certainly couldn't write a song'.[12]

In spite of the writer's block, there was still a certain amount of soul-baring – most in evidence on the punchy version of 'Claudette', with Roy spitting out every word.

More subliminal were his interpretations of 'Two of a Kind'
– written by Bob Montgomery and Earl Sinks – and Melson's
'If You Can't Say Something Nice', which was presumably
about Claudette. On the back cover, Orbison was depicted
astride one of the three motorbikes that he and Claudette
had once ridden together. Now he rode alone – like the
freewheeler in the album's promotional single, 'Ride Away'.
Indifferent to rather than celebratory of his bitter freedom,
he zooms into a prairie sunset soaked in violins. Though
couched in romantic allusion, the lone rider – not surpris-
ingly – is on the look out for a bit of frivolity. There were
plenty of pretty girls after a bit of frivolity too . . .

Possibly because the brake had been applied to the monu-
mental operatics of old, 'Ride Away' furthered the wane of
Roy's hit parade fortunes. It really may have been 'too good
for the charts'. Fred Foster did not share this opinion, of
course. 'There's an old saying over here – "Don't disturb a
winning combination" – and he and I obviously were a
winning combination, and I think while getting adjusted to
a new producer or producers, his writing suffered. Whether
or not it was because he was then the possessor of the biggest
contract ever given an American artist at the time and
he lost his incentive, I don't know. I don't think he even
knew what happened, but he started doing things that,
to my mind, weren't prudent things to do to build his
career.'

The next item to be cast adrift on the vinyl oceans,
'Crawling Back', tended to support this argument in an
industry where sales are arbiters of success. It reached the
brink of Britain's Top Twenty, but only dithered for seven
weeks around the middle of the Hot Hundred in America –
and that's where it counted. Recounting the tale of some
poor, uncomplaining fool who always comes back for more
abuse, it was a perfectly reasonable song of its kind, but its
comparative failure was caused by too much subtlety in the
instrumentation. Acoustic arpeggios had replaced the crude
Gibson drang; instead of sawing bows, there was fairy dust.

The half-crazed howler of 'It's Over' was now beseeching his insensitive bitch with a box of chocolates.

This soft-sell attitude coloured much of the album from which 'Crawling Back' and the even less profitable 'Breakin' Up is Hard to Do' were lifted. Co-author with Dees of most of the songs on *The Orbison Way*, Roy's increased creative input intimated a more cheerful frame of mind. In Orbison's sweeping estimation there were only three subjects worth writing about: 'boy-girl relationships, one's fellow man and a relationship with God. All the rest anyone writes about means nothing.'[13] *The Orbison Way* concentrated exclusively on the first, apart from Dees' 'This Is My Land' which strayed beyond lovey-dovey tribulations to a lost Texas in which an oil well had yet to be dug. A lesser utopia, 'Time Changed Everything,' had a traveller returning to one still constant. Elsewhere, there were more complex explorations. With expansive flamenco strings, for example, 'The Loner' tackles a girl's illicit meetings with a town's ne'er-do-well.

As its sleeve notes spell out, nothing on *The Orbison Way* was alien to 'emotions any listener has experienced and can understand', but fans would still interpret lyrics like 'Breakin' Up is Hard to Do' and the sardonic 'It Ain't No Big Thing' as a commentary on their idol's private life – which was still unsettled. Like most divorced fathers, his access to the children brought him in contact with their mother. No matter how much Roy may have feigned aloofness, he was concerned about Claudette's welfare. He noticed how she had lost her old vivacity as she would be on the verge of tears each time they said goodbye. Come the New Year, he'd be back in Europe, he told her – but he'd write anyway.

After a trip to Scandinavia, he'd be engulfed in another UK tour by the spring. Because of his more modest ratings in the charts, there was again a danger of his being eclipsed by a support act. Omnipresent in Britain then were the Walker Brothers, three unrelated Americans who had become pin-ups in girls' magazines, filling the space left by the Byrds, another equally fascinating US act. Walker Brother

John Maus' assertion that 'being on a bill with him has brought fantastic luck to other artists'[14] came true when, mid-tour, his group's fifth single, 'The Sun Ain't Gonna Shine Anymore', started a four-week reign at No.1. Moreover, Maus' fellow long-haired heart-throb, Scott Engel, had the range, projection and impeccable control of a coltish Sinatra – and an Orbison too for that matter. Not only was he another proverbial 'pop singer who can really sing', but his also was an aura – real or imagined – of one who has known sadness.

On the opening night at Finsbury Park Astoria, the battle of the billing seemed a foregone conclusion. Smothered by hysterical screaming, the Brothers' energetic gyrations were impeded when fans broke through the barricade of shirt-sleeved security manning the front of the stage. After this display, Roy risked a dismissal as archaic – especially as his latest record was nowhere near the Top Twenty. Collected and professional, this veteran of pop went the distance with his old favourites, exacting their habitual sweet surrender to justify his closing the show.

It would be 'a tour I remember more than any other,'[15] he said later. At the Walthamstow Granada on Easter Monday, the curtains would divide on a seated Orbison with his left foot in plaster. Without a worried wife to deter him, he'd been competing in celebrity motorcycle scrambles since the previous autumn. Surprise gave way, therefore, to delight when an invitation to a meet at Hawkstone Park (near Shrewsbury) was delivered to his suite at the Westbury Hotel.

Three hours before the first race, a loophole in Roy's £250,000 insurance policy was brought to his attention. It stipulated that he wasn't to take part in any scramble if it was windy. With a gale lashing the racecourse, Orbison in belted overcoat glumly resigned himself to flagging in the winners. By mid-afternoon, however, the excitement overcame him and he begged champion rider Dave Bickers to lend him his 250 cc Czechoslovakian machine for a lap of

honour. In order to be identified more easily beneath the
peaked helmet, the foolhardy pop singer did not remove his
otherwise unnecessary sunglasses. Two hundred yards after
kick-starting the machine, it skidded off the track, throwing
him onto the grass. In front of 15,000 astonished spectators,
Roy gamely remounted. Back in the paddock, a mob clam-
oured for autographs. Amongst them were leather-clad
rockers whose greasy steeds roared with fiercer menace than
the hated mods' phutting Lambrettas. Roy's 'Ride Away' –
a precursor to 'Born to Be Wild', was a fixture on jukeboxes
in cafés frequented by Rocker gangs.

Escorted from the Hawkstone Park meet by a cavalcade
of mounted rockers, nothing seemed amiss until Roy's Rolls-
Royce glided into east London as street lights flickered. In
Thorpe Coombe General Hospital near the Granada, a duty
doctor in casualty treated the broken ankle. Within Orbison's
hearing an hour later, a theatre lighting technician muttered
'He doesn't have to sing with his foot, does he?' A stool was
provided and, at showtime, a wincing Roy, with knuckles
whitened round the neck of his Gibson, began a 'Running
Scared' that pain honed to razor-sharp poignancy.

Of course, the tabloids latched onto the 'irony' in the title
of his current single, 'Twinkle Toes', but this unlooked-for
publicity wasn't enough to lengthen its chart life of a month.
A discotheque floor filler with manufactured 'party' ambience and trendy fuzz-toned 'Satisfaction' guitar as its irritant
factors, the feverish 'Twinkle Toes' was 'about a dancing
girl . . . pretending to be happy and gay but I think she's
lonely and covering up'.[16] Apparently, the idea for it came
to him while he was watching a line of chorus girls at the
Palladium on the Sunday he'd announced his divorce.

It was now a year after that strange day. News of his
injury reached Claudette in Houston – seven hours behind
Greenwich Mean Time. Before nightfall, she had boarded
a flight to England. Knowing Roy to have performed with
streaming colds, she was concerned that his insistence that
the show must go on would not let the bones heal, and

irreversible complications would set in. He could be an obstinate so-and-so. With old affections flooding her heart, it had also crossed Claudette's distressed mind that she might win her husband back.

After Walthamstow, the host had descended on Chester for a concert in an 800-capacity cinema. That Tuesday, in a hotel on the city's outskirts, Claudette caught up with Roy. Muzzy with painkillers, he rose up on his crutches to embrace a 'pretty little pet' with travel-tousled hair and rings under her eyes. 'We both suddenly realized we didn't want to be apart – and that was it. It was wonderful to see Claudette again.'[10]

After the tour wound down, the cast re-assembled in Soho's La Dolce Vita restaurant on St George's Day to witness Roy slicing a guitar-shaped thirtieth birthday cake. A further cause for celebration was that Claudette and Roy – too late to cancel the decree absolute – had resolved to re-marry as soon as it could be arranged. The ceremony back in America would be as discreet as the divorce. 'It was all a hush-hush affair. Only the essential witnesses were there.'[17]

The best man was Bill Dees, who was continuing to work on songs for the film with a working title of *The Fastest Guitar Alive* while the lovebirds took themselves off on a second honeymoon in Florida. Though they'd lost the knack of writing smash hits, Bill and Roy were as prolific as the Orbison/Melson team had been. On the latest LP, *The Classic Roy Orbison*, the only non-original had been a drum-heavy version of 'Never Love Again' by Cajun brothers, Rusty and Doug Kershaw. A new lyrical aggression, hardening the general climate of the album, was instanced by a more pronounced emphasis on percussion. There was the usual quota of old-style, string-laden love ballads – 'Where is Tomorrow', 'Losing You', 'Going Back to Gloria' – and 'Growing Up' had a pretty-but-nothing bounce. Nevertheless, some of the faithful may have been alienated by clumsy attempts to address contemporary issues – as in the rushing agitation of 'City Life' or 'Pantomime', which was devoid of melody. Because you weren't quite sure how to take it, more fascinating was the whimsical quasi-rockabilly of '(No) I'll Never Get Over You', which namechecked 'Mary Lou', 'Peggy Sue' and 'Suzie Q'. However, this paled into insignificance beside 'Just Another Name For Rock and Roll', which ran a gauntlet of such US-only phenomena as the Mashed Potato and Ubangi Stomp in the same breath as it referred to the Hippy Hippy Shake and 'Twist and Shout'. Three years out of date, it was a kind of 'Orbison Goes Merseybeat' outing.

Roy and Bill had their moments as composers, but nobody expected them to be the next Lennon and McCartney. In its pooling of so many of the accessories of mid-sixties pop, the neatest conclusion would be that *The Classic Roy Orbison* wasn't so much 'classic' as typical of prevalent cultural trends. Weighing its mistakes against some startling breaks with the past, this final album of 1966 reveals an artist in uncertain transition – and it is worth a listen for that reason alone.

On the domestic front, however, much of the old routine had been re-established. As if nothing had happened, he'd make time to accompany Claudette to the ski club, while she'd be hand-in-hand with him at the annual country festival in Nashville. As he'd done in the poor-but-happy era before 'Only the Lonely', he'd traipse behind her with the trolley in the supermarket. With a relief that he did not articulate, Roy had cut down on work – though, with Claudette as prompt, he was trying to memorize his lines for *The Fastest Guitar Alive*. During the few weeks left to them, the Orbisons were savouring just being together again.

After sorting out a sitter for the children, Claudette and Roy packed for a June weekend at the National Drag Races near Bristol, a resort two hundred miles away on the Virginia border. With another couple, they travelled as befitted the occasion – Roy on his gleaming 120 mph Harley Davidson; Claudette on a slower BMW. Thundering homewards on 7 June, dusk found the four riders slowing down to pass through Gallantin, a small town only a few miles north-east of Old Hickory. A thirty-year-old truck driver named Kenneth Herald – later charged with involuntary manslaughter – pulled out from a side turning. With a screech of brakes, Claudette Orbison vanished beneath the articulated lorry's double wheels on her BMW as her husband watched in helpless horror.

In the hospital an hour later, she was pronounced dead, 'and then it was left to me to tell our three boys. I explained to Roy Duane and he seemed to understand.'[18] The eldest son would be permitted to attend the interment at Nashville's Woodlawn Cemetary.

So ended the first act of Roy Orbison's tragedy. As in Guy Pellaert's well-known illustration, 'Rock Dreams', myth would paint the ugly and cruel release of Claudette's spirit in the bright, pre-Raphaelite sentiment of a death disc: with his crash helmet on the tarmac beside him, a kneeling Roy wearing his stage gear looks thoughtful as one crystal tear drops to the unblemished face of Claudette, who is cradled in his arms. She gazes back up at him peacefully, as beautiful in death as she'd been in life.

Notes

1 *Melody Maker*, 23 May 1963
2 *New Musical Express*, 18 September 1964
3 *Punch*, 23 December 1988
4 *Melody Maker*, 13 August 1966
5 *Melody Maker*, 20 February 1965
6 *New Musical Express*, 31 May 1963
7 *New Musical Express*, 30 April 1964
8 *On the Beat*, Radio Merseyside
9 *Daily Mirror*, 8 March 1965
10 *Daily Express*, 30 March 1966
11 *Daily Express*, 1 April 1966
12 *New Musical Express*, 20 December 1980
13 Concert programme, 1979
14 *Daily Sketch*, 1 April 1966
15 *Disc*, 25 June 1966

16   *Melody Maker*, 26 March 1966
17   *Melody Maker*, 26 March 1966
18   *Daily Sketch*, 27 April 1970

7

Cry Softly, Lonely One

Nothing would ever be the same again – not even the past. So many of his old songs – 'Only the Lonely' and 'Leah', for example – would now carry prophetic meaning to the most casual Orbison listener. This morbid search for profundities in such lines as the following from 'Borne on the Wind' – 'Between the sunset and the dawn/so tenderly/your memory/lingers with me all night long' – anticipates the idolatry that was already beginning to elevate pop from ephemera to Holy Writ. Soon we would be entering what Roy Orbison called 'the crazy late sixties; not 1966–7, but after that when it got real weird – politics, music, fashion. Everything went crazy, sort of.'[1] Crazy was the man whose obsessive analysis of Bob Dylan's lyrics was such that, in order to prove one pet theory, he placed a wanted ad in a New York underground magazine for a Dylan urine sample.

At the dawn of this Age of Aquarius, one of pop's eternal verities still held water. From Buddy Holly's No.1 in 1959 to John Lennon's one 'Starting Over' in 1980, it was accepted that a death in pop sells records. In the week following his wife's burial, Roy's latest single jumped from thirty-six to eighteen in the British charts, his biggest hit for more than a year. That it was the hoary old 'Lana', dragged from Monuments' vaults by Fred Foster, didn't matter. With all the publicity generated by the Orbison tragedy, it couldn't miss.

Within a fortnight, the widower faced the press. 'That really is wonderful news – especially now,' he replied, when told the news about 'Lana'. Yes, he was keen to get to grips with *The Fastest Guitar Alive* next month. 'In fact,' he continued, 'I aim to do a whole heap of work for the next few months. It'll help.' Too polite to change the subject, he answered that he hadn't been put off motorbikes, because 'people have accidents in automobiles, in airplanes, just as much . . . at least, I'd like to feel this way about it. I don't know yet that I really do. My thinking just isn't connected at the moment. I think it's a bit early to say how I feel.'[2]

Hot on the heels of Monument, MGM had also nipped in with a new single infinitely more tear-jerking and profitable than 'Lana'. Leading off with Chopinesque piano arpeggios and the statement, 'It's too soon to know if I can forget her,' this despondent number was a heaven-sent means by which Orbison could be propelled into the public eye again after a perturbing chain of flops. After all the company had practically gone into hock to sign him up.

While his handlers, past and present, derived what gain was possible from the situation, Roy coped as best he could. The black melancholy which now held him in its grip seemed to reduce to caricature the words in which he had veiled most of his hits. It penetrated his exhausted slumber with fragments of memory, disjointed thoughts: 'in dreams I walk with you, in dreams, I talk to you . . .' So often they were of trivialities – the canteen queue at college; a drizzling car park; dumb anguish in Houston; in her biker leathers at Bristol. Jerked awake again, dawn seemed a year away as the grievous truth replaced the balm of ignorance: 'memories like falling leaves just fill the air'.

Among sympathetic ears at that time were Fred Foster, whose childhood had ended with his father's sudden death, and, when back home in Memphis, Jerry Lee Lewis, whose son had drowned. Next door to Roy lived another insomniac. Fresh from a failed marriage, Johnny Cash had a police record for drug-related offences. The latest one had been a thirty day suspended sentence in January for possession. Once nearly a goner through overdosing, it hadn't been unusual for Cash to come down from amphetamines in a cell, unable to recall the circumstances that had led him there.

Unalike temperamentally – Johnny a man of extremes versus mild-mannered Roy – they became intimates as each faced up to and mastered his own inner chaos. Johnny, whose mouth had once turned the air blue with his swearing, was now, through the love of a good woman, ripe for religion.

Already a practising Christian, Bill Dees – a pallbearer at the funeral – had been another on hand day or night when Roy needed to talk. Although his colleague did not attend church as regularly, Dees gathered from their discussions that, true to his background, Roy 'didn't just believe in God; he had a personal relationship with him'. Though he would never demean himself with albums of musical Bible-bashing like Elvis, many of Roy's songs – alone or with a co-writer – were as devotional in their boy/girl way as hymns.

In the autumn of 1966, however, as always happened in the dark hours of his life, nothing would come. Almost eagerly, he'd sit down to compose with Bill but, after strumming a bit, all the fragments of song would sound the same to him, infantile vibrations hanging in the air, then fading away. A glazed languor would set in and he'd drift off to the lake, the television, the refrigerator – anywhere but back to the job in hand. Bill said nothing. Roy would get over it. He always would.

Already written, the soundtrack album for *The Fastest Guitar Alive* had to tie-in with its première. Therefore, both to satisfy MGM and provide occupational therapy, Orbison plunged into a project that, when suggested to Fred Foster, had been shrugged off as 'an exercise in futility'. MGM, thinking otherwise, were most enthusiastic about a twelve-track Orbison album of songs written by Don Gibson. That any product at all could be squeezed out of the bereaved star was enough.

As a taster, 'Too Soon to Know' had come within an ace of topping the UK chart – though it had only hovered around the middle of *Billboard*'s Hot Hundred. Produced by Jim Vienneau, *Roy Orbison Sings Don Gibson* did not re-invent its raw material to anything like the extent of New York's Vanilla Fudge, who would grab the Supremes' 'You Keep Me Hangin' On' by the scruff of the neck and wring the life out of it a few months later. Much of Roy's most public declaration of his artistic debt to Gibson adhered unambitiously to the original arrangements. Opening side one, for instance, 'I'd Be a Legend in My Time' was pleasant enough, but it sounded listless against an earlier Frank Ifield version, not to mention Ray Charles' gravelly recording, also from 1963. Most of the LP's most inspired brushstrokes occurred when unusual instruments were brought into the faster items – such as the balalaika in 'What About Me' or the kazoo in 'Lonesome Number One'. In fairness, while 'Roy Orbison Sings Don Gibson' is less than spectacular, it added up for Orbison – with his appearances in the US charts now all but spent – to give his still potent overseas markets songs by a composer of whom the majority had never heard. It was all new to them.

His moods had fluctuated but, as the Gibson sessions had progressed, Roy had contributed more to their outcome than simply singing along to Vienneau's ideas. Day by day, he was coming to accept the loss: 'teach your heart to smile/ and live a little while in memories'. As happened so often in his life, the balance was quickly restored. 'I had reasoned it out that if you take all that is good in life, you must accept tragedy if it comes along.'[3] He wasn't the only single parent in the world. His own elderly but supportive parents had taken charge of the children splendidly, even uprooting themselves from Texas and coming to live in Hendersonville so that their famous son could 'get on with all the work I had to do. I wanted to be able to remove myself and look at what had happened objectively before I retired, before I quit, before I dropped out or became convinced that life was not worth living. I just turned away.'[3]

Looming largest on the agenda was *The Fastest Guitar Alive*, whose script had been re-written in a more light-hearted vein at the request of its producer, Sam Katzman. Katzman, a man without highbrow pretensions, was a Donald McGill among film-makers who, by the mid-sixties, could dash off an Elvis vehicle in less than a month, each one a quasi-musical of cheery unreality usually more vacuous and streamlined than the one before. Roy Orbison thought so too. 'Once I started seeing his movies, other than *King Creole* and *Jailhouse Rock*, I thought they were mistakes.'[4]

Shortly after the cameras began to roll, Roy suspected that *The Fastest Guitar Alive* wasn't a taut espionage drama any more. In lieu of their nervous leading man's economic acting ability, Katzman and his director, Michael Moore, had re-modelled the story as a 'rollicking Western comedy-drama . . . in which all kinds of hot and hilarious adventures ensue.'[5] At MGM's insistence, a last-minute cameo had been written for Domingo Samudio who, as 'Sam the Sham', was picking the bones from *Wooly Bully*, a gloriously dim worldwide smash of 1965. MGM thought he needed the exposure. As Samudio was a Texan Mexican, Katzman could surely fit him in somewhere.

Another obstacle to overcome was that of Orbison's mousy countenance. Thanks to a daily cosmetic miracle, Roy would walk onto the set as Johnny Banner, Confederate officer. In contact lenses, processed hair and beautified almost beyond recognition by an hour of make-up, he was every inch a gigolo – if not a film idol. As if auditioning for the Merseybeats or Los Paraguayos, he posed for a syndicated publicity shot in a bat-winged blouse that looked like whipped cream. Seated, he held an acoustic guitar in mid-strum.

This was no ordinary six-string though – more a six-shooter. Just as a boulevardier's walking cane could be converted into a duelling rapier when convenient, so Johnny Banner's guitar turned into a rifle to fight off marauding

Indians – a frequent obligation throughout the film. 'Based on actual historical fact',[5] Banner and his comic sidekick, Steve – played by Presley regular, Sammy Jackson – rob the US mint in San Francisco to finance the beleaguered rebel forces with the blessing of their superiors. Fleeing with the wagonload of gold bullion – to the tune of 'Heading South' – they learn half-way to army headquarters in El Paso of Robert E. Lee's surrender at Appomattox courthouse in April 1865. Downgraded from soldiers under orders to common crooks, the honourable Johnny and Steve elect to return their prize of war. They are hampered in their attempts by bandits, pistoleros and other dastards who cast covetous eyes on the loot. However, it would have been an odd Katzman potboiler if Banner and his Tonto hadn't cleared their good names – just in the nick of time.

Though apparently capable of 'rattling strings like a Gatling gun', Banner in fact ignites no nimble fretwork fireworks during the film's musical interludes. The essentially rigid structures of the plot would bring forth a soundtrack album that can be seen as either an aberration or a refreshing change from a stylistic diet unbroken since 1960. From time to time when he could smile, Roy seemed to have had fun recording it. There are traces of an earlier Orbison in some of the pieces – most markedly 'Borne on the Wind' and 'Whirlwind'; but, as you might expect, its cover portrait of a gunslinger mowing down a horde of whooping savages in hot pursuit is an accurate guide to its content. It encompasses elongated tunes and lyrics to complement particular scenes – as epitomized by 'Good Time Party', with its gambolling clavicord and bandstand brass, and the homespun philosophizing of 'Best Friend': 'a diamond is a diamond, a stone is a stone but a man's not all good or all bad'. In one number, Roy actually breaks into Spanish for a couple of verses prior to a pistolero's incarceration 'six feet underground'.

According to the actor/composer, the title song, was 'supposed to describe my way of life, but I had a problem living up to that'; while 'Rollin' On' was written 'because I had to tell these girls we had to leave with the gold, and I guessed the only way to get out was to sing a song.'[6] From the cantering of 'Pistolero' to the shivering strings of 'Whirlwind' and the lazy hobo's saddle trot of 'River', it was the sound at any given moment that seemed to matter rather than individual pieces. Like any semi-incidental music, little was designed to divert attention from the action. Nonetheless, the enduring influence of *The Fastest Guitar Alive* was keenly felt by England's Dave Dee, Dozy, Beaky, Mick and Tich who borrowed from it for 'The Legend of Xanadu' – all bullwhips and ruined haciendas – which, in 1968, became their only UK No. 1.

Citizen Kane it wasn't, but critics were kind to Roy when the film went out on general release. Perhaps their pens were blunted in sympathy. The general verdict was that, as a thespian, Orbison had coped quite well with what had been, admittedly, an undemanding role. If not a natural actor like Presley, he'd put up a better show than Ricky Nelson, Dave Clark and other pop stars who over the years had fancied themselves as cinema attractions. Obviously, Roy's cinema-going hadn't been wasted.

It was noted by some that Johnny Banner's embraces with his female lead, Maggie Pierce, had been shot in non-committal shadow; Roy's ingrained Pat Boone-prudity made him disinclined to exchange lingering kisses with a married woman, no matter how above board the situation. Though one wasn't in evidence when he attended the film's New York premiere on 15 January 1967, there were, however, whispers of a lady friend. A few weeks later, the paparazzi named Francine Herack, a twenty-three-year-old air hostess from Los Angeles, as the 'new pretty woman in Roy's lonely life'. Even so, there was no hint of any impropriety – other than whatever sleazy conclusion could be drawn from Orbison's forlorn hope that the busy Miss Herack might visit him on tour. Unfortunately, 'it looks as though it's impossible – so we're thinking of spending a holiday in Jamaica instead when we can really get to know more about one another'.[7]

After a moment's pause over the typewriter keys, some hacks even found similarities between Francine and the late Mrs Orbison. This new one, she's American – and a brunette too. Weird, eh?

Roy's romance with his TWA girl may not have been as serious as some of the more trivial tabloids tried to make out, but the root cause of its collapse – and it was the same with other 'constant companions' – may have been the three boisterous young strangers in need of a mother. 'A father isn't enough. I can only take them part of the way.'[7] After that eerie Christmas of 1966, Orbison sifted through over 2,000 applications from all over the free world for the well-paid but exacting task of nannying Roy Duane and his brothers.

By April, he'd whittled these down to a matronly English-woman, Mrs Dorothy Cook who, to her advantage, also had secretarial skills, having risen to head typist with an insurance firm. Sharing her apartment in the Orbison mansion would be thirty-year-old Mrs Cook's husband Bob, who had been taken on to maintain the fleet of vintage cars – and to act as occasional chauffeur. When the childless couple were installed, Roy Orbison embarked on a round of international commuting more hectic than any he'd undertaken before.

It was the overall drop in Orbison's record sales that had necessitated this more intense focus on touring. Monument's compilation, *The Best of Roy Orbison*, would always sell steadily. There was also the unforeseen jackpot with 'Penny Arcade' in Australia. But for the next few years, Roy would largely ignore the United States – as its pop consumers were ignoring him: 'I tended to fulfil commitments around the world and then come home to rest.'[8]

On his own soil he was something of a has-been by 1967, lost to a nether world of Midwest three-thousand seaters and thence to the supper clubs. As early as January 1966, Roy Orbison had played his first cabaret date. In that Atlanta night-club, customers in their obligatory ties punished pricey liquors and guzzled food, while the sunken orchestra discreetly sight-read musak as showtime crept closer. Sickening him more was a return to engagements in the Nevada desert city where he'd once lost at roulette. 'If you do well in Las Vegas, they cut the show short because they want to get the customers to the tables. Vegas is there for the gambling; it's no place for an artist despite the big money you can make.'[4]

Other than the occasional trip to New York, Los Angeles and back to Atlanta, Roy's North American stock-in-trade had boiled down to small-town cinemas, civic halls and the larger social clubs – where he'd be subjected to a build-up by some buffoon of a compère who'd just regaled the audience with gags that would shock a drunken marine. On the same bill, there might also be some fallen Bobby with a strange musical concoction of old-style rock 'n' roll and third-rate renderings of Sinatra numbers. He might even throw in the one or two hits of his own from way back when.

Yet even in these desperate backwaters, Roy Orbison invariably brought the house down. Running through his best-loved songs for the people who loved them – and him – best of all in some back-of-beyond palais in Missouri or Nebraska might not be such a bad place for anyone to be in 1967 after all. Just think of the wretched fates of Gene Vincent, Frankie Lymon and others trapped in a vocation founded on short-lived novelty. Orbison's greater chart grandeur would guarantee work for good money for as long as he could stand. 'I'm making more money now than I did before; I play to more people than I did before, and I sell relatively as many records,'[9] he said in 1967. On such a plateau, a hit record can only be a sideshow. Perhaps the Roy Orbison story should have ended there.

Of the Orbison merchandise ranged in the foyers of these oases of entertainment, you could bank on *The Very Best of Roy Orbison* selling briskest of all. As he didn't bother with much beyond the hits, it hardly seemed worthwhile displaying *Cry Softly, Lonely One* (his latest album) or *The*

Fastest Guitar Alive soundtrack, issued within weeks of each other to the detriment of both.

Cry Softly, Lonely One paralleled *There Is Only One Roy Orbison*, which had likewise masked a non-productive trough. Leaving aside the album of Don Gibson numbers, this was the first post-Claudette collection. Like the 'divorce' album, it showcased only five Orbison/Dees compositions out of twelve selections. Otherwise, there was the heavy-hearted 'Just One Time', left over from the Gibson masters, plus another half-dozen from the vaults of Acuff-Rose. These included 'Here Comes the Rain', a slow waltz from Mickey Newbury, first of a new breed of Southern writers, and, from the old firm, Joe Melson's title track. Though he'd composed this with Jim Gant, who would produce the avant-garde 'Southbound Jericho Parkway' for Roy in 1968, Melson couldn't resist inserting some antiquated nonsense syllables in the style of 'Only the Lonely' and 'Blue Angel'.

The technical virtuosity of the later sixties impinged as much on this reconstruction as anywhere else on the LP. In its varying degrees of acoustic overspill and minor intricacies such as the reptilian piano glissando in 'Memories', Orbison's voice floats effortlessly over layer upon layer of treated sound. Gadgetry and constant retakes intrude upon the grit; it was perhaps that non-retractable margin of error that had put teeth into some of the early records.

Rolling like treacle over 'Girl Like Mine' is a Hammond organ whose warm purr was to the sixties what the polysynthesizer would become to a less innocent pop generation. Cropping up too are fragments of jive talk – 'groovy', 'a gas' – peculiar to the age. The sequence of moods on 'Cry Softly, Lonely One', however, belong to Orbison alone. He censures his woman for flirting in 'That's a No No'; but finds his home empty without her in 'Time to Cry', on which Floyd Cramer's note-crushing commiserations are echoed by the strings. In this track, as on 'She' and 'Memories', Claudette's spectre effuses from the speakers.

In 'Memories', however, the sentiment is not laid on with

a trowel. Had this song existed in the summer of 1966, MGM might have thought it too mawkish to release as a single: 'Even in the darkest night when dreams fade away/ when your love has gone, you'll never be alone with memories'. Accompanied only by piano, bass and drums, Roy's elegant resignation is as loaded as the sonorous wailings of 'It's Over'. Probably Orbison and Dees' most fetching libretto, 'Memories' satisfies every qualification required of a 'standard' like 'September Song' or 'Yesterday'. For all that, it was consigned to a B-side, while lesser songs like 'She', 'Cry Softly, Lonely One' and the hard-talking 'Communication Breakdown' were lifted from the album as top sides. They all, needless to say, sold like hot cakes in Australasia and the Far East, if nowhere else.

In the British Top Twenty, he had signed off with 'There Won't Be Many Coming Home' which, unhappily, had sloped off the charts at the beginning of his tour with the Small Faces in March 1967. Luckily for Roy, this Cockney quartet's current single, 'I Can't Make It', lived up to its title.

'There Won't Be Many Coming Home' (along with 'Best Friend') had been 'composed when *The Fastest Guitar Alive* was still regarded as a serious film. Its actual subject matter was the American Civil War but it could equally well apply to a Third World War – or even the fighting in Vietnam.'[9] Despite – or perhaps because of – Orbison's clean, conservative image, 'There Won't Be Many Coming Home' earned him, albeit briefly, the approbation of the blossoming hippie sub-culture. Though not as multi-purpose a protest as 'Eve of Destruction' by Barry McGuire or Hedgehoppers Anonymous' 'It's Good News Week' of the same year, Roy's contribution to the anti-war effort was seen as a rebuttal of RCA's fastest selling disc of 1966, the jingoistic 'Ballad of the Green Berets' by fellow Texan, Sergeant Barry Sadler.

Orbison's lyrics may have been less perfunctorily boy-meets-girl these days, but they did not coincide with the

accelerating musical complexity of another sergeant, whose
Lonely Hearts Club Band had helped more than any other to
turn pop from harmless entertainment into egghead activity.
The Beatles, the Rolling Stones and other humble beat
groups were now pseudo-mystics, dictating shifts in musical
– and social – consciousness that had even penetrated below
the Mason-Dixon line. As far south as Texas, there were
psychedelic combos whose very names – Infinite Staircase,
Mechanical Switch and the Thirteenth Floor Elevators –
intimated more abstract leanings than those of the Wink
Westerners and the Teen Kings. While sitars whined, tapes
looped and Frank Zappa inquired, 'Who are the Brain
Police?', Roy Orbison 'didn't hear a lot I could relate to so
I kind of stood there like a tree where the winds blow and
the seasons change, and you're still there and you bloom
again'.[10]

For most of 1967, it was business as usual. After the Small
Faces' stint, Roy was Down Under again. Greeting him
backstage at the first engagement were the familiar faces of
the Walker Brothers. Like Roy, their predominantly slowish
ballad style made them sound archaic to the younger hip
audience during that Summer of Love. Worse still, they
were too young and long-haired to cut much ice with admirers
of 1967's paradoxical chart buster – stardust-and-roses
crooner, Engelbert Humperdinck, whose syrupy 'Release
Me' had kept the Beatles' 'Strawberry Fields Forever'
off the No. 1 spot in Britain. This and other counter-
revolutions of schmaltz were of course applauded by Tin
Pan Alley and Sixteenth Avenue during that watershed
year.

Cause for milder celebration had been the fall from grace
of another act which had supported Orbison in Australia.
Innovative though it may have been, the Yardbirds' highbrow single, 'Happenings Ten Years Time Ago', had recently put the tin lid on to their chart career. Some
considered it an aural nightmare, while others shared one
pundit's claim that it was 'possibly the greatest single ever

released'.[11] Shaking baffled heads in the wings, Orbison and his Candy Men inclined towards the former view – while Yardbirds' drummer Jim McCarty's concentration wandered as the star 'seemed to do all his old hits in chronological order'.

Neither faction seemed aware of their underlying similarities. Whereas Orbison had superimposed Ravel, flamenco and the balalaika onto his musical grid, the Yardbirds made use of Gregorian chant, Indian ragas and other erudite obscurities. Each had made use of symphonic tempo changes and dynamics. In two years' time, Roy would record the surreal 'Southbound Jericho Parkway', aswarm with jarring vignettes of music spliced together beneath his sung narrative. In retrospect, the chasm between 'In Dreams' and 'Shapes of Things' does not seem so great, but in 1967 the Yardbirds played 'rock' – which only the finest minds could appreciate – while Roy Orbison was regarded by *Rolling Stone*, *International Times* and other 'groovy' journals as an outmoded perpetrator of vulgar 'pop'. Nevertheless, the Yardbirds and Roy parted cordially enough, with the headliner presenting one of the quintet's guitarists, Jimmy Page, with some Fender Telecaster accessories from Nashville. By 1967, however, the coast-to-coast package tour had had its day. Because they'd ceased to perform on stage, the Beatles were spared having to be 'real' musicians. These days, 'bands' – not groups – that carried any weight were demanding public attention for lengthy concept albums, rock operas and other epics that couldn't be crammed into a ten-minute spot between the Terry Young Six and Erkey Grant. There was also growing respect for instrumental proficiency as outlines dissolved between rock and jazz. Instead of the swooning hysteria of old, there was serious 'appreciation' of guitar heroes like Jeff Beck, Alvin Lee – the 'fastest guitar alive' – and Eric 'God' Clapton, whose high-decibel trio, Cream, could spin out a three-verse blues for nigh on twenty po-faced minutes to tumultuous applause. This was as much a case of the Emperor's New Clothes as screaming at Brian

Poole had been, but the divide between rock and pop had become such that mismatched pairings like Roy Orbison and the Yardbirds were no longer mutually beneficial.

If there was room for another act on the same bill as Cream, the Jimi Hendrix Experience or the Rolling Stones, it couldn't be someone who just stood up and sang fiddly two-minute singles without embellishment. Not only had it become uncool for a collegiate youth to own up to liking him, but hitting Roy harder was the realization that he couldn't get an American pop hit to save his life. Apparent already were dwindling returns everywhere else. The prospects seemed so depressing that Orbison no longer studied the charts.

Physically, he was none too hale either. Noticeably tubbier, he'd also had to cancel several engagements in the autumn of 1967 because of a severe throat infection. Moreover, by the New Year, he'd been in hospital twice for the removal of a kidney stone. Apart from these enforced rest periods, he hadn't taken a holiday since 1959.

Why not pack it in? Wise investments had ensured that he could live quite comfortably into old age if he retired at his present age of thirty-two. But, although he would tell reporters that he was 'really doing it for the people who made me a millionaire',[12] what he could not articulate – not even to himself – was that he enjoyed the life of a travelling celebrity. How would he have felt if he hadn't been recognized during his surprise appearance in the 1966 London-to-Brighton Historic Commercial Vehicle Run? There he was in green-tinted specs, fingers festooned in diamond rings, behind the wheel of a bright maroon 1920 Maxwell charabanc with its roof peeled back for all to see. More uncomfortably conspicuous beside him was a blonde in an Edwardian picture hat.

He called the bluff of another American star who'd been 'complaining to me that he couldn't get away from his fans. I felt like telling him to go home to the States if he wanted to go unrecognized.'[13] However awkward the time or place when autograph books were thrust his way, Roy would still sign and smile. Like deified Caesar in Gaul, he'd never offend by refusing votive offerings – like the piece of fabric from Baron von Richthofen's Fokker Triplane received from his New Zealand fan club. Then there were the birds awaiting his collection from Britain's Budgerigar Information Bureau during the tour of 1968. He'd intended them as a coming-home present for the boys. Instead, they went to the fan club in London.

One of the cheapest intrinsically valuable gifts was the demo tape of 'Penny Arcade'. With deceptive casualness, this musical record of an idle hour was pushed onto Orbison's table in a Beefeater grill in Leeds by its composer, Sammy King. 'It's the only time this sort of thing has happened to me,' Roy would recall a couple of years later, 'and it turned out a winner'.[14]

'Penny Arcade' would almost – but not quite – do the trick. Unfashionable though he was, Roy Orbison was quite prepared to stick it out, as he'd done often enough before, in the firm belief that another big record would surface, because 'when I hear a favourite artist of mine who is not getting hit product, I can still hear what I love about the artist in there. There comes a saturation point where people like to move on to newer things, not necessarily better. It's the way it should be – then if you're into something new, you can look back and say, "Was this really as good as I thought it was?" And in many cases, it is, and in a lot of cases you say, "That's better than I remember it being and it's still part of my life." So it could be that people move on temporarily.'[15]

With good reason, Orbison would rate much of his output of these lean years as at least the equal of his earlier smashes. 'Walk On' was a 'Running Scared'-type crescendo ballad, but its production clearly belongs to the multi-track ethos of the later sixties. More 'poetically' perhaps, the themes once explored in 'Growing Up' and 'You'll Never Be Sixteen Again' recur in 'Yesterday's Child', while 'Sugar Man' is a

rather derivative re-write of – you guessed it – 'Candy Man'.
'So Good' may not have been quite up to scratch either, but
the male backing counterpoint of 'Heartache' is every bit as
breathtaking as some of the Beach Boys' choral convolutions.
So disappointed was Roy by its dismal public reception that
he would try again with a slicker re-make six years later. On
a more adult tack, 'My Friend' predated C & W's new-found
popularity amongst the middle classes by its twist-in-the-tale
depiction of a harrowing domestic crisis.

This creative peak was motivated perversely by unresolv-
able tensions between Dees and Orbison. For the past two
years, Bill had been up there on stage to the far left of Roy,
harmonizing on the lines and choruses he'd sung on the
records. However, the show was never the high point of the
day for Dees. It was the new songs that mattered – but not
so much to Roy these days.

Orbison didn't seem to have many ideas of his own any
more. Mind you, he hadn't had much encouragement of
late. When they heard him do 'Blue Angel' for just short
of three minutes, Mr and Mrs Average turned back into
teenagers in high school, lovestruck and irresponsible. Was
the sole purpose of Roy Orbison to remind them of the good
old days? In this large scale of re-runs like the post-'Ooby
Dooby' slump a decade earlier, Roy found himself living on
past glories.

One consolation was that, freed from the constraints of
trying to sustain a run of hits, he was able to indulge himself
in a patchwork of different musical styles on record. Wilfully
uncommercial, the unprecedented 'Southbound Jericho
Parkway' lacked a single discernible melody line as it darted
from section to section, utilizing every instrument available.
A production rather than a song, this psychedelic soap opera
about a divorced father's suicide and its consequences was a
revelation to those who unearthed it on the B-side of 'My
Friend'.

Roy was not the composer of 'Southbound Jericho Parkway', but by dipping his toe into the oblique in this way,

he became trendy enough to be approached by arty Italian film director, Antonioni, to contribute a number to the soundtrack of *Zabriskie Point* to be sung at the closing credits. A hip 'catch us if you can', this fantasy about a group of wonderful young people who run away from over-civilized old squares would also feature items by the likes of the Pink Floyd, the Rolling Stones and the Grateful Dead. Talk of a second film starring Orbison had fizzled out – as had his attempt to form a London-based movie company with Peter Walsh. Responding eagerly to Antonioni's tangible incentive, Roy's 'So Young', though dependent, to a certain extent, upon its context in the film, was a self-written ballad – with help from Mike Curb and Roger Christian – in which youth is celebrated from the perspective of manhood. Although it showed the distance he had travelled from the 'twixt-twelve-and-twenty' agony uncle of 'Growing Up' in 1966, the song did not, however, mark the beginning of a return to form.

Now very much in the easy-listening bracket in the States, his *Roy Orbison's Many Moods* album was not thought worth releasing elsewhere. Nevertheless, the beautifully sung readings of chestnuts like 'Unchained Melody', 'Try to Remember' and, complete with shimmering mandolins, 'More', gave genuine pleasure to many listeners. 'What Now My Love', a bolder choice from the early sixties, hung on a familiar bolero rhythm. These nestled among three Orbison/Dees originals plus a handful more from the stable of Acuff-Rose. Two of the latter, 'Amy' and Mickey Newbury's 'Good Morning Dear', are reminiscent of the menacing and emotional work of Belgian composer Jacques Brel and, since the break-up of the Walker Brothers, his foremost interpreter, Scott Engel.

By contrast, 'I Recommend Her' smacked of Motown. This track was written by Mark Mathis, mainstay of the Newbeats, who was Bill Dees' new songwriting partner. Like Joe Melson before him, Bill was beginning to tire of his role as Orbison's sidekick. 'Writing needs to come from

the heart not the pocket' was his muttered maxim whenever
Roy asked for help in knocking out a new single for MGM
– nor did he like the prolonged absences from his wife and
four children. There'd also been a falling-out with Orbison
when Bob Montgomery – then riding high as the producer
of Bobby Goldsboro's 'Honey' – offered Bill an opportunity
to cut a single. With Roy's creative malaise quashing loyalty,
Dees quit the road and retreated back to Tennessee. Signed
up to a label of no great merit, he restarted a recording
career held in abeyance since the Whirlwinds. Shamelessly,
he'd plug his own version of 'Oh! Pretty Woman' when on
stage at local venues.

   Though Orbison's work spectrum was on an international
scale, his records had become almost incidental to a liveli-
hood which depended more and more on personal appearances on the supper-club circuit – the hard-bought screaming
had all but stopped. Nowadays he appealed to those who,
having satiated their appetites for novelty, had been turned-
off by all this marijuana-smoking crap – they didn't know
about 'Southbound Jericho Parkway' and yearned for a bit
of 'decent' music. Roy's new audience contained ageing
Teddy Boys, parents with teenage children, and young
marrieds. There were incorrigible old rockers too who didn't
mind mothballing their leathers and jeans to squeeze into
Sunday clothes or smart casuals that were the norm at
Wigan Casino, Caesar's Palace in Luton and other citadels of
'quality' entertainment – above bingo but a long way from
Glyndebourne. In these places, there were rarely less than
capacity crowds even if Roy Orbison's presence didn't turn
a town on its head any longer.

   His own head had been turned one night when, after
finishing a show in Batley, he was persuaded to string along
with a party who were off to a discotheque in nearby Leeds.
This time, the city offered a more personal joy than the
'Penny Arcade' tape. Worth more than a second glance was
a girl – German, you say? – with waist-length black hair on
the dance floor. What struck him as odd about the girl was

that she seemed so bored by the music – and yet she was moving so beautifully . . . Eighteen-year-old Barbara Wellnoener-Jacobs had never been crazy about pop singers. Other dancers may have found Roy Orbison's descent into their midst impressively disturbing, but not Barbara, whose knowledge of him began and ended with 'Oh! Pretty Woman'.

When he introduced himself, Barbara's daunting Teutonic directness put him on his mettle: 'I was wearing a denim jacket at the time, and the first thing she said was what a terrible jacket it was. I told her it didn't belong to me, that I'd just borrowed it to stop catching cold. But I said that if she turned up at the show the next night, I would show her my best suit.'[16]

Sartorially he was spoilt for choice. A few days before the start of this particular British tour, he'd ventured out of the Westbury Hotel 'to get me some suits – around forty or so – and to see a little Scots fellow who makes my shirts. I need a few of them too – like around fifty or so. You have better workmanship in England – better materials too.'[17]

These leisurely preliminaries were typical of Orbison's revised attitude to work. On doctor's orders, he could no more dismiss a thousand miles between engagements as a few inches on a map. Hanging over him were mopping-up operations in unvisited minor territories like Crete and Taiwan, but to reduce the self-imposed strain of twice-nightly performances and battling with adverse acoustics in different auditoriums, 'it seemed easier to sit in one place for a week and do the show than to hop, skip and jump.'[18] After eight years of being forever on the move, he could sell out a month's residency at the prestigious Talk of the Town – only a walking distance from the Westbury. Arguably the highest-paid cabaret artist in Britain, he sang his songs to faces tanned on the ski slopes, bow-tied tuxedos, pearly adornments and drinks like melted crayon.

Like Enrico Caruso before the Great War, each Orbison classic would hush worshippers like a mass bell in Madrid.

Puccini had praised Signor Caruso's rapturous warbling as god-like; a London critic's more measured opinion of Orbison was that his 'secret seems to be understatement . . . his programming is exquisite . . . a hypnotic attraction.'[19]

Though he acquitted himself admirably before metropolitan swells, Roy wasn't above promoting his current single on the radio. It made just as much sense to amble down Memory Lane as well. On almost the final edition of the BBC Light Programme's pop showcase, 'Saturday Club', recorded in July 1968, 'Walk On' – in the charts by a whisker – was cushioned not between tracks from a new album but by 'Oh! Pretty Woman' and 'Only the Lonely'.

When recording the transmission in Birmingham, he'd been backed by the vocal trio and small orchestra from the Talk of the Town. Under the baton of Barry Booth, the girls had been requested to 'simmer a bit more. Camp it up a bit'.[18] For all his jocularity, Barry was dispirited by too much work. Between his Orbison commitments, there were demands for his services from London theatres – and these would draw him back to England permanently. Dissatisfied with his own efforts under pressure during the Talk of the Town season, he named a deliberately unrealistic figure for future work, an ultimatum that he knew would provoke Acuff-Rose into paying him off.

For Roy to take Barry and the orchestra on the road was impractical anyway. As well as the logistics of shunting such an operation from place to place, the expense would be so great that there'd be hardly any profit margin. Besides, would there be room for everyone on the stage of Wakefield Theatre or at the Double Diamond Club in Caerphilly? By exercising thrift, you could still put on an acceptable show. Partly through restrictions imposed by the British Musicians Union and partly because he'd an option on a cheaper alternative, Orbison had dispensed with the Candy Men, four of whom had then been absorbed into the Atlanta Rhythm Section, a studio session band; while the sharp-eyed might have spied other ex-Candy Men sweating it out with the McCoys and Buffalo Springfield. No matter how far he may have drifted into show business proper, the respect for former Orbison sidemen in rock circles was thus affirmed.

For the next few years, Roy would be backed mostly by the Art Movement, an English sextet recommended by Acuff-Rose's New Bond Street office. Modelling themselves vocally on the Beach Boys and the Four Seasons, and instrumentally on Blood, Sweat and Tears, their Decca single, 'Loving Touch' had been bland enough for a spell on the playlists of the BBC's two new national pop radio stations, whose cautious programming was beginning to make the UK Top Thirty shallower and less subversive in content. Harmless purveyors of popular song in outsized bow ties and dung-coloured stage costumes, the Art Movement were granted their own spot before the Big O's grand entrance.

After the gruff taciturnity of the Candy Men, Roy was refreshed by the Art Movement's easy professionalism and cheerful dedication to their craft. Indeed, with drummer Paul Munday as principal protagonist, he was even amenable to their suggesting changes in his time-honoured set. Little by little, the acts began to merge. Once he'd broken up the ballads with ravers like 'Mean Woman Blues' and 'What'd I Say'; now he was inserting Art Movement mainstays between his hits. As well as done-to-death set pieces from the beat boom, some onlookers were nonplussed when Roy also slipped in 'Help Me Rhonda' and even the drippy 'Loving Touch'.

The zenith of this collaboration was the appearance of an album recorded in London called *Big O*. This product – as their photo with freshly shampooed hair on its cheap beige sleeve testifies – was as much the Art Movement's as the Big O's. It made for tedious listening too. The unmistakable lead voice apart, there was the discomfiting suspicion that had *Big O* been offered anonymously to record companies, it might have courted rejection. This seemed to be confirmed by its non-release in the States. Shrill and neatly dovetailed accompaniment was not a recipe for excitement. As well as the new up-tempo numbers, there were flaccid renderings of 'Only You' from the Platters and Harry Belafonte's 'Scarlet Ribbons'. For good measure, some Acuff-Rose bagatelles were thrown in such as John D. Loudermilk's over-vocalized 'Break My Mind', issued as a single. *Big O* was supplemented further by 'Penny Arcade', in which the Nashville session players' smooth handling of its tricky switches of tempo puts the pointless frenzy of other tracks in a bad light.

Roy Orbison seemed to be plodding a well-beaten path from maturity to dreary repetition, making the most of every chance that came his way. He even admitted himself that he was 'just basically working. I didn't know where it was leading'.[20] By 1969, he didn't care much either. The scapegoat for his broken fortunes became MGM itself. 'In the first five years of the contract, there were six different presidents, and then someone bought the company and then sold the real estate, so they were not in the record business, so I don't know what I could have done had they been really solid.'[15]

For their part, the powers at MGM blamed Orbison's decline on more family traumas. This time though, there was no compensation in the form of a big hit – just the headlines in the newspapers. When he returned to public life, he was not a common-or-garden pop star on stage but a man from Hell.

On the morning of 16 September 1968, road manager Bob Blackburn phoned the Art Movement at their digs in the Midlands to inform them that the Bournemouth Pavilion show that night – the last of a six-week tour – had been cancelled. As he spoke, Roy was already halfway across the Atlantic, remembering another death, fuzzy-headed with an injected sedative.

Backstage in Birmingham, he'd missed the news by minutes. Discovering that he and Blackburn had decided to drive through the night to Bournemouth's Royal Spa Hotel, the London office had even left messages in motorway service stations en route, but the limousine didn't stop once during the two-hour journey to the seaside.

Leaning back into the deeply upholstered seat speeding along the open road made Roy feel positive. That German girl had showed up for the second night at Batley. Away from the disco's flashing lights and deafening row, their eyes had met and something had clicked. Before she left, they'd exchanged addresses and promised to keep in touch.

Business-wise, things were a bit slack right now, but people were still paying to see him regardless of passing trends. When MGM's time was up, he'd get back on course. Hadn't 'So Young' proved he could still do it? He couldn't wait to see the film. For all anyone knew, a chance to hit the big time again might be lurking just round the next bend.

Nearer the coast, it started to rain pretty heavily. He hit the sack as milk delivery vans wafted along the promenade. At around 5 a.m., Bob Blackburn was roused – someone on the line.

Bob shook Roy gently and came straight to the point. 'I can remember the exact words. Bob said, "Your house has burnt down. Roy and Tony are gone".'[21]

Devoid of will, he was steered downstairs; cases were packed before the town woke. Eyes bloodshot with fatigue, Blackburn hurtled through the downpour towards Heathrow with poor Roy Orbison. 'I was totally shattered,' said Roy, 'probably because I was not close to them. I was here. They were there. I didn't know about my mother, my father or my youngest son until my [road] manager put me at ease about them an hour later.'[21]

In the middle of the American night, the limpid waters of Old Hickory were still alive with the brightness of the blaze that the wooden structure and air conditioning had accelerated. Shivering despite the heat, the boys' grandfather was trying to explain as a cop jotted down facts. Orbie Lee had been the only adult in charge. Early that evening, after Wesley had nodded off at last, the other two boys had been messing about in the basement where the petrol was stored for the antique cars. Alerted by the first of a series of explosions down there, Orbie Lee, still clasping the bawling baby, had managed to shepherd Roy Duane and Tony up the steps as the fire gained hold. Only a few yards from the front door, there was the loudest bang of all. Glancing back, the old man froze in shock as his grandsons were snatched from him forever, disappearing 'in a wall of flame'.[22]

Brushing aside a pitiless woomph of flashbulbs, Roy Orbison crossed the tarmac of Kennedy airport. He waited in the VIP lounge, knowing that the internal flight to Tennessee would be his final sanctuary before he'd no longer be able to stifle the images of those who had been so mercilessly swallowed by the horror.

By the time he arrived, the rubble and the blackened remains of his automobile collection were still belching smoke, but most of the fire engines had gone. At first, he was a detached spectator with no interest or stake in the disaster. Then the truth that he had refused to avow inflicted itself upon him. He could no longer not believe it.

Notes

1   Radio 2, 20 March 1980
2   *Disc*, 25 June 1966
3   *Daily Sketch*, 27 April 1970
4   *Melody Maker*, September 1987
5   Sleeve notes to original soundtrack album (MGM SHU8358)
6   *Melody Maker*, 13 August 1966
7   *Daily Mirror*, 9 March 1967
8   Press release, Clifford Elson Publicity, 1979
9   *Melody Maker*, 7 January 1967
10 *The Face*, February 1989
11 *Rare Records*, Tom Hibbert (Proteus, 1982)
12 *Daily Star*, 8 December 1988
13 *Melody Maker*, 26 April 1969
14 *Melody Maker*, 8 May 1971
15 *Daily Sketch*, 28 April 1970
16 *Melody Maker*, 24 August 1974
17 *Daily Sketch*, 24 July 1968
18 *Melody Maker*, 27 July 1968

19 *Greatest Hits of Roy Orbison* (Acuff-Rose, 1970)
20 *The Sunday Times*, 21 June 1987
21 *Daily Sketch*, 27 April 1970
22 *Daily Express*, 16 September 1968

8

I Wanna Live

The funeral in Hendersonville's Philip Robinson Chapel would be the last that Roy Orbison would ever bring himself to attend. One day he'd be able to assimilate this second tragedy without thoughts of suicide. With extraordinary resilience, he'd conquer his own desolation by anchoring himself to the notion that he would live. He'd cry his tears, then would come catharsis and a dull ache. It couldn't be now though – not for a while yet.

Wesley and his grandparents had left for the recently-purchased home-away-from-home high in the hills overlooking California's Malibu beach, while, in a Nashville hotel room, Roy Orbison was shrouded in darkness and squalor, waiting for the madness to subside. Anxious friends would brave his depression to check up on him. In the midst of leftover food, crumpled bedclothes and overflowing ashtrays, some would even quote the Scriptures, but 'if you weren't religious before, then I think it would be hypocritical to start praying'.[1] That would come much later.

A gesture or a word would set him off: 'someone will use a particular phrase and I'll recall that Roy Junior used to say that too'.[2] The most vital source of solace during these care-worn days was Barbara Wellnoener-Jacobs, who would ring him from her home in the Rhineland. He bared his soul to her. 'Perhaps the most important thing she has done for me is to help me talk about Claudette and the boys instead of it all being bottled up inside me.'[3]

Gradually his rising from half-death became perceptible. One of his session musicians, Harold Bradley, was summoned to that gloomy suite to discuss the merits of a new make of guitar. The wheels cranked further into motion as a tour – and even recording dates – were pencilled in. The ravaged site of his former home was sold to Johnny Cash, who planted an orchard there. Cash's lead guitarist, Luther Perkins, had also perished in a Nashville house fire.

A few hundred yards along the peninsula, building commenced for a Bavarian-style chalet for Roy and his surviving son: 'I know it is close to where my old home used to be, but your own life can't stop. You can only go on doing the things you did before and learn to live with memories.'[4] As well as a view of the lake from each window, the new house would have alarms hooked up directly to the fire station. Roy also gave the go-ahead for work to begin on 'US Recording', his own studio.

He'd coped by burying himself in his career before but, when the music was over for the day, sorrow would flood his already overloaded mind. He'd long to be at rest but sleep wouldn't come, no matter how many medicines were prescribed. But down the motel corridor were those who understood that what was just a tour for them was occupational therapy for Roy. In the months prior to their respective resignations, Bill Dees and Barry Booth were the ones who were closest to Orbison during the period of emotional convalescence. Barry's recollection of their part in the healing is worth reiterating at length:

> He wasn't exactly a Bible-basher or even a practising churchgoer, but he had as many questions crossing his mind as any thinking person. He could do no more than voice those that presented themselves – such as why anyone should have so much bad luck in one go, and what were the implications? How do you relate to that? How do you come out of it? What was the driving

force, the personality, the spirit, the soul, whatever you call it? What is the reaction meant to be? What is the best thing to learn? It is an experience, after all, that is denied most people: certainly very unpleasant. It was the old 'what is the meaning of life?' I couldn't say that either Bill or myself would be preaching, but I think that the three of us would find ourselves in long discussions, asking questions and offering possible answers. Roy did intimate as such that it was a great help at the time to talk through rather than having to bear that amount of grief in solitude. I also found it better – from my point of view – that we could talk about it rather than just keep a respectful silence. I would be the one to ask, 'What are you thinking? What are you feeling about it? What's it doing? Let's be open. Let's use our intelligence rather than keep separate on it.' After a period of self-examination, he came through all right. The point is: he kept on working.

Bill Dees may have commented on Roy's troubles in the song, 'If Only For a While'. Tactfully, Barry Booth decided not to submit the second song he'd written with Orbison in mind, the premonitory 'The Last Time I Saw You Was Tomorrow'. The press, however, had no such inhibitions about quizzing Roy at every available opportunity on his dead wife and children – just as they'd been there taking photographs at Kennedy airport. Yet, without yielding any of his self-esteem, he'd always give unblinking copy. 'It was a long, long time ago, but I'm trying to reach back and really give you what went on as opposed to what I would like to have had happen. It was a devastating blow but not debilitating. I wasn't totally incapacitated by events – and I think that's stood me in good stead. You don't come out unscathed, but you don't come out murdered, you know'.[5]

In the hungover morning after the Swinging Sixties, this topic seemed to close the case on Roy Orbison. In common with other pop stars well past their sell-by date, he'd answer perfunctory enquiries about whatever current record the reporter might or might not have even bothered listening

to. Then he'd have to retell the old, old story of his distinguished past for the umpteenth time. He'd heard that
even the Sun material – stuff that he'd only listen to under
sufferance – was being sought after these days. There were
groups around who were trying to recreate the old sounds,
too – and even perform like the Teen Kings all over again.
British Teddy Boy revivalists like Crazy Cavan and Shakin'
Stevens were even getting 'street level' acclaim. Across the
Atlantic, fifties rock 'n' roll specialists such as Sha Na Na
and Flash Cadillac were paving the way for a resurgence of
rockabilly in the late seventies, spearheaded by the Cramps
and the Stray Cats, whose concert set would include
'Ooby Dooby'. Meanwhile, managed by vintage record
shop proprietor, Malcolm McLaren, the Sex Pistols'
exploratory rehearsals in 1974 would hinge on forgotten
Mod classics.

Along with the retrospectives in pop journals and the
proliferation of more erudite 'fanzines', these archivists and
performers appealed to Roy's well-developed sense of historical perspective: 'We didn't play our Sun records on stage
for a long time – until about 1970, I think, when it became
instant history, you know. All the information coalesced to
the point where everybody thought that was a beginning –
and so I took it more seriously myself because I had a few
years to reflect – and Presley started singing "That's All
Right" and I started singing "Ooby Dooby".'[5]

Though he was no longer ashamed of his Sun discs,
Orbison was rated a lowly twenty-seventh – below even such
doubtful contenders as Adam Faith and Brenda Lee – in a
British fanzine poll devoted to classic rock.[6] At home, he'd
already set his face against appearing on nostalgia revues
with the likes of Bill Haley and Little Richard – but no
doubt he'd have seized the opportunity had he been a spent
force everywhere else as well. As there were plenty of Monument re-issues in the shops, he hadn't been tempted to
re-record any of his big hits either, as had Gene Vincent
with 'Be-Bop-a-Lula '69' or Carole King's 1971 reworking

of 'Will You Still Love Me Tomorrow', which she'd written for the Shirelles eleven years before.

This song had been the highlight of *Tapestry*, an album that belongs to the early seventies' school of 'self-rock' – singer/songwriters who infested both college bedsits and the hit parade. The drab uniformity of most of its practitioners was just one symptom of the post-sixties' doldrums. Typical examples are James Taylor, Melanie or the many others who whinged cheesecloth-and-denim songs at outdoor festivals, television specials and sold-out-stadiums. They'd caught the general tenor of the bland 'Woodstock Generation' – a re-run of 1967 without overwhelming colour, daring or humour – whose anthem was Simon and Garfunkel's 'Bridge Over Troubled Waters'; these were the people who flocked to see *Zabriskie Point* and adored Neil Young, a self-rock colossus.

What had been merely implied by Roy Orbison, Young carried to ridiculously morose lengths, as demonstrated by his rehash of Don Gibson's, 'Oh Lonesome Me'. Nevertheless, with Young's known admiration, Roy's own contribution to *Zabriskie Point* and the generally downbeat musical mood, the hour may have come for Roy Orbison – a precursor of the singer/songwriters if not of self-rock itself – to regain a toehold in the States as an album artist on the university circuit. Heaven knows, he could probably outsing any self-rocker. On stage, you didn't have to do much except sing to the guitar and give a coy, sad smile every now and then. They especially liked it if you sat on a stool.

It was even cool to dig Andy Williams these days, the Mister Wonderful of easy listening. Hadn't some hip names been printed on one of his LP sleeves? If, like Williams, Roy Orbison had adapted enough of this trend not to turn off his older fans, he might have had a walkover if he'd had new songs of his own to sing then. As always, however, personal problems had severely curtailed that aspect of his creativity – hence the Art Movement hotchpotch and, for US ears alone, an album of 1971 entitled, *Hank Williams, the Roy Orbison Way*.

Tributes to Hank Williams over an entire album had been recorded by other artists in the past, the most reverential being that of rockabilly balladeer, Jack Scott who, in 1960, sang the tunes 'as though he'd inhaled the Nashville air for months on end'.[7] Orbison, a Nashville resident of many years' standing, and a Southerner to boot, felt entitled to take more liberties with the original arrangements – such as grafting the riff from Johnny Ray's 'Such a Night' onto 'Jambalaya', and imposing jarring accent shifts on 'Cold Cold Heart' and 'I'm So Lonesome I Could Cry'. Elsewhere, there were mid-song key changes, lavish orchestration and insertion of modern guitar distortion devices – most prominent on 'You Win Again' and 'Cold Cold Heart'. The most innovative updatings occur on the opening tracks. With a stomping rhythm section, 'Big Country' strings and tough guitar-harmonica interaction, Orbison's 'Kaw-liga' is arguably the most impressive Hank Williams cover ever recorded, while 'Jambalaya' rides roughshod over the Carpenters' hit-single version of 1974. Most of the other selections, however, are merely passable and, like 'Jambalaya', blemished by jaunty big-band brass and slushy cinematic strings. Nevertheless, Roy, who knew the songs backwards, is in excellent voice throughout.

When issued in Britain ten years later – as 'Big O Country' – three old Don Gibson interpretations were added to make up the needle time. To the chagrin of overseas enthusiasts, two other Orbison albums were confined to North America too. Sales there were enough to make such projects a practical proposition, but elsewhere new records became even more a mere adjunct to Roy's roaming the earth in cabaret. These days, 'Mr 1960', as one reviewer described him in 1974,[8] had no wish to foist on ticket holders anything but his greatest hits, a compilation of which would top the album charts in Australasia, Britain and Canada in 1976. Unfortunately Orbison's market killing exacerbated a shortage of new, original talent. This was reinforced by similar triumphs of repackaging from the likes of the Beach Boys, Glen

Campbell, the Dave Clark Five and even Perry Como. In the seventies, there were also attempts at rebirth by the Byrds, the Animals, the Spencer Davis group and Small Faces.

With nostalgia as his calling card, Roy Orbison had become an archetype and the only serious practitioner of his particular genre of pop. Therefore, it made more sense to plug the seemingly timeless sixties' chartbusters, while leaving what was now the annual new single – recorded almost for form's sake – to fend for itself. Unsurprisingly, no one was interested in the latest from Little Richard, Bill Haley or, for that matter, the Beach Boys either.

Turning his back on the contemporary stage, Roy submerged himself in a world where current chart status had no meaning. As predictable as the sunrise were the annual world tours. He'd pride himself on knowing an oft-visited country's geography better than most of its inhabitants. Finding himself back at the same venues time and time again, he at least had the opportunity to form genuine friendships rather than play backstage host to starstruck fans: 'Whether I'm in London, Sydney or Hong Kong, it makes no difference. There is always someone who knows me . . . I must be one of the unloneliest people in the world'.[3]

During this less hectic phase of his stardom, he would take up conversations begun the previous year with night spot managers, catering staff and patrons, who now realized how reclusive and ordinary – even boring – was the icon they'd once worshipped from afar. Reserving a little of his Southern charm for everyone in this orbit, he'd ask after their families, notice whether they'd lost weight or grown a beard, and bring them up to date with the new car collection or Wesley's reading. Yet, for all this hail-fellow-well-met familiarity, he was quite used to them suddenly falling silent in the manner that every old star comes to identify – an awestricken sense of *déjà vu* mingled with a touch of scepticism – as if he wasn't quite real.

To the doting members of his fan clubs, it was as if time had stopped in 1966. No matter how mundane he appeared to others, how long he'd been without a hit, how unrecognized he was in restaurants, 'to say he looked incredible would be almost an understatement', ran *Texan Star*, one club magazine, 'tanned, slimmer than for ages, smiling from behind his dark glasses, with his black hair completing the picture as he stood there, unmoving himself, but moving every emotion in every member of the audience, resplendent in his gold-studded black regalia. This was . . . this is . . . Roy Orbison 1975!'[9]

Nobody was getting any younger and, though he could still belt out the old magic, he was now weighing in at an unhealthy fifteen stone. More often nowadays, he'd wake up feeling groggy and out-of-sorts. Nevertheless, he'd salvaged contentment from the shambles of recent years since plighting his troth to Barbara, his long-distance comforter, in March 1969. As besotted as a man in middle life could be with a shapely, beautiful girlfriend fourteen years his junior, Roy would swing from gloom to breezy vitality, amazing those who found it hard to believe he'd ever been a rock 'n' rolling Teen King: 'she has helped me make a new Roy Orbison – and, when this happens, you find very quickly that you don't want to be your old self.'[9] At Barbara's suggestion, he even began brushing his hair forward like a teenager.

Actively looking for a mother for Wesley, he'd flown to Germany for the dual purpose of meeting the Wellnoener-Jacobs and inviting their daughter to his homeland to see if she'd fit in there. As well as a spell as Honorary Consul for Panama, Barbara's aristocratic father also owned Bielefeld's dress factory. The success of each of Baron Wellnoener-Jacobs' occupations depended on keeping up appearances and creating good impressions. Was it so strange, therefore, that after a girlhood in such surroundings, Barbara should elect to make her way in the world of fashion after finishing school? A career in catwalks and cloth had still been on the cards the night she met her husband-to-be.

However odd a choice this American pop singer may have seemed on first encounter, her parents raised no objections when, on returning home, Barbara announced that she wanted to marry the man. A month after the wedding, Roy presented his brand-new wife at a Westbury Hotel press conference to publicize three weeks of English cabaret dates.

He'd got these down to a fine art these days: one week up north, the next in the Midlands, and the last down south. On one visit, his band played the 'Star Trek' theme as its overture – as Presley's orchestra in Las Vegas had used 'Also Sprach Zarathustra' from *2001*. However, starting with 'Only the Lonely', it was often the same set in the same order as the previous outing – but this never affected the takings, and he'd be rebooked for the next season before he even left the building. If unqualified to appear on BBC's 'Top of the Pops', there was still the occasional showcase like 1974's 'Roy Orbison sings Roy Orbison' – and he was more than welcome to guest on 'Sez Lez', 'Saturday night at the Mill' and other light entertainment programmes that flashed the beery joviality of a working man's club into your living room. The stand-up comic around whose personality the series was built would complete the sort of facetious introduction that an uninterested Roy would hear over and over again these days: 'Without further ado, ladies and gentlemen, I'd like to bring on a grrrrrreat entertainer I know you're all going to enjoy – well, my late grandmother was quite fond of him . . .'

He'd even endure singing a medley of oldies so that nobody could complain that he hadn't sung his or her favourite. Taking this and other lines of least resistance, he played 125 concerts on 105 consecutive nights in 1974 – the road really did seem endless. 'In the seventies, I got to the point where I just didn't want to go on. You'd begin another tour; you'd get a bit ill and a bit confused and, finally, you can't see the point in either touring or not touring. It was only around '75, after I'd called a halt to the whole thing and reassessed the point of it all, that it started getting to be fun again.'[10]

Closing the show after a string of vile comedians and corny variety acts, he'd become the epitome of Adam Faith's assertion that 'the worst thing in the world is to be an ex-pop singer doing the clubs'. Yet Roy Orbison played them all, from England's heavily industrialized Black Country to outback towns in western Australia. On one such evening in Batley, Barry Booth was saddened to see his old boss cutting corners with only a guitar/bass/drums backing group. 'I don't want to sound disparaging, but the band was a bit lacklustre after the kind of entourage he'd been used to when you'd get a small orchestra on stage.'

He'd become rather commonplace. Like a London bus, if you missed one performance, another would come along if you waited. Orbison was always a 'forthcoming attraction', spoken of in the same breath as Les Dawson (of 'Sez Lez'), Freddie and the Dreamers and pianist Mrs Mills – all thoroughly diverting entertainers in their own fields. Around a thousand pounds a time would buy Roy Orbison – more than he'd ever realized as a chart contender. And if he wasn't available, how about Del Shannon?

Each passing year was a little shabbier, a little less respectful. The 'house full' signs would still go up, but small paragraphs in evening newspapers would also mention the High Court writs Orbison or Acuff-Rose had served on club owners and agents for breach of contract. Roy was said to have suffered 'substantial loss of reputation',[11] for example, when the Sands in Brighton cancelled a widely advertised four-night run in 1972 at short notice. Damages were also awarded in that same year because army manoeuvres had wiped out a ten-day tour of US military bases in Germany.

Another vocal aesthete, Scott Engel, had found himself in similar circumstances. As well as working the clubs, the former Walker Brother had lapsed from Brel translations and his own stream-of-consciousness creations to middle-of-

the-road LPs of film songs and standards, both mainstream
and C & W. Roy Orbison would never sink so low, but
there was, nevertheless, a feeling that he was marking time
musically in the three collections that saw out his MGM
commitments. The overall atmosphere of each album might
vary from the three-o'clock-in-the-morning 'Roy Orbison
Sings' to the more buoyant 'Memphis' and 'Milestones', but
the musical direction was governed by what was known as
'country pop', a genre engulfed by the silent majority.

Although traditionalists like Charlie Pride, Hank Snow
and Roy Acuff still kept the faith in Music City USA, by
the seventies Nashville had embraced pop music of a more
generalized kind – albeit not uninfluenced by C & W's
lyrical preoccupations and melodic appeal. One particular
preference of Orbison's was Lynn Anderson's 'Rose Garden',
written by the outspoken country-rocker, Joe South, whose
reply to his own rhetorical question, 'Do they love country
music in the South?' was: 'They sit around in the studios
cutting hot licks to assure each other, "Man, I don't play
this country stuff. I just do it for a living." Then when the
tape comes up, they go real country-and-western. They all
hate it. There are no country pickers left. They all died and
passed away. How can anyone be a real country picker who
was born and raised in the middle of a city?'[12]

C & W may have died of old age, but it wouldn't lie
down. The Grand Ole Opry was now broadcast from a
purpose-built concert hall, while tourists could stay at the
kitsch Opryland hotel with its stadium-sized atrium of palms
and cascading rivers. They could also touch Presley's gold
Cadillac in the Country Music Hall of Fame, and torture
their eyes in Conway's 'Twitty City' with its 'million colored
lights at Christmas'.

Twitty's magnum opus 'It's Only Make Believe' had been
revived in 1970 by Glen Campbell, who was among the first
to profit from the commercial viability of countrified pop.
(He followed this, incidentally, with his own version of
'Dream Baby'.) Jumping on the same bandwagon, one of

Roy's Sun stable mates, Charlie Rich, came in for an unexpected chart bonanza in 1974 – despite the silver hair. Jerry Lee Lewis too had risen anew as a country star. In 1972, Del Shannon was recording a country/pop album in Nashville. Elvis had also got wise with 'Kentucky Rain', Tony Joe White's 'Polk Salad Annie', Neil Diamond's 'Sweet Caroline' and others – either hit singles or highlights of his pageants at Caesar's Palace. The last most people would ever see of him would be in the white garb of a rhinestone cowboy *sans* stetson.

Taking their cue from both Nashville's spellbinding gaudiness and its revamped music, licensed premises throughout the world transformed themselves during the seventies into parodies of either Wild West saloons or truckers' roadhouses. Barging through the swinging half-doors of a Canberra bar or an Oxfordshire pub, you'd bump into Calamity Jane lookalikes, Vegas Presleys and buckskinned quaffers of Southern Comfort. Belying their daytime guises as clerks or teachers, conversations would be peppered with Deep South slang – 'mess of grits' for 'plate of food' – picked up from Merle Haggard albums and 45s like C. B. McCall's Citizen's Band monologue, 'Convoy' from the film of the same name starring Burt Reynolds. In the film *Roadie* four years later, Roy Orbison and Hank Williams Junior as singers in a bar band would hush a brawl with 'The Eyes Of Texas Are Upon You', but more likely inclusions in such a group's repertoire would be 'Sunday Morning Coming Down', 'Okie From Muskogee', 'I'm the Man on Susie's Mind', 'Crystal Chandelier' and Kris Kristofferson's 'Help Me Make It Through the Night'. Even if these hadn't made the Top Ten, they were as well-known as many that had.

'I'm the Man on Susie's Mind' had been co-written by Joe Melson, with whom Roy had now resumed his songwriting partnership. With Don Gant, Joe had also been the brains behind 'Run Baby Run', which had restored Mark Mathis' Newbeats to the hit parade after a long absence. Roy recorded both this and 'I'm the Man on Susie's Mind' on

Memphis, which he and Melson produced at US Recording – as they had four tracks from *Roy Orbison Sings*.

Like *There is Only One Roy Orbison* and *Many Moods*, this album had been another of Orbison's mixed bags, released to keep investors sweet while he found his bearings. From the same session as 'So Young' came 'It Takes All Kinds of People', while Wesley Rose and Don Gant joined the movable feast of producers for the remaining selections. In order not to short-change British buyers, 'Yesterday's Child' (from *Many Moods*) was tacked onto the end of side two. Though Orbison disclosed in 1969 that 'I've never really had the time to devote to albums like I wanted to and they usually wind up being twelve singles,'[13] there was little discernible difference in quality between *Orbison Sings*, *Memphis* and *Milestones*.

Elvis had beaten him to 'Sweet Caroline', but Roy was first to the sentimental 'Danny Boy', a mainstay of cabaret. Moreover, the title track of *Memphis* stole a march on the King's rediscovery of Chuck Berry in 1975. The rendering of 'The Three Bells', however, sticks as close to the Browns' 1959 hit as Brian Poole's version had in 1965. Apart from the phased drumming, the outlaw lope of 'I Fought the Law' likewise emerged intact from the Orbison studio. Nevertheless, this song, 'Memphis' and 'Run Baby Run' were light relief against the mature country ballads that were the backbone of this final MGM trilogy. What Roy had merely alluded to in 'My Friend' came out into the open in Gene Thomas' 'Ring of Gold' (her adultery) and Roy and Joe's own 'Help Me' (his). Sex rears its head again in the spicy 'Cheyanne', though it's laced with love in another Orbison/ Melson original, 'Harlem Woman', about a mother forced into prostitution by poverty.

In a friskier vein is Eddy Raven's 'Plain Jane Country (Come To Town)', a Beverly hillbilly without the money. More country-rock than country-pop is Jerry McBee's 'Run the engines Up High'. Roy also taped McBee's 'Why a Woman Cries' and 'Take Good Care of Your Woman', both of which vaguely confirm Roy's views about the role of women: 'I think equal pay for equal work is fine, but I think the majority of women would like to be treated like a woman, and I don't think it can be any other way. I think they are entitled to more fairness, but I wouldn't go along with some of these radical Women's Libbers who think that they can lift the same amount that a man can – which is impossible – or that they can control their emotions under certain situations. Certain women could but not women in general.'[14]

For those who were in the habit of tracing Roy's feelings through his songs, it now seemed if 'God love You', and 'I Wanna Live' were to be believed that he'd not only come through his trials sane and philosophical, but his new life with Barbara was joyful. As was the case with 'Claudette', an eponymous song he'd written for her was given away to a duo – not Don and Phil Everly this time but Don Gant and Joe Melson. *Roy Orbison Sings*, his interpretation of Mickey Newbury's 'Remember the Good' helps to put Claudette in perspective – as had 'Memories' in 1968: 'heaven knows I've learnt to live without her . . . for all she meant to me, I'll remember the good'. No potential hit singles stick out from the three albums but, unlike *Big O*, Roy was no more a listless passenger, a pliant executor of another's ideas. However, assuming that most listeners would have a glimmer of its maker's personal history, the juxtaposing on *Memphis* of 'The Three Bells' before the 'Danny Boy' finale was most insensitive. Who could prevent a knotted stomach – even tears – when, after the third bell ushers in the lines 'one rainy morning dark and grey/a soul singed its way to heaven/ little Jimmy Brown had passed away,' another graveside ballad – now from a father to a son – follows. 'Danny Boy' was among Roy Orbison's most magnificent performances on record but his domestic tragedies and the tragedy yet to come have bequeathed it a piquancy as unbearable as that of John Lennon's 'Beautiful Boy' after the ex-Beatle's pavement assasination in 1980.

    That Roy found the emotional detachment to tackle songs
so close to the bone is testament to his emotional equilibrium:
'I have the balance in my life to see what the bad is, what
the good is and where the in-between lies.'[15] There had been
another death – his brother Grady had died of a coronary in
1973 – but, against all the odds, 'my outlook is optimistic.
I always look on the brighter side of life. If I were describing
myself, I would say that I am a man who has to wear several
hats; an artist, sometimes a songwriter, a business man'.[14]
He was also the father of two more sons, Roy Kelton Junior
born in October 1970, and Alexander who arrived four
years later. Though more removed from public gaze than
Claudette's children had been, the two well-favoured, blond
boys could not help but become aware of their father's
celebrity, but their mother wisely assured them that 'it is a
job just like other dads have . . . like doctors, lawyers,
train drivers or anything else. If they think their father is
something special, something different, too soon in life, it
can destroy their sense of values.'[16]

    'She has done many things for me,' remarked Orbison of
his wife, 'and she has not failed me in any one of them.'[11]
As well as her maternal virtues, he was fortunate in having
a wife with an instinct for the commercial and economic
machinations of the music industry. Negotiations with ac-
countants, attorneys, managers and agents were not mysterious for long to the daughter of an important government
official. With an icy ruthlessness formidable to those accustomed to Roy's glib bonhomie, Barbara took charge of the
day-to-day running of the family's business enterprises.

    Of these, the studio complex was proving a worthwhile
investment. By the mid-seventies, it was attracting a few
famous names, such as Jerry Lee Lewis, Floyd Cramer and
Tom T. Hall – who, like the Killer, was signed to Mercury.
Hoping to repeat the same success they'd had with Jerry
Lee's immersion in country, the same company took on Roy
Orbison in 1974 for a one-shot LP when, at long last, he
had extricated himself from the clutches of MGM.

The result, *I'm Still in Love With You* (not released outside America), paints a rosy picture in its sleeve notes, promising that the three singles derived from it were all sure-fire hits. Yet in spite of this and the flashiness of its cover portrait, the music of this first and last Mercury album was something of a false dawn. Orbison's singing seems strained or unimpassioned as he went through the motions once more. With Jerry Kennedy, one of his former guitarists, as producer, and arrangements by an even older colleague, Bill Justis, Roy cranks out a Don Gibson cover version, a token ballad, the re-make of 'Heartache', a remodelled C & W oldie ('Crying Time', complete with flutes and robotic drumming) and a couple of new country songs, Bud Reneau's 'All I Need is Time' and Larry Gatlin's 'Circles' – the record's strongest track. Orbison and Melson's makeweight 'It's Lonely' – one of the singles – recalls the Searchers minus the smooth Scouse harmonies. The other three new compositions have more substance, though 'Spanish Nights' a holiday romance with stock castanets, flamenco twiddling and Costa del Nashville strings is a pastiche that Joe and Roy could have written in their sleep.

Mercury neglected to pick up an option on a second album. Why had he gone so stale? Since their reunion, he and Melson had been unduly worried about surpassing their previous standards. Back in the suffocating emptiness of Odessa in the fifties, they'd had ideas nonstop. Now hours would go by without a ghost of a tune or a lyric. The songs that did get underway all hovered round the same formula melodies and buzz words. Like the alchemists, they'd explore the same worn-out themes over and over again from new angles in the wrong-headed expectation of finding gold. 'If I try to write for Roy Orbison,' Melson complained, 'it doesn't work. It takes forever and is no good anyway.'[17] Occasionally they'd break out of their old habits – the capricious humour of 'Changes' on *Roy Orbison Sings* has a breath of new life in it, for example. With the scanty critiques of the Mercury album lukewarm at best, neither could convince the other that they'd ever equal or better 'Running Scared', 'Blue Angel' and all the rest of them.

Roy Orbison confessed as much to Fred Foster, with whom he'd been in touch again recently. During a Canadian tour of 1975, Roy had been badgered by K-Tel, a conglomerate specializing in re-issues, who wanted him to re-record all his hits for worldwide release on its Arcade subsidiary. On the verge of consenting, he checked first with the keeper of the original masters. Quick on the uptake, Fred Foster knew that there was no need. Though Monument's own compilations of its old Orbison tracks had been pressed in largish quantities since 1966, Fred saw greater fiscal opportunities in leasing the rights to K-Tel, whose budget stretched to saturation television advertising, perking up sales from tens of thousands to close on a quarter of a million a year.

Since parting with Roy, Fred's company had diversified from pop into country and black music, although several of its signings had crossed over into the Hot Hundred – Robert Knight with 'Everlasting Love' in 1968, for example. Among whites who had also managed this were Kris Kristofferson and Tony Joe White, Southern singer/songwriters considerably less well-mannered and artistically self-centred than the Melanies and Neil Youngs of the North. From Elvis downwards, their compositions attracted numerous cover versions. Broadly speaking, these two individuals could be described as exponents of 'country-soul'.

Fred Foster realized that Roy Orbison – divested of all the schmaltz he'd recorded lately – could fit into that category too. It abruptly made sense for Roy, now a free agent, to return to the fold. That he didn't have any new material didn't bother Monument. Fred was certain that a well-produced album of other writers' songs would restore Orbison's confidence – and that's when his own numbers would start coming. They could go on the next one.

To symbolize both this intended renaissance and the prodigal's homecoming, the first project would bear the title

Regeneration. White and Kristofferson were each delighted to pen a song for Roy – as were two lesser lights on Foster's file, Bob Morrison and the many-sided Dennis Linde. Along with the cream of Nashville session players, imported from Alabama would be the crack in-house horn section from the trendy Muscles Shoals studios. Their beefy riffs had serviced many a soul smash. All Roy had to do was sing.

In deferring to Foster, Roy became a challenger again. With punk's distant thunder out of earshot, the American pop scene was still glutted with idols from the Woodstock generation. Even if there was no immediate sales animation, *Regeneration* was therefore 'contemporary' enough to suggest that the reinstatement of Orbison in the charts was not improbable.

The hero of *Regeneration* was Dennis Linde, provider of nearly half its songs – including 'Belinda,' the first promotional single. His contribution was mainly country-rock, but, with clipped guitar chukka-wuskka, 'Under Suspicion' soul stew, was as implausible a setting for Orbison as 'Southbound Jericho Parkway' had been. Nonetheless, for a piece better suited to 'Godfather of Soul' James Brown, Roy coped admirably. As always whatever he sang sounded like Roy Orbison. He was also convincingly out of character as a wine-drinkin' hedonist 'makin' love in the pale moonlight' in Tony Joe White's steamy '(I'm a) Southern Man'. More typical fare included Morrison's stately 'Born to Love Me' and Kristofferson's 'Something They Can't Take Away' – which wasn't a million miles away from 'Memories'. Though there wasn't much love lost between Foster and Wesley Rose – from whom Roy was also gradually becoming estranged – a smouldering work-out of Fred Rose's 'Blues in My Mind' led off side two. All on tape within a few days, every item on *Regeneration* was enacted with more guts and conviction from both artist and musicians than anything on the insipid Mercury album.

Admittedly, Roy had been almost a cipher on his own album, but *Regeneration* was made of harder metal than the soporific country-rock wafting in from the West Coast. Then in vogue were the likes of John Denver, Linda Ronstadt and the Eagles, whose 'Greatest Hits' collection would stay in the US album chart for most of 1976. Also popular that year (and in succeeding years) was Bruce Springsteen from New Jersey with his deep vibrato and energetic vitality. Prudently Mercury had quoted a line about Roy Orbison singing 'For the Lonely' from *Thunder Road* – Springsteen's latest 'Orbison-soaked album',[18] – in the press release for *I'm Still in Love With You*.

Subtler traces of mid-period Orbison had infiltrated the classical rock fusions of such best-selling British bands as Queen and the Electric Light Orchestra. Bryan Ferry, leader of the arty Roxy Music, was also a big Orbison fan, while the ghoulish Alice Cooper's 'Only Women Bleed' relied structurally on a Big O crescendo – as did 'Don't Cry for me Argentina', *the* hit song of 1976. The following year, 'Blue Bayou' would shift ten million – nine million more than that of the original – for Linda Ronstadt. Meanwhile, Don McLean's version of 'Cryin'' was rejected by his record company as 'too slow'. However after singing it on a Dutch television programme, McLean's 'Cryin'' became more popular than his 'American Pie'. A UK Number One, it also clambered into the US Top Five.

Suddenly, Roy Orbison became a name to drop in hip circles, prompting favourable critical notices for *Regeneration*. Though this album wasn't as tidy as he'd have liked, there was talk of him performing a couple of its titles when he hit the road again. In from the cold, he could now tour the States on grounds other than nostalgia. In one audience at an exploratory engagement in California were members of the Eagles, the futuristic Steve Miller Band, current chart-toppers Jefferson Starship and comedy band, the Tubes. Some of these worthies could not restrain themselves from joining the Big O onstage for the encore – a snippet noted in the glowing report of the show in the *Los Angeles Times*.

Returning to Tennessee, he was introduced by Fred Foster to another big name of the later seventies, Emmylou Harris, whose band comprised many revered country-rock figures, some of whom had been hired in the past by Elvis. Though her own records sold well, Emmylou's harmony vocals were so admired that she became just as renowned for her duets with other artists. These included John Sebastian, the ubiquitous Linda Ronstadt, Johnny Halliday and, a singular honour, Bob Dylan. Possibilities of another such liaison may have crossed Emmylou's mind when she invited Roy to 'one of those picking parties that happens sometimes. Everybody was passing the guitar and he sang. I remember commenting that I'd probably never sell that house because Roy Orbison had sung in it.'[5]

The moment couldn't have been better for a comeback, but it was lost when he went into hospital for a triple-bypass heart operation in January 1978.

The doctor had told him that the chest pains he'd suffered from during the recording of *Regeneration* were no cause for alarm. Watching a football game in the company of the Presley clan at the Liberty Bowl in Memphis a few weeks later, he was in agony again after dashing up several flights of stairs for refreshments. Not long after during a holiday in Hawaii, he reeled to a pay phone explaining the symptoms to a local doctor, who advised an immediate return home for another checkup. Further tests – involving camera insertion – revealed extensive arterial blockage, 'but that didn't bother me too much, thank goodness. The doctor said, "Roy, we're going to have to have open heart surgery," and I said, "Well, be sure to leave a nice scar because I wear open-necked shirts".'[19]

He was warned to avoid stressful situations in future. Roy was not so keen to cut down on cigarettes, nor did he appreciate the recommended diet designed to reduce both his weight and blood pressure. Nevertheless, the freeing of his arteries and the consequent increase in brain oxygen spurred a renewal of professional activity. By April, a livelier Orbison was back on stage.

It was now a false economy to employ second-rate backing groups who couldn't – or wouldn't – reproduce the original arrangements. He could afford to pick and choose nowadays. The group he had his eye on were Skwydro Heegie, an Oklahoman sextet who'd worked at US Recording. Five members of Skwydro Heegie (a name derived from a water pump component) were brothers called Price. The eldest, forty-one year old Ron, had been one of the Velvets – a group that had also been signed to Monument. They'd even twice cast their shadow in the Hot Hundred in 1961. The Velvets' third single contained 'Laugh', one of the better Orbison/Melson compositions not appropriated by Roy himself. Like the Art Movement before them, Skwydro Heegie's liking for the Beach Boys would be evident whenever they were required to play their own spot. They did not presume, however, to impose their own ideas and personality. Skwydro Heegie knew their place: 'We followed his career and we never dreamed we'd be playing with him one day. We took his "Greatest Hits" album and played the songs exactly like the records.'[20]

The group were not alone in finding Mrs Orbison rather intimidating. Since Wesley Rose's retirement, Barbara had become very much the power behind the throne by the late seventies. When in London, the family would now stay at the Mayfair Hotel rather than the Westbury because she had taken offence over an incident involving Roy Kelton Junior and a harassed chambermaid. A more absolute alienation would take place in 1982 when the Orbisons, claiming lost income from royalties, sued a shocked Wesley Rose for thirty million pounds: 'Barbara and I felt we had to put everything in order in my career. We never had the right management, the right agency, the right record company all at once.'[5]

The outcome of this re-evaluation was a two-year silence after *Regeneration*. During Roy's recuperation after the heart operation, he informed Fred Foster that he 'didn't want to do any more records for a while, so would I release him from his contract? This I did'. In relinquishing this and other commitments, Roy came as close as he'd ever been to a pain-free existence. With a lovely and supportive wife, three adorable children and such riches – he was a sterling millionaire – work was a diversion, not a necessity. Could anyone begrudge Roy his bliss?

Never a miserly fellow, his new home matched his income. Its six bathrooms and three kitchens alone occupied thousands of square feet. The rosewood from which expensive guitars are made lined the master bedrooms. The carpets underfoot were *objets d'art*, never mind the one on the wall: 'Yes, I suppose I have a feeling for the aristocratic way of life' he said in 1970, 'and to have been in Berlin and Paris in the 'twenties would have been my cup of tea.'[16] The electronic speaker system in Roy's leather-padded writing room enabled him to communicate with any part of the house. At the push of a bedside button, a meal would be automatically delivered for the couple to eat while watching the fitted giant-screen television.

With no obligation to rise from his silk sheets, what did Orbison do all day? Well, there was the swimming pool, the guitar-shaped radio, the workshop where he constructed his model aircraft. Sharing this childlike enthusiasm, guitarist Benny Birchfield – later Roy's tour manager – would spend jolly afternoons with Roy in the open air sending their radio-controlled toys soaring into the endless blue.

Orbison took a more impersonal pride in his replenished treasury of vintage vehicles. As before, he was contemplating their storage in a museum that would be open to the public. He'd accumulated so many old cars now that he'd had to sell some to make space for more valuable purchases – such as a 1937 Jaguar and a Mercedes ten years older. After acquiring the latter's chassis in 1969, the task of rebuilding its bodywork was entrusted to an English mechanic, Peter Gray, whose Worthing garage had serviced antique vehicles for Orbison since 1965. Roy had been dismayed that procrastination had allowed another collector, Jimmy Page, to outbid him for an American Cord rarity.

As with Claudette, Roy had introduced Barbara to the thrills of motor-biking – as he would the teenage Wesley. Like his late elder brothers, Wesley had inherited musical skills, and was showing promise as a songwriter. Alexander was a bit of an enigma as yet but, to Roy, the other two were 'a reflection of me. They both like what I like and are very, very busy right now having a lot of fun.'[14]

On the surface, therefore, Roy Orbison seemed much the same as he'd always been: 'You should not give up the things to which you are accustomed. If you keep late hours, for instance, you should continue. If you have a hobby, you should continue – or, at least, try to continue your interests and career and let time take care of everything else. If you get off the track and give up this and that, you will never find yourself again.'[15]

The most profound change over the decade was his drift back to religion. He'd begun with what he knew. Soberly attired, the family attended matins at the Church of Christ in nearby Madison for several years before rededicating themselves to Hendersonville's Baptist ministry. As other famous worshippers there included Kris Kristofferson, Johnny Cash and Skeeter Davis, a sign would appear at the lychgate, warning: 'Absolutely No Autographs Or Pictures Taken Inside This Sanctuary'.

Even at the extremities of despair and elation, Roy had never lost touch with the simple Christianity of his childhood – the 'religion' he'd figured out at the age of six. But regular affirmation of his faith had been impractical during his global wanderings. His recording of 'I Belong to Him' with Waylon Jennings and Jessi Coulter would be, however, Orbison's most public declaration of faith. He would never be as evangelical or pious as Johnny Cash and Jerry Lee Lewis. Instead, his moderate personality made him reticent to talk about the subject unless specifically asked: 'I don't have a pure statement, but I believe in Jesus Christ and try to live by the rules of morality and conduct and a certain faithfulness in all things. That helps a great deal – so does common sense. It's very important to me. Your mind is created by a higher power and common sense will often tell you what to do.'[15]

A more illustrious contemporary coped less well. 'I know Elvis had a strong faith, but it was just that there was no one close enough to him, that loved him enough, to tell him what he was doing to himself.'[21] Prey to obesity, hypochondria and paranoia, the self-destructive King's reign was drawing to its close – and there would be no replacement. However, if (as some of his chroniclers would allege) he was crazy behind closed doors, nothing had seemed amiss when, in December 1976, the mutual admiration society of Orbison and Presley met for the last time. Roy had already taken a bow from the audience when, up on stage at Caesar's Palace, Elvis introduced him as 'quite simply, the greatest singer in the world'. This opinion, unaltered since 1959, may have been pleasing, but the Big O suffered for the compliment when mobbed for two thousand autographs after the lights went up at the finish of the first house. Laughing it off, he slipped backstage to pay homage: 'We hadn't seen each other in years. He hugged me. We talked about everything – Jerry Lee Lewis, touring . . . he was a little overweight but looked really good'.[21]

So impressed was Orbison with Presley's appearance that, back in Britain the following March, he appeared on stage in a *white* leather-fringed jump suit, rather like the one into which the ailing Elvis had stuffed his podgy bulk in Vegas. Roy – no stick insect either – was now filling many of the theatres he'd first packed out in the mid-sixties. Some nights, there were even a few screams. Plainly, the lay-off had been worth it.

Augmenting Skwydro Heegie were string and horn sections in black evening dress to contrast with the star's sartorial volte-face. The hour-long performance was nothing if not vulgar. A line of choreographed dancers, for example, were more prominent than Roy himself during 'Land of a Thousand Dances'. Nevertheless, the already converted had to admit that he was taking more trouble this trip.

Needless to say, Orbison was despised by those journalists whose living seemed to depend on toadying to Johnny Rotten of the Sex Pistols. In Britain – and, to a lesser extent, in the States – the punk-rock storm had broken. It was a fierce time and no mistake. The musical content of 'Anarchy in the UK', 'Sheena is a Punk Rocker' by the Ramones, Generation X's 'Wild Youth' and other two-minute bursts of self-conscious racket was irrelevant. What really counted was that, more so than skiffle or rockabilly, *anyone* could do it – even if most punk outfits looked and sounded just like the Sex Pistols, with their ripped clothes, short hair and safety-pin earrings – plus the three chords thrashed at speed to machine-gun drumming behind some shouted denigration of the old, the wealthy and the established. In August 1977, when news of Elvis Presley's bathroom death reached a basement club frequented by London punks, some even cheered.

That was a bad year for Grand Old Men like Roy Orbison. 'We're another generation,' scowled Joey of the Ramones. 'They're rich and living in another world altogether . . . to them, it's just another way of making money.'[22] Buried amongst the fawning coverage given to this new wave in the music press, a review of the Orbison show at the Bristol Hippodrome seemed to corroborate Joey Ramone's jaded appraisal: 'There can be few businessmen around building themselves such a large pension fund with such ease.'[23]

Benignly, Roy refused to bitch back, seeing only 'a bunch of fresh, new people trying to do their thing like we did in '54 . . . disgraceful we were, degenerated because we played that kind of music and everything. So that's exactly what they are, what we were then.'[24] As with rockabilly, the grubbing show business industry stole punk's most viable ideas and persuaded the more palatable new wave entertainers to ease up, grow their hair maybe, talk correctly, and prepare to take the States for every cent they could get. The aptly-named Billy Idol of Generation X, for instance, was groomed as an updated Ricky Nelson. With one of his songs absorbed into Linda Ronstadt's canon, one of the first British new-wave ambassadors to clean up over the Atlantic was a weedy young man in glasses who'd been given the name of 'Elvis Costello'. Not content with an affinity to the King, Costello also borrowed Roy Orbison's uncommunicative stage persona.

Crucially, the real Roy's voice was still a thing of wonder. A running joke with Skwydro Heegie was his poker-faced, 'Cover me for any notes I don't hit' just before showtime. Orbison's vocal resonance was now closer to its natural baritone, but the hits were still played in their original keys. Sometimes he'd need to muddle through the 'Only the Lonely' opener to switch into gear. In a televised performance of 'Running Scared' during his 'white period', he appeared to be struggling a little too.

It wasn't that he'd become a bad singer – just an old one. Tiredness may not be so discernible in a rapt auditorium – but it made a marked difference when, in 1978, he was cajoled by the fashionable Elektra-Asylum – the Eagles' label – into cutting another album. 'When I was making my older records, I had more control over my vibrato. Now, if I don't want to have the vibrato in the studio, I have to do a session earlier in the day because, by the evening, it'll be there whether I want it or not.'[5]

Roy's 'miraculously singular voice' and the final track, 'Hound Dog Man', were deemed by *Rolling Stone* to be the only salveagable aspects of the new LP, which was otherwise 'an embarrassing travesty . . . maybe the most soul-less album ever recorded at Muscles Shoals.'[25] Other criticisms of *Laminar Flow* – named after an aeronautics term – were just as harsh, and Orbison himself felt it 'was like a half-finished project to me'.[5]

It was, indeed, easy to pull to pieces. Hardly any of the

songs would have stood up had their orchestration been pruned down to just voice and piano. There was a velvet-smooth helping of the moderato soul style – more feathery than Stax or early Motown – that had emanated from trend-setting Philadelphia from the likes of the Stylistics and Jerry Butler. At its worst, 'Philly Soul' would have limpid sweetening of strings, vibraphone and woodwinds plastered over a muted but jittery rhythm. This would be crowned by vocal burbling of lovey-dovey mush to a gambolling flute or saxophone obligato. As Roy processed 'Under Suspicion' on *Regeneration,* so he made the best of Terry Woodford and Clayton Ivey's productions of 'I Care', 'We're Into Something Good' and 'Tears'. No doubt these exhaled from many a late evening stereo, facilitating the winning of maidenly hearts by smitten young executives in penthouse apartments the world over.

From Philadelphia too had come David Bowie's 'plastic soul' album, *Young Americans,* from which, in 1975, was taken his first US Number One, 'Fame'. A laughable theft of the riff central to 'Fame' cropped up in the tedious funk exercise 'Lay It Down', while plunging Orbison further into disco were 'Warm Spot Hot' and 'Easy Way Out' – though this began with an unsettlingly funereal string passage.

More foreign to Roy was Chris Price's libretto to 'Movin''. Though this put some realism into the overworked myth of the rock 'n' roll lifestyle, it was somehow disappointing to hear that nice Roy Orbison drooling over 'those front row women' and – albeit sotto voce – twice interjecting an oath you'd never have imagined his using. It wouldn't have mattered so much had not Ivey and Woodford's session crew been so gutlessly precise. Perhaps the rowdier edge of Skwydro Heegie might have saved the day.

Almost as deplorable was when Roy sang in 'Friday Night' of picking up a female hitch-hiker who 'put her little hand on my knee' to encourage nature to take its course – and him a God-fearing, happily married man and all. You wouldn't read about it – except that, for the first time on a Orbison disc, the words were printed on the inner sleeve.

Meaning did not take precedent over phonetics in 'Warm Spot Hot' and 'Lay It Down' but 'Love is a Cold Wind' and the vengeful 'Poor Baby' – tracks closest to the Orbison of the sixties – betray some lyrical flair, though neither overdid the insight. Possibly because it didn't have a weather eye on passing trends, the stand-out *Laminar Flow* song was the Elvis eulogy, 'Hound Dog Man', from an idea of Barbara's in 1974. After cash-ins such as Danny Mirror's 'I Remember Elvis Presley' and the ghastly 'The Greatest Star of All' by Skip Jackson, it 'was long enough after all the exploitation. It's on an album for sale but it wouldn't bother me if no one heard the song. I really did it from me to him. Also, I've got the credentials to sing it.'

Coming after all the sequencers, synth-drums and other treated clutter, the no-frills arrangement and unvarnished narrative of 'Hound Dog Man' only compounded the artistic mismatch and loss of direction that was *Laminar Flow*.

Composing credits were split roughly between the Muscles Shoals house musicians and, at Roy's request, Skwydro Heegie. Though he'd only contributed a few melody lines to this album, Roy had decided that 'if I did record new things, I would have a hand in the writing of them – because it makes me feel responsible. If I wrote them and they weren't successful, that's OK. It was my responsibility.'[23]

During the year of Don McLean's 'Cryin'', Roy's role in the film *Roadie* went part of the way towards overcoming his writer's block. On a varied soundtrack – which also included contributions by Jerry Lee Lewis and Alice Cooper among others – he duetted with Emmylou Harris on his and Chris Price's 'That "Lovin' You" Feelin' Again'. Originally on the B-side of the spin-off single, it picked up more airplay on C & W radio than its coupling, Craig Hundley's 'Lola'. By the autumn of 1980, it had not only topped the country chart, but had also earned the pair a Grammy award – a pop-music Oscar – for 'best country performance by a duo or group'.

Partly on the strength of this, Orbison found himself touring California with the Eagles. Winning over their largely adolescent following, it was almost a throwback to days when he'd had the onerous duty of preceding the Beatles or Stones on stage. 'But it was a modern day thing and a lot of fun'.[24] There wasn't much time left but he wasn't wasting it. 'Things are moving at a very good pace. I got this feeling around '54; I got this feeling around '59, and I get this feeling now that what I want to do is going to happen.'[26]

Notes

 1 *Daily Sketch*, 27 April 1970
 2 *Daily Express*, 8 December 1989
 3 *Sunday Express*, 3 September 1972
 4 *Daily Mirror*, 24 April 1971
 5 *Rolling Stone*, 26 January 1989
 6 *New Rockpile No. 5*, May 1977
 7 'I remember Hank Williams', Jack Scott (Top Rank BUY 034)
 8 *Melody Maker*, 24 July 1974
 9 *Texan Star*, 1975
10 *Melody Maker*, September 1982
11 *Evening News*, 7 October 1972
12 *Beat Instrumental*, July 1969
13 *Melody Maker*, 26 April 1969
14 *Women's Choice*, 21 September 1974
15 *Evening News*, 3 June 1972
16 *Daily Sketch*, 28 April 1970
17 *Melody Maker*, 26 March 1977
18 Greg Mitchell's sleeve notes to 'I'm Still in Love With You'
19 'Tribute to the Big O', Radio 2, 5 January 89
20 *Sunday Times*, 21 June 1987
21 *Melody Maker*, 27 August 1977
22 *Rock Quotes*, ed. J. Green (Omnibus, 1977)
23 *Sounds*, 26 March 1977

24   *New Musical Express*, 20 December 1980
25   *Rolling Stone*, 23 August 1979
26   Veronica Television (Dutch)

9

Not Alone Any More

The Grammy (his first) had been an unexpected but
deserved accolade. A resurgence of desire for an old
flame, 'That "Lovin' You" Feelin' Again' had been a well-
integrated duet with sure-footed harmonies. Of course, its
success owed much to cinema exposure, and, as commodity
began to take precedence over creativity, more work of this
kind fell into Roy Orbison's lap.

Planned for the spring of 1980 had been *The Living
Legend*, Roy's authorized film biography: 'I want to avoid
people having a wrong account of my life',[1] he said in 1982.
Martin Sheen of *Apocalypse Now* had been wooed for the
title role, and Orbison completed two songs for the soundtrack with Chris Price. However, unhappy with the low
budget and long delays, Roy withdrew from the project.
This was considered regrettable by its backers – but by no
means disastrous. With hardly a break in schedule, *The
Living Legend* was remodelled as a generalized fiction about
a pop star more like Elvis than anyone else.

That Orbison could dismiss such an opportunity said
much about his new-found standing – the history of pop had
been seized upon as an avenue for selling records. 'Teenagers
were no longer pop's most vital consumer group, having
been outmanoeuvred by their Swinging Sixties' parents.'
Even the *Wink Bulletin* now defined rock 'n' roll as 'a type
of music preferred by teenagers aged thirteen to sixty'.[2] No

matter how it was tarted up – as a twelve-inch megamix or recorded on polkadot vinyl – the pop single had become a loss leader, a mere incentive for grown-ups to buy an album – hopefully on compact disc.

In the mid-eighties, for instance, Britain would be consumed with nostalgia for the sixties. At one stage, every fourth record in the charts was either a re-issue or a revival of an old song. In the States, jumping out of albums as the sampler single would be an act's disposable revamp of an oldie – as exemplified by Cheap Trick's ham-fisted 'Don't Be Cruel' (also recorded by the Judds) and Michael Bolton's Top-Forty cover of Otis Redding's 'Dock of the Bay'. In 1982, heavy metal men Van Halen hit No.12 with a version of 'Oh! Pretty Woman', which only the year before had been in the UK Top Ten as part of Tight Fit's 'Back to the Sixties' medley.

Nor was it any longer out of the question for older stars to re-enter the hit parade with their latest releases, holding their own amidst entertainers of the post-punk me-generation. After the Kinks had re-emerged in 1983, other second comings included Tom Jones, George Harrison, the Bee Gees (for the umpteenth time), Steve Winwood and, too late, Roy Orbison. More than ever, the words of John McNally of the Searchers rang true: 'You don't have to be young to make good records'.[3] For all their wrinkles, they were a source of perpetual fascination to the young. 'Looking back on both the Presley era and the Beatles and Stones era, those two bursts of energy were quite amazing,' surmised Roy Orbison. 'It was like people had something to say and they really loved saying it. I don't know whether there's been so much of that since then. The energy's still there in some ways but there either isn't so much of it or there are so many different kinds of artists now that the energy has been dissipated.'[4]

Among many salutes by the young to a more vibrant past were ABC's 'When Smokey (Robinson) Sings' and 'Godstar' – about drowned Rolling Stone, Brian Jones – from Psychic

TV. The generations even joined hands. Two singles by the Art of Noise were collaborations with, respectively, Duane Eddy and Tom Jones, while one of George Michael's biggest sellers was a duet with Aretha Franklin, a soul singer well into her forties.

Although he'd rest on past laurels until the eleventh hour, Roy Orbison's name would come up too. On a par with Chuck Berry and Duane Eddy in a *Record Collector* popularity poll, he could look down on the likes of Johnny Cash, Del Shannon and Carl Perkins. In April 1982, he and Jerry Lee Lewis had been major attractions at London's Country Music Festival. This was the first time they'd appeared on the same bill for nearly thirty years – though there had been a close shave in the seventies when both had been booked for a televized 'Johnny Cash Christmas Special'. However, Cash's objection to Jerry Lee referring to himself by name in the third person – 'I'm dreaming of a white Christmas/ just like the ones old Killer used to know' – caused the Lewis section of the show to be edited out.

There would be no hard feelings, however, when the three old campaigners convened with Carl Perkins to record an album together at the now much-modernized Sun studio back in Memphis. The idea for this had been conceived four years earlier when Sun issued a jam session from 1956 allegedly involving the 'Million Dollar Quartet' of Lewis, Cash, Perkins and Elvis Presley. More of documentary interest than anything else, this thirty-minute sing-song nonetheless provoked sufficient response for a premeditated eighties' reconstruction of the 'Class of '55' – with Roy filling in for the departed Presley.

If short on spontaneity, *Homecoming* was a likeable enough sentimental journey, rife with tuneful reminiscences, slices of autobiography in song, a commemoration of Elvis – 'We Remember the King' – and three numbers with 'rock 'n' roll' in the title. Cash and Orbison seemed the least active of the chicken-necked principals, submitting only one solo turn each against the others' two. The remaining four tracks were communal efforts, with verses doled out more or less equally and everyone in raucous harmony on the choruses.

At opposite poles were the voices of Jerry Lee – darker and bereft of all ingenuity – and Roy, forever sweet and innocent, especially on 'Coming Home', his own ballad soliloquy. Opening the second half, this had a separate life from the rest of the album. The first half of its melody was not unlike Nilsson's 'Without You' of 1972 but, free of the name-dropping and 'Memphis beat' that seemed compulsory on other tracks, 'Coming Home' – if not a masterpiece of song – conveyed the required back-to-the-roots aura without too much olde-tyme retrogression.

In the LPs eight-minute 'party' number, 'Big Train (From Memphis)', the four legends and their backing musicians' guests spanned all ages of pop. In Sam Phillips and Jack Clement, there were the opinionated console sages whose musical conditioning process had primed four country boys for greener pastures. Ricky Nelson was there too, as were the noted songwriter Toni Wine, and John Fogerty, composer of 'Big Train' and the mainstay of Creedence Clearwater Revival. Another revivalist was Welsh guitarist Dave Edmunds, whose adolescent imagination had also been captured by rockabilly and its offshoots.

Lending a hand too were the Judds, a mother-and-daughter team from Kentucky who, for better or worse, had been marketed as part of the 'new tradition', a late development in C & W. To a greater extent than the Glen Campbells and Lynn Andersons of the decade just gone, the differing aptitudes of the Judds, k.d. lang, Randy Travis, Dwight Yoakam, the Sweethearts of the Rodeo and others were rescuing country from its decline by forsaking much of its rhinestoned tackiness for a leaner, more abandoned approach. In North America anyway, it found favour with a younger audience, for whom C & W had been the corniest genre in pop. Inherent in its very name, new tradition maintained respect for country's down-home maturity and veneration for its elder statesmen. As Jason Ringenberger, leader of Texan new traditionalist group the Scorchers, explained: 'we're not trying to slaughter country or walk over it. We feel we have a lot in common with singers like Hank Williams – obviously not in sound but we're out there on a certain edge.' Putting action above debate, Dwight Yoakam collaborated on an album with Buck Owens. For the film *Hiding Out*, the passage of k.d. lang into the US pop chart was assisted by her formidable duet of 'Cryin'' with a figure from recent past – Roy Orbison.[5]

Making up for lost time perhaps, the homeland that had written him off as a has-been was now beating a path to Roy's door. 'It seems as though America is saying, "We loved you back in the sixties and we still love you today".'[6] With Elvis dead, he was surely one of the next best things. Given the right song, Orbison would be ripe for another conquest.

One record that had all the qualities of a smash but never actually grabbed the public was 'Wild Hearts' of 1985, another film souvenir. The commission from the reputable Nicolas Roeg – of *Performance*, *Don't Look Now* and *The Man Who Fell to Earth* – was something of an honour for Roy. Pleasing too was the release of 'Wild Hearts' in various mixes and sizes by ZTT, then on the crest of a wave with Frankie Goes To Hollywood who – in Britain at least – were swamping the Top Ten. Teetering on the edge of the charts in Britain, 'Wild Hearts' may have been issued in the States by ZTT had the rather pretentious movie, *Insignificance* – 'the story of life, death, sex and the universe' – done better at the box office. Instead, 'Wild Hearts' faded – like the film itself – from general circulation. Unfortunately, it was Roy's strongest single for years.

Orbison's songwriting partner on 'Wild Hearts' (and others) was Will Jennings, a professional lyricist. His lyrics also graced the music of the Crusaders – a revered jazz rock outfit from his native Texas – and, recently relocated to Nashville, Steve Winwood, whose *Arc of a Diver* LP of 1980 had rescued a deflated career. Approaching tunes with detached efficiency and the reasonable argument that the words should blend both with the music and the singer's personality, Will would 'look for an identity between myself and the person I'm working for.'[7]

If his 'Coming Home', written for Roy Orbison, was repetitive, it nevertheless rolled off the tongue without pomp or affectation. As Winwood was Jennings' main concern (and source of revenue) his work for others, though competent, tended to pay the mortgage rather than sate him with pride. 'Wild Hearts', for example, repeated a key phrase – 'in the sunshine of your mind' – first heard on Winwood's 'Help Me Angel' three years earlier. However, another Orbison song 'Life Fades Away', written for the soundtrack of *Less Than Zero*, was a succinct intimation of mortality pertinent to the death scene in the script.

Though it upset Barbara when he smoked, it didn't occur to anyone at the time that Roy's days might be numbered. Nevertheless, Orbie Lee's sorry decline after heart surgery had brought home to his son what a fatal weakness he – and Grady – had surely inherited. His favourite fizzy drink was also frowned on by the doctor, but Rick Rubin, producer of 'Life Fades Away', recalls, 'it was time to do the vocal and he was in the booth, and he made us get him a Coke – because he'd never made a record without having a Coke.'[8] The chest scars had been discreetly airbrushed out, but the sleeve photographs of *Laminar Flow* – taken a year after treatment – were pictures of health. He even tried to stick to his diet – 'not meaning a restricted food intake but the proper food' – and even exercise 'from time to time'.[8] Nevertheless, beneath the fringe that he still dyed, the face grew chubbier, the chin doubled, and the waist thickened – though he became noticeably thinner in 1988.

Whereas once the show might have gone on, minor illnesses now prostrated him. An attack of flu would write off a televised return visit to the London Palladium on 15 November 1987. At another British concert a couple of years earlier, Michelle Booth (a very special fan) 'knew he was unwell because he had to be helped from the stage – but I didn't know how serious things were'.

Barry Booth saw him at Croydon's Fairfield Halls, during that tour, and couldn't help comparing the present with the past. 'I was very struck by the sense of continuity. The act was – apart from two recent additions – the same. It was really strange to be sitting there in a box, looking down and watching the performance with a synthesizer player doing the orchestral bits. I could not avoid making comparisons. The economic considerations that dictate that the synthesizer player will actually take the place of a string section was a shame. Although the show was wonderfully well received – that comparison that there was a time when he was touring with woodwinds, brass, strings, a full rhythm section and three girl singers still held – and that was what he deserved.'

The 'two recent additions' were the resurrected 'Ooby Dooby' and now its B-side 'Go! Go! Go!' – alias 'Down the Line'. Otherwise, 'I do all the more popular songs in my stage show. I get asked many times, "Don't you get tired of singing those old songs?" and I say, "Gracious, no, because I've worked a lifetime to do a show of just my own material."'[9]

While 'Wild Hearts' and 'Life Fades Away' boomed out in half-empty cinemas, a re-cut of 'In Dreams' was mimed by actor Dean Stockwell during an eerie sequence in the more acclaimed Blue Velvet, directed by David Lynch, who'd also been responsible for the cult movie, Eraserhead. Lynch was so delighted by the new 'In Dreams' that its sound would engulf the cast and crew at fixed intervals throughout the shooting of the film.

David Lynch would also produce re-makes of another eighteen Orbison numbers for release by Virgin America, the company with whom Roy, after much wavering, came home to roost in 1985. 'I decided on Virgin because of the personalities of the people behind it and their attitude and gusto.'[10] Roy's enthusiasm was shared by other negotiable names – amongst them Bryan Ferry, Scott Engel and the

Sex Pistols, all of whom had fallen under the spell of founder Richard Branson. After being with Island for over twenty years, Steve Winwood had also defected to Virgin. Not prone to excessive thrift, the company's publicity department would not stop at simply mailing a pre-release copy of so-and-so's latest record to a *Rolling Stone* reviewer. Far better to make money work by taking half-page advertisements in the national dailies, TV commercials and street hoardings.

Thus, *In Dreams – the Greatest Hits* was presented to the populace. Another re-issue of the Fred Foster masters had been more difficult by legal problems following Monument's liquidation in 1981. But re-recordings of well-loved smashes can leave a peculiar aftertaste – especially if the original had some emotional significance for the listener. Mercifully, the producers remained faithful to most of the original arrangements in Orbison's case. Some indefinable element may have been missing, 'but God has a way of giving you the lyric and the melody and, if it stands up over the years, that adolescence, that innocence helps to keep its intentions pure. That innocence is the big ingredient that keeps my songs alive, that makes them stand tall.'[11]

On the Tuesday before the cancelled Palladium spot, a feverish Roy Orbison, in the dark, double-breasted suit that he would still be wearing, jet-lagged, hours later on breakfast TV, walked onto a British stage for the last time at Harlesden's Mean Fiddler. Because of the nation's obsession with the sixties, Roy felt 'a bit awkward about being in England at this time. It looks like a set-up to me'.[12] As the sound balance evened out, his voice shimmered over the sea of bobbing heads before him. From the barrage of applause that splintered the silence after the second number – 'Leah' – onlookers and singer meshed as the jigging crowd assumed the role of rhythm section, stamping and clapping on the off-beat, right through 'Dream Baby' and other up-tempo numbers. Roy's guitar picking was a revelation – he seemed to be attacking the strings with a raw intensity that night.

Though he didn't respond to a bawled request for 'Borne on the Wind', he was still quite chatty. 'That was the first record I ever made,' he announced after 'Ooby Dooby' – and then, 'This is the first song I ever wrote' before the lengthy instrumental introduction to a 'Down the Line' that embraced shades of Bill Haley. Later, he introduced the band by their first names and thanked the audience for being wonderful.

He'd drooped slightly during 'It's Over', almost overwhelmed by the backing vocalists, but he had more than recovered for the big finish of 'Running Scared' and its reprise. Over the play-out, Roy Orbison grinned, waved and vanished into the wings forever. It was such an easy, unceremonious parting as he left forever the people who had never stopped adoring him.

'Running Scared' lent its name to a US cops-and-robbers film in 1986, while in the BBC series 'Tutti Frutti', the Majestics – Glasgow's self-styled 'Kings of Rock' – would include 'Only the Lonely' and 'Love Hurts' amongst their salaams to departed glory. Younger artists pounced on the Orbison songbook too. As well as recording 'Cryin'', T'pau plagiarized the title of 'Only the Lonely' for one of their own creations. In the States, John Cougar awoke a tired 'Oh! Pretty Woman' while, back in Scotland, 'It's Over' was sung by the Associates' Billy McKenzie. Delving even deeper, Australia's Mental As Anything released their version of 'Working For the Man'.

Most sincerely garrulous in praising the Big O was Bruce Springsteen. In January 1987, he had inducted Roy at the second Rock and Roll Hall of Fame ceremony. On the podium of his New York's uppercrust Waldorf-Astoria Hotel, 'he was saying that I had been part of his life when he was in New Jersey in that little room. He said I could make it seem like it was any place in the world . . . and so many flattering things that I can't repeat them all.'[13] In the presence of the cream of the American music business, Roy felt he had at last been 'truly recognized, you know, justified.

"Validated" might be the word."[11] Dumbfounded when accepting his ovation and statuette, Roy afterwards requested a copy of Springsteen's speech, which had finished with an explanation of his aims when writing *Thunder Road*. 'I wanted a record with words like Bob Dylan that sounded like Phil Spector – but, most of all, I wanted to sing like Roy Orbison. Now everybody knows that no one sings like Roy Orbison.'

Springsteen would demonstrate that *he* didn't when, months later, he made his presence felt on an Orbison television spectacular in California. He wasn't alone in this most public patronage of pop's methuselahs. Lately, the sixtieth birthdays of both Fats Domino and Chuck Berry had been celebrated before the cameras with musical attendance by some of the famous who'd grown up to their music. Roy's turn came on 30 September 1987 in the Coconut Ballroom of Los Angeles' Ambassador Hotel. This glittering extravaganza was the brainchild of Barbara and its baggy-suited musical director, Joseph 'T-Bone' Burnett, an owlish Texan who had assisted David Lynch on Orbison's *In Dreams* collection.

Flying back from a more orthodox concert on the same day, Roy had but the haziest notion of who would be accompanying him. At the afternoon rehearsal, he found not only Springsteen but also Elvis Costello, one of T-Bone's clients, who was now looking more like the Orbison of 1960 than ever. Polarized round Presley's Las Vegas rhythm section, the mixture of west coast show-business periphery eager to get in on the act and those with some actual affinity to the main event would include a backing chorale of k.d. lang, musical archivist Ry Cooder, J. D. Souther – who had helped Roy and Will with 'Coming Home' – and Eagles' associate Jackson Browne. Darting about, too, was bearded, post-beatnik, Tom Waits.

What could have been a self-congratulatory disaster was in fact a triumph, partly because everyone wanted it to be. At Roy's vocal entry with 'Only the Lonely', an almost palpable wave of goodwill washed towards him from an audience whose jewelled celebrity took him back to the Talk of the Town. They loved him for wanting to please them. Not for nothing had he spent over thirty years perfecting his craft. For the remainder of his hour-long performance, they'd worry if he showed signs of strain, cheer when he rallied, and glow when, ultimately, he went down well.

No one in the rank-and-file could upstage him – not even the animated Springsteen whose little 'hah!' was heard in the two-second gap after the fake ending to 'Dream Baby', who had shared Roy's microphone on that one, and also on 'Uptown'. Hovering in the background, he mouthed Roy's words, wrinkled his nose, clenched his teeth and grinned. Costello and Waits elbowed in with a minimalist organ solo each; Costello also played the harmonica on 'Candy Man'.

Orbison's cohorts had done their worst, but it was far from a death touch. At least they had the grace to keep out of the way on the ballads – and on these Roy sang his heart out. The public may have preferred a more characteristic recital, unencumbered by the famous friends who had given Roy Orbison another contemporary seal of approval. Harder to take was the topsy-turvy camerawork on Virgin's subsequent video in sixties monochrome. Despite this, 'Roy Orbison and Friends: A Black-and-White Night' was seen on over fifty thousand domestic viewers within weeks of its release in May 1988.

The film, as expected, re-ran the old hits – but 'The Comedians', written by Elvis Costello, does not seem out of place amongst the customary goods. In fact, it ranks with the best of Orbison's eighties' swansongs. This song would be one of T-Bone Burnett's production contributions to Roy Orbison's posthumous *Mystery Girl* LP that would be two years in the making. Its sleeve credits were voluminous. In the forefront was Jeff Lynne, studio boffin, former leader of the Electric Light Orchestra, and an Orbison admirer from way back: 'I finally got a tape with all his songs on and played it non-stop for, like, five years . . . it's still hard for me to believe that I got to work with him and have him trust me.'8

Lynne was much in demand at the time after his co-production of George Harrison's *Cloud Nine* album had helped to put the former Beatle back in the spotlight. Jeff had had to postpone work on *Mystery Girl* in April 1988 to oversee one final, and trifling detail of his prior commitment to Harrison – a bonus number for a European twelve-inch single. Tagging along while the two Englishmen discussed this matter over lunch in Los Angeles was Roy Orbison. George was astounded that Roy seemed so well versed in British comedy – he'd had only sporadic contact with Roy since the ravages of Beatlemania: 'Roy knew every word to every Monty Python song and the dialogue to all the movies and the TV series. I mean, he was a gentle person but he had a good sense of humour.'8 George was elated when, over dessert, the jocular Orbison volunteered to sing with him on this extra track.

As it wasn't worth booking anywhere expensive, Harrison rang his pal Bob Dylan whose unsophisticated studio garage in Malibu was available the next day. Duly turning up at the agreed hour, Roy shook hands with guitarist Tom Petty whose group the Heartbreakers had backed Dylan on his last world tour: 'Well, George had to stop by Tom Petty's house to pick up his guitar and Tom said, "Hey, I'm not doing anything. Can I come along?"'14

By the evening, flesh had been put on the bones of a piece entitled 'Handle With Care', onto which had been grafted what Harrison called a 'lonely bit' for Roy – while Dylan wheezed his trademark mouth organ on the fade. This gathering was not meant to be a 'super-group' in embryo. More like Roy's 'Class of '55', it was just the gods at play over a long afternoon. Orbison spoke for everyone: 'We all enjoyed it so much. It was so relaxed. There was no ego involved and there was some sort of chemistry going on.'14 Apart from his and Dylan's distinctive voices, no one would suppose that 'Handle With Care' was special. Would they?

The next day, Dylan continued preparing for his summer tour, Roy left for a one-nighter in Anaheim near Long Beach, and Harrison drove round to his record company with the new tape. It was pronounced too potentially profitable to hide under a twelve-inch single. In conference with Lynne afterwards, George warmed to the idea of cutting an entire LP with the 'Handle With Care' line-up. Petty jumped at the chance; while, over the phone, Dylan's affirmative was more brusque.

That evening, Tom, Jeff and George plus their wives drove down the coast to Anaheim, and put it before the Big O. In the dressing room, Petty would remember, 'he was so calm – "Sure, sounds like a lot of fun". Then we went out and watched the show.'[8] As Orbison went through his paces, it may have struck the party that as a singer he outclassed all of them – and Dylan too. He may not be a prolific songwriter any more, but he could certainly pitch the notes way beyond their own two octaves.

Safe in this knowledge, the album was completed over the summer. Most of the composing – with everybody on acoustic guitars – took place at the LA home of the hospitable Dave Stewart of the Eurythmics, then Dylan's producer. Sustained by a continuous running of barbeques, this companionable atmosphere bred matey abuse, coded hilarity and mutual reminiscences about the old days. Jeff and Tom, for example, had on different occasions recorded with Del Shannon – as Bob had with Johnny Cash, and George with Duane Eddy. Roy and George both knew Michael Palin, Barry Booth's lyricist and one of the Monty Python team whose *Life of Brian* feature film had been floated on a loan procured by Harrison. The Beatles may have integrated the riff from 'Oh! Pretty Woman' into their concert version of 'Daytripper', but would Bob bring up the demo of his 'Don't Think Twice It's All Right' that was sent to Roy in 1963? 'I must have been thinking of something else at the time because I turned it down. Next thing was "Blowing in the Wind" on the radio and then I knew I'd made a mistake'.[4]

Early on, George and Jeff had made up The Traveling Wilburys – referring to studio gremlins – as a name for the pretend group. 'We wanted a lighthearted name as opposed to anything serious,' Orbison would tell the *Boston Globe*. 'We were thinking of the Beatles in *A Hard Day's Night* – something along those lines.'[15] With his Handmade film company one of the pillars of the British cinema, Harrison would later think aloud about a full-length movie based on the sleeve notes (attributed to Michael Palin) to the album. Masquerading as half-brothers born of the same father (Charles Truscott Wilbury Sr) the five would be name-checked on this cover under their chosen pseudonyms, Roy's being 'Lefty Wilbury' in recognition of Lefty Frizzell. Entering further into the spirit of this elaborate joke, the oldest Wilbury sibling would remark, 'Some people said Daddy was a cad and a bounder but I remember him as a Baptist minister.'[8]

As to the 'group' going on the road, 'we did sort of discuss it but really only got as far as discussing the order we'd go on stage – and there's no second album planned. The "Volume One" on the first record was just, well, in the spirit of the Wilburys. Anyway, we couldn't repeat the ploy on the record companies the second time round.'[14] None of the labels involved had raised any fuss when *The Traveling Wilburys Volume One* was presented as a *fait accompli*. Nobody wanted to be unpopular. One executive simply muttered something about not standing in the way of history before hanging up on the Wilbury concerned.

Out of step with the march of hip-hop, acid house *et al*, the release of Volume One was like a Viking longship docking in a hovercraft terminal. After the songs had been written, only ten days could be set aside for the actual taping owing to Lucky Wilbury's forthcoming tour, but any lifting of this restriction may have detracted from the proceedings' rough-and-ready appeal. Though it was still the product of gentlemen who could afford to muck about, minor experiments such as hired drummer Jim Keltner whacking a refrigerator's wire grille with brushes reflected the LP's uncomputerized, do-it-yourself air. Closer in execution to skiffle or rockabilly than even *Homecoming* had been, Harrison went on about the Wilburys being 'like the Green Party. You've got to battle against all these whales stuck in ice – namely the music industry – to release all these people from feeling guilty for not using a synthesizer and not being able to programme it' – which Lynne capped with, 'Don't even bother learning – just *play* the bleeding piano'.[16]

Swimming with the tide, Roy's contributions were more or less equal in quantity to those on 'Class of '55'. He'd been featured singer on 'Winged Serpent' – inspired by William Blake's 'The Sick Rose' – but this had been tossed aside to leave 'Not Alone Any More' as Roy's sole lead vocal contribution, while Dylan had four. Within the off-the-cuff climate of the situation, 'Not Alone Any More' re-cast Orbison as the cuckolded boyfriend turning up when he isn't wanted. As always, his singing makes him a being apart, as Lynne observed during Orbison's vocal takes: 'Everybody just sat there going, "Wow! It's Roy Orbison!"' In the booth, with one hand steadying the headphones and the other with the inevitable Coca-Cola, 'even though he's become your pal and you're hanging out and having a laugh and going to dinner, as soon as he gets behind that mike and he's doing his business, suddenly it's shudder time.'[8]

After recording 'Not Alone Any More', Roy took a back seat for the other tracks – backing harmonies, the odd bridge, a verse or two. On 'Dirty World', he unfurled his 'Son of Paleface' growl like a conjuror reproducing a popular effect to amuse the children.

In tying up the Wilbury loose end, Roy not only managed that long-threatened return to the charts, but also brought the aura of a fresh sensation to those young enough not to have heard of him before. In a way, it was the same old scene. In Virgin's soft-focus publicity shots, teenagers saw not a portly dotard or even the oldest swinger in town. He was a mysterious but unthreatening man-of-the-world, a wellspring of supercool. In other words, he was as he'd appeared to the mods and rockers of yore – apart from a few modern touches like the wine-red spectacles and a lately grown pigtail. With an old-young countenance drained of colour and unmarred by perceptible hair loss, only Orbison's known maturity distanced him from the current incumbents of the hit parade.

Those who remembered felt vaguely reassured that his cowboy-operatic larynx was still going strong. When 'You Got It', the first single from *Mystery Girl*, reached the counters, some would try to will it to No.1 as a verification of the lost value of someone singing a song as opposed to producing a production.

Roy Orbison's era as an outsider was over. No more would he have to reaffirm his credibility as a contemporary artist by so gladly supporting an act like the Eagles. Who the hell are they anyway? Now he could fill stadiums on his own again. Leaving them wanting more, he'd bound off stage wreathed in smiles, but some noticed that his eyes were full of tears: 'I've been taken aback by the way things are going. It's very nice to be wanted again but I still can't quite believe it.'[17]

During this most gratifying transition, musicians years younger than any Wilbury had been buzzing round him. The most staggering conversion was that of guitarist Steve Jones, formerly of the Sex Pistols, who as both songwriting partner and person was, according to Roy, 'just a sweetheart; real open and honest.'[6] There wouldn't be an Orbison/Jones opus on *Mystery Girl*, but 'She's a Mystery to Me', composed and produced by members of U2 – then an even bigger hit in North America than the Eagles had been – would be its second hit single.

Backtracking from their punk beginnings, this Irish quartet had tumbled into Orbison through the soundtrack of *Blue Velvet*. Of 'In Dreams', vocalist Paul 'Bono' Hewson enthused, 'It breaks all the rules of pop music. I hadn't realized he was such an innovator – and I'd never heard a voice like it . . . there seemed to be all the dreams and nightmares in there, all mixed up.'⁸

In common with 'Dream You' and 'In the Real World' – a Will Jennings number in possible homage to Jacques Brel – 'She's a Mystery to Me' was another angle on Roy Orbison's fantasy world of sleep – that's all he ever sings about, isn't it? The romantic utopia of U2 inhaled a breath of the Orient to Orbison and Hewson's droning guitars beneath the vocal understatement of the 'poetic' couplets – bleeding hearts, fallen angels crying out from hell and all that.

While in collusion with these newcomers, Roy did not renege on his past. *Mystery Girl* includes a song entitled 'Windsurfer', co-written with Bill Dees. Throughout the seventies, Roy had made a point of regularly recording songs Bill had written with other collaborators. From the lesson of his irresolute reconciliation with Joe Melson, the reunited Orbison and Dees knew better than to block out new ideas by trying to supersede 'It's Over' and 'Oh! Pretty Woman'. Though one new song, 'The Way is Love', had to be discarded, 'Windsurfer', with a tinge of the Beach Boys in its backing vocals and swooping Hawaiian guitar, suggested there was at least half a chance of the old firm being back in business. With Bill back in Amarillo, further collaboration between Orbison and Dees might have been hampered by distance. Just as remote was Joe Melson, who had returned to Odessa. In November 1988 Roy had called Joe from Malibu – just for a chat. Roy, Barbara and the two youngest were off to Europe next week, Roy to collect a Wilbury video award in Holland while Barbara and the boys visited the in-laws. Wesley was staying at his grandmother's. At twenty-three, he was now old enough to start a career. He was going to be a songwriter but, though having a famous father opens doors, it also increases expectations. Nevertheless, he was shaping up really well. Some might call it nepotism, but Roy was even considering one of Wesley's songs for inclusion on *Mystery Girl*. With Steve Cropper on guitar and doubling as conductor of the Memphis Horns, a master had already been recorded. George Harrison had played on another track. Actually, 'You Got It' had been mixed in George's private studio in Henley-on-Thames by Jeff Lynne. He and Tom Petty had helped Roy with some of the *Mystery Girl* originals. Maybe Joe and Roy ought to try once more.

Like riders on the old frontier, the two old comrades went their separate ways without formal goodbyes. In Midland's Chaparral Centre, not far from Melson's, Roy Orbison had already settled his score with the land that bore him. On 25 April 1987, he'd headlined an 'Oil Aid' charity concert for those caught up in the industry's recession. This had been the real homecoming – infinitely more so than the 'Class of '55'. However trying his Wink adolescence may have been, Roy's earlier years had overflowed with happiness. For all his wanderings since high school, his regional loyalty and identity had often brought him back. In 1981, he'd sung during the festivities in Lubbock that had surrounded the unveiling of Buddy Holly's statue.

Well, here he was again – the local boy made good. Chatting backstage before the concert, he learnt from the editor of the *Wink Bulletin* that the town council had voted to rename Langley Way in his honour. Thrilled as he was, the Big O perversely chose to open the show with 'Cryin'' but, as the *Bulletin* reporter said, 'As anyone could guess, the loudest and longest cheers for "Ooby Dooby" came from those of Wink and formerly of Wink'.[18] Despite his good nature, the Wink High School boy could not be blamed for thumbing his nose at those who had once belittled and embittered him.

After an Elvis Presley Memorial Concert in Atlantic City two months on, there was a reminder of a later and better disposed condescension. As they posed in the dressing room for a snapshot, Gordon Stoker whispered something to Roy. He'd just remembered an instruction he'd been given by Chet Atkins in 1958 to sing along behind a bag of nerves in his early twenties. It had been on a number called 'Seems to Me'. With that same orphaned smile of thirty years before, Roy seemed quite overcome with rose-tinted sentiments – unusually so, thought Gordon, because 'he didn't show his feelings too much'.

A few mornings later at Nashville airport, who should Orbison bump into but Mr Guitar himself. Chet Atkins had remained close to Roy in spite of the teacher/pupil gulf of the RCA sessions: 'I feel lucky to have been associated with him in his early years. He is a truly great artist and just as great as a person. I am one of his greatest admirers.' On equal ground now, Chet graciously accepted a Roy Orbison lapel badge during a cordial conversation with its giver.

During the last month of his life, Roy was back at Old Hickory with the custodian of what would forever stand as his best-remembered testaments. He couldn't help liking Fred Foster as the waspish old rascal confessed to enjoying 'That "Lovin' You" Feelin' Again'. That was praise indeed. 'We made a lot of good music, didn't we?' replied Roy, with a look that would haunt Fred through the years.

To those who knew him less well, Orbison had seemed strangely contemplative in those last months. Shortly before he and Barbara flew to Europe, Roy apparently told Los Angeles record producer Tony Pastor that 'he thought the end of the road was near and he didn't really care; that his life had been a series of ups and downs that didn't really make sense. His exact words were: "If I go tomorrow, it don't make no difference to me."' Perhaps it was merely that he was still apprehensive about air travel. There'd been quite a few accidents recently.

Landing in the Netherlands in one piece, he performed his Wilbury duty and returned to Nashville via London, where he was photographed wearing a chic dancer's sombrero and geometrically patterned cloak. He was also button-holed by journalists who learnt that he was 'totally centred', meaning that he was at peace with himself at last. Although it was great to be back in the limelight, he was too long in the tooth to make predictions: 'my life is a never-ending dream. I take one day at a time and never look too far into the future.'[19]

Orbison did admit that it was time for his autobiography. Like Chuck Berry, he'd write it himself. There'd be no ghosts. He'd already waited too long. One British publishing house, Sidgwick and Jackson, had been seeking the UK rights to the Roy Orbison saga since September 1986. 'Why Roy Orbison?' a bemused London monthly had enquired of Susan Hill, one of the firm's directors. 'Because he's actually done something, and has something to say,' she replied. 'It always helps if someone's had a few experiences, gained a bit of wisdom, and is capable of telling a story with some drama.'[20]

Roy also dared to predict that *Mystery Girl* would keep up his present run of success. 'It's not like this is the only album I'll ever make,'[11] he continued, dropping the names of Dylan and Springsteen as certain donors of songs for the next album. Yes, he'd be adding about thirty minutes of *Mystery Girl* to his act when he rehearsed for the world tour starting in March. He was sorry for neglecting his faithful British fans lately but there was now 'too much ground to cover'.[14] Nevertheless, he'd be back in England nearer Christmas for the shooting of a video for the second Wilburys' 45. One direct quote – 'at the moment, it's like the Devil chasing me around'[21] – would provide a chilling headline for one British daily within a fortnight.

The first few days of December, however, were relatively quiet. As Barbara was yet to jet in from Germany, he stayed with his mother and Wesley – whose song 'The Only One', had made it onto *Mystery Girl*. Simultaneously universal and personal, its lyrics are a dissection of self-pity after an unspecified tragedy. The view expressed was one shared by its singer, who had concluded years before that, 'If you take a good look at life, it teaches you that you are one of billions in the world with problems.'[22] The three generations of the family under the same roof that fateful week had had more than their fair share of those.

On Tuesday 6 December, Benny Birchfield and Roy spent a hectic afternoon out of doors with their miniature aeroplanes. 'They were having a hell of good time,'[19] remembered country singer Jean Shephard the day after. Puffed out, Roy called a halt and wended his way back to Nadine's to eat. During the evening, he complained of a tightness and shooting pains across his rib cage. Maybe they would pass – as they had at the Liberty Bowl in Memphis. He'd obviously had too much fun today. Close to eleven o'clock, however, his exhausted heart finally came to a standstill after a series of shuddering gasps.

Panic-stricken, his mother summoned an ambulance. In the bathroom where he'd collapsed, the paramedics tried cardiopulmonary resuscitation and other procedures for half-an-hour before rushing the unconscious patient to the hospital in Hendersonville. In the emergency room, there was nothing the doctors could do. While the town slept, Roy Orbison was pronounced dead.

Mid-morning in Bielefeld, the distraught Barbara must have known something of the disbelieving helplessness that her husband had felt that day in Bournemouth. Closer to home, Bill Dees turned over in bed, having been wrenched from sleep at 6 a.m. by the telephone. With phlegmatic detachment, he'd taken comfort in John v, 24: 'He that heareth my word, and believeth on Him that sent me, hath everlasting life, and shall not come into condemnation but is passed from death unto life.'

Later that Wednesday, journalists were more inclined to lean on yellowed, dog-eared cuttings from the sixties than the Bible as they cobbled together over-hasty obituaries and tributes. Most were aware that Roy Orbison had been big in the mid-sixties and had just made a comeback. What had he been up to in-between? Old rumours were distorted even more: 'Too Soon to Know' was said to be about Claudette's motorcycle crash; he advertised for a second wife and arraigned the best-looking applicants at the Westbury Hotel; and he wore a toupée. One misguided provincial hack even confused him with Gene Pitney.

Despite Springsteen's warning at the Waldorf-Astoria, audiences were bombarded with Roy Orbison numbers by singers such as Steve Harley, who had a go at 'Not Alone Any More'. US outfit Little Feat tried to dispel the gloom in London's Town and Country that Wednesday night by dedicating their 'All That You Can Dream' to the Big O. The Art Movement decided to wait a decent interval before recording a tribute to their old boss. Major Bill Smith was already in his Fort Worth studio taping a monologue entitled 'Big O'.

That same morning, Virgin shipped out advance copies of *Mystery Girl* and began pressing 'You Got It', which was destined to be Roy's first Top Five entry since 1966. This was accompanied by a video showing him very much alive. In accordance with the widow's wishes, none of the scheduled release dates were altered.

The Sun compiled a dial-a-tune megamix of six Orbison hits at thirty-eight pence a minute; estate agents wondered who would be doing the probate assessment; and publishers liaised with biographers. A less self-interested celebration of Roy Orbison took place in a Los Angeles theatre exactly a week after his passing. This was the music industry's equivalent of a wake. Among its highlights were Stray Cat Brian Setzer's frenzied 'Ooby Dooby' and a touching speech by Joe Melson. Fresh from the funeral in Malibu, Barbara also managed a few words, as did Will Jennings. Not quite so moving was a prepared panegyric from Virgin-America.

In Nashville, Vernon and Wink, flags waved at half-mast. Hendersonville's collective grief was partly exorcised by a memorial service in the Baptist Church the Sunday after. Neither Johnny Cash nor Waylon Jennings were able to make it. Both were in intensive care in Nashville's Baptist Hospital with heart conditions. A proclamation was issued in Wink by Mayor Maxie Watts declaring that 9 December would henceforth be Roy Orbison Day. In February, the Chamber of Commerce launched a subscription scheme for the erection of a bronze statue of one – the only one – who had put the town on the world map. A possible site was the vacant lot of North Roy Orbison Avenue where the family bungalow had stood. By June 1989, however, only a paltry $554 had been donated to its estimated cost of $30,000. Many of the town's inhabitants claimed not to remember Roy Orbison.

As he might have wished, Wink's most renowned son had died with a record in the charts – albeit as one of the knockabout Traveling Wilburys. It was to be expected that the morbid publicity would boost sales for 'Handle With Care' (which was slipping down when he died) and its LP – particularly in the States. Elsewhere, a more common Christmas gift was one of the sixties compilations that had reappeared all of a sudden. In Britain, *The Legendary Roy Orbison* would start the New Year heading the album list, while the Top Forty singles chart would not see the back of Roy until the second half of 1989.

During that final round of press interviews in London, he'd trotted out the remark about his best records being yet to come. When *Mystery Girl* came out in mid-February, many could see Roy's point – even if, as with 'Danny Boy', it wasn't easy to be entirely objective. His singing was as ageless and glorious as ever. It had all the virtues and some of the faults of a virtuoso performance, but at least it was an artist doing something he was good at, even if he was too old to learn new tricks. There'd never have been another 'Southbound Jericho Parkway'.

Most of the material was affiliated to some aspect of the Orbison mythology. Sardonically, he'd speculated whether anyone would offer him a song entitled 'Blue Dream'. On *Mystery Girl*, as well as a surfeit of dream references, love is lost in 'A Love So Beautiful' and found in 'You Got It' while 'Careless Heart' has Roy attempting to make the same amends as in 'Falling'. Far apart geographically, both 'Blue

Bayou' and 'California Blue' are, nonetheless, home thoughts from abroad.

The *Mystery Girl* songs are not in themselves devalued by these comparisons. 'You Got It' and the lush 'A Love So Beautiful' are two that might have made the charts circa 1962. Like all Orbison's best work, 'Mystery Girl' is not so 'modern' that it will sound dated by the turn of the century. It's just that the sixties hits will always have a head start of up to thirty years of availability and airplay. They are associated with pop's most unpretentious and optimistic period. In those days, Roy Orbison could steal the show single-handedly.

Notes

1 *Evening Standard*, 8 April 1982
2 *Wink Bulletin*, 8 December 1988
3 *Zabadak No. 7*, December 1988
4 *Melody Maker*, September 1987
5 *Format*, April 1988
6 *Evening Standard*, 12 September 1987
7 *Q*, February 1989
8 *Rolling Stone*, 26 January 1989
9 Radio 2, 20 March 1980
10 *Today*, 8 July 1988
11 *The Face*, February 1989
12 *The Sunday Times*, 21 September 1987
13 Veronica Television (Dutch)
14 *Time Out*, December 1988
15 *Melody Maker*, 11 March 1967
16 *Kaleidoscope*, Radio 4, 30 November 1987
17 *Daily Mirror*, 8 October 1988
18 *Wink Bulletin*, 30 April 1987
19 *Daily Mail*, 8 December 1988
20 *Q*, December 1986
21 *Today*, 8 December 1988
22 *Daily Sketch*, 27 April 1970

Epilogue
Memories

Though his albums were filed in the 'Rock and Roll' section in record stores, Orbison's was not a name that sprang immediately to mind when discussing the behemoths of classic rock. Had he not overcome an essentially retiring disposition and snapped into the idiosyncratic style that, from 1959, would sell over thirty million units, his good-in-parts rockabilly inventory might have been a body of work desired for its very obscurity rather than any intrinsic worth. Without needing to hear 'Ooby Dooby', 'Rockhouse' et al., rock 'n' roll connoisseurs might have mentioned him in passing alongside Warren Smith, Johnny 'Peanuts' Wilson, Charlie Feathers, Malcolm Yelvington(!), Sonny Fisher – the list is endless of those who flowered momentarily in the wake of Elvis Presley. Instead, Roy Orbison's later achievements infused his earlier outpourings with a considerably greater historical interest.

By day a Kentish landscape gardener, seventeen-year-old Stephen Howe had been bitten by the rock 'n' roll bug. Through the influence of his elder brother Mick, this sandy-haired youth's favourite singing star came to be Roy Orbison – whose first hit records antedated Steve's birth. Accompanying himself on guitar, one of the first Orbison songs mastered by Steve Howe was 'The Clown', one of the 1957 demonstration recordings never intended for release. From the elementary fretboard chords he'd taught himself, he began to compose songs after the manner of his idol. Steve's faith in his not inconsiderable vocal talent would be justified when his facsimile of Roy's 'Danny Boy' received high commendation in a talent contest organized by the *Evening Post*.

This newspaper was local to Reading, home of Steve's girlfriend, Michelle Booth. In her final year at Highdown Comprehensive, Michelle's musical tastes had run to Elvis Presley and, a long way behind, Bryan Ferry. Unlike other girls of her age, she'd been quite unmoved by the outrages of the Sex Pistols, Generation X and other punk rockers who, by 1978, had become rather passé anyway. After pairing off with Steve during a fortnight in a Bognor holiday camp, her previous preferences were tested and found wanting by the magic of Roy Orbison – whose old records Steve had been systematically buying up from his brother.

Early one Friday evening in March 1978, Michelle left Reading by train to spend the weekend with Steve and his family in Gravesend – a destination too appropriately named. After waiting in vain to greet her at the station, Steve informed the police before driving home to spend a sleepless night. At 5 a.m. on that chilly morning, a squad car pulled up to whisk Steve to the Middlesex hospital where Michelle was on a life support system. She'd sustained near-fatal injuries when flung from the speeding Inter-City just past Brentford. Her broken body had been spotted beside the track by a railwayman on an early shift.

In the intensive care cubicle, Steve could only identify her by a mole on her left shoulder. In the thick of inserted tubes and drips, her wounds were so numerous and serious that you wouldn't have known she was a human being. From the first, there was almost no hope of recovery. However, though that pitiful, helpless life could have been taken without effort, the Grim Reaper decided to spare Michelle Booth.

Foul play was suspected but confirmation of this would have to hang fire until the patient stirred – if she ever would

– from a deep coma. To improve the chances of arousal, she was spoonfed with familiar sounds. Her twin sister, Sharon, chattered about school; Steve whispered sweet nothings, and, from a cassette player for hours on end, Roy Orbison sang.

Hearing of the schoolgirl's plight, certain show-business celebrities made thoughtful gestures. Comedian Spike Milligan sent flowers. From rock 'n roll revivalists, Darts, came a signed photograph. A letter even arrived from high society gadfly-turned-pop singer, Roddy Llewellyn. Michelle's eyes opened but there was no flicker of understanding yet. A shot in the dark was someone's idea to contact Roy Orbison. Perhaps a personal message from him might lift her closer to the brink of consciousness.

There are not untrue stories of stars employing secretaries whose job it is to rip open fan mail, extract any cheques, cash or the more useful gifts and throw the unread letters away. Roy Orbison, however, was of a different stamp. In his Tennessee fastness, the Big O acted immediately on Michelle's behalf. Seating himself before a tape recorder microphone, 'I was recovering from heart surgery myself and I was hoping that if I could say something on a tape without referring to hospitals or accidents or anything that she might not relate to, then it might help.'[1] For what it was worth, he wished her all the best for the future and invited her to be his guest of honour when his concert itinerary next reached a convenient venue in southern England. 'I was hoping that she would have that in her mind and just sort of be wanting to come to that concert but I think that her own strong will-power brought her through.'[1]

Though she couldn't recall hearing Roy during her oblivion, Michelle was convinced that his pre-recorded presence was of subliminal benefit 'because when I came home from the hospital and the tapes were played again, I could remember a lot of the words to songs I'd never heard of before.' She also recalled being first offered a cigarette in the train corridor by her ill-favoured assailant whom she described to the police as resembling a penguin. Enraged by her spirited resistance to his sudden and thuggish embrace, the sex maniac threw her out of the train.

Technically, the case remained unsolved. After a reconstruction of the crime – with Sharon standing in for her sister – several witnesses came forward and an Alan George Westlake was charged. As he waddled to the dock at the Old Bailey, you could appreciate the penguin allusion, enhanced further by a domed forehead and pear-shaped body.

Through the oratory skills of his barrister, Westlake was acquitted but only painful months of therapy and further operations would enable Michelle Booth to re-enter the world outside: 'I don't think I'll ever recover completely but physically I'm getting on quite well. My walking's not half as good as I'd like it to be but I'm coming along.' Scotched, nonetheless, was her ambition to become a nurse. No stranger to life's hard knocks himself, Roy Orbison would advise Michelle that 'it's not getting over it. It's getting used to it' when, on 20th March 1979, he more than kept his promise.

Straight from a television appearance in Los Angeles, he'd flown to Heathrow where he touched down around lunch time that Thursday. The British tour was scheduled to start in Manchester in two days. Despite a lost night's sleep, he instructed his chauffeur to go not to the usual West End hotel but to bear left down the M4 motorway towards Reading. Turning off at the A329, the limousine nosed through the lugubrious suburbs of a university town reckoned by makers of television documentaries to be the most 'average' in the United Kingdom.

Nothing would deflect Orbison from his iron purpose. Off the roaring A4 to Bath stood Fawley Road, a forlorn cul de sac where vehicles like his were seen only on formal occasions. When the car braked outside Number 45, Roy Orbison – an American legend for nearly thirty years – took a giant leap for Michelle Booth.

Ten years later, Michelle cried when the news of Orbison's death came: 'he played a major part in bringing me out of my coma and I will always remember him for that.' Steve – now her husband – had been told after it had been heard on a workmate's transistor. That evening, the Howes mourned not the star but a modest, easy-going fellow who'd spent the afternoon at Fawley Road just relaxing over a nice cup of tea. Afterwards had been the limousine gliding to a meal at the London Hilton and the VIP guided tour of Broadcasting House by Radio Two's bow-tied director. Next came the chat shows before which Roy assured an apprehensive Michelle with the sweet lie, 'I don't feel all that comfortable on radio or TV after all these years.'

As their words were transmitted across the nation, Steve looked on, seated between a stetsoned Sammy Orbison and Michelle's younger sister, Debbie. He'd been too starstruck to press his compositions on his idol as Sammy King had done with 'Penny Arcade'. It hadn't seemed the time or the place.

Steve's requiem to Roy had been a poignant 'Only the Lonely' in Reading's moribund folk club. He even drew participatory 'dum-dum-dum-dummy-doo-wahs' from an audience who joined in partly because of the glowing obituaries they'd read in the more liberal newspapers. Apparently, Orbison was cool nowadays. Illustrative of this had been one reaction in 1987 to his arrival in England without a suitable guitar for that jettisoned Palladium spot. Unwilling to expose his treasured Gibson to the pitfalls of airline cargo, he had been appalled to learn that the only identical guitar in the whole of London belonged to one who sensibly refused to let anyone *look* at such a rare instrument let alone *play* it. 'Who's it for?' the owner asked the desperate telephone receiver. 'Roy Orbison,' pleaded the Virgin executive. 'Well, in that case,' came the reply after the briefest pause, 'where do you want it delivered?'

The chicness that had been Roy's at his departure might have fallen away after a few months as such obsessions do.

U2 had now cottoned on to blues sexagenarian B. B. King. While the veteran guitarist's blistering obligatos tore at their latest single, perhaps Bono and his boys tacitly wondered what they'd ever seen in a cloying old balladeer like Roy Orbison.

Of course, the Big O's time would have come again as it always had – and the classic records will endure regardless, even the *Mystery Girl* postscript. Though he'd been a most unlikely-looking rock star, his image and approach – 'Caruso in sunglasses and a leather jacket'[2] as Tom Waits put it – was both tangential and capable of full integration to any pop era. Forever, his voice on the radio will bring butterflies to the stomach. Forever, the image will eclipse the man. 'I may be a living legend,' agreed Roy Orbison in one of his final interviews, 'but that sure don't help when I've got to change a flat tyre'.[3]

Notes

1. *The John Dunn Show*, Radio 2, 20 March 1979
2. *Rolling Stone* 26 January 1989
3. *Daily Express* 8 December 1988

Discography

SOLO SINGLES

		UK	US
1956	'Ooby Dooby'/'Tryin' to Get to You'	Not released	Je-Wel JE 101
May 1956	'Ooby Dooby'/'Go! Go! Go!'	Not released	Sun 242
September 1956	'Rockhouse'/'You're my Baby'	Not released	Sun 251
March 1957	'Sweet and Easy to Love'/'Devil Doll'	Not released	Sun 265
December 1957	'Chicken-hearted'/'I Like Love'	Not released	Sun 284
September 1958	'Seems to Me'/'Sweet and Innocent'	Not released	RCA 47–7381
December 1958	'Almost Eighteen'/'Jolie'	Not released	RCA 47-7447
September 1959	'Paper Boy'/'With the Bug'	Not released	Monument 409
February 1960	'Uptown'/'Pretty One'	Not released	Monument 412
June 1960	'Only the Lonely'/'Here Comes That Song Again'	London HLU 9149	Monument 421

September 1960	'Sweet and Easy to Love'*/'Devil Doll'*	Not released	Sun 353
October 1960	'Blue Angel'/ 'Today's Teardrops'	London HLU 9207	Monument 425
March 1961	'I'm Hurtin''/ 'I Can't Stop Loving You'	London HLU 9307	Monument 433
May 1961	'Running Scared'/'Love Hurts'	London HLU 9342	Monument 438
September 1961	'Cryin''/'Candy Man'	London HLU 9405	Monument 447
February 1962	'Dream Baby'/ 'The Actress'	London HLU 9511	Monument 456
June 1962	'The Crowd'/ 'Mama'	London HLU 9561	Monument 461
October 1962	'Working For The Man'/'Leah'	London HLU 9607	Monument 467
February 1963	'In Dreams'/ 'Shahdoroba'	London HLU 9676	Monument 806
May 1963	'Falling'/'Distant Drums'	London HLU 9727	Monument 815
September 1963	'Blue Bayou'/ 'Mean Woman Blues'	London HLU 9777	Monument 824
November 1963	'Pretty Paper'/ 'Beautiful Dreamer'	Not released	Monument 830
February 1964	'Borne on the Wind'/'What'd I Say'	London HLU 9845	Not released
April 1964	'It's Over'/'Indian Wedding'	London HLU 9882	Monument 837
June 1964	'You're My Baby'*/ 'Rockhouse'*	Ember EMB 5197	Not released

September 1964	'Oh! Pretty Woman'/'Yo te amo Maria'	London HLU 9919	Monument 851
September 1964	'This Kind of Love'/'I Never Knew'	Ember EMB 5200	Not released
November 1964	'Pretty Paper'/ 'Summersong'	London HLU 9930	Not released
February 1965	'Goodnight'/'Only With You'	London HLU 9951	Monument 873
March 1965	'Sweet and Easy to Love'/'You're Gonna Cry'	Ember EMB 5209	Not released
July 1965	'(Say) You're My Girl'/ 'Sleepy Hollow'	London HLU 9978	Monument 891
August 1965	'Ride Away'/ 'Wondering'	London HLU 9986	MGM 13386
October 1965	'Crawling Back'/ 'If You Can't Say Something Nice'	London HLU 10000	MGM 13410
January 1966	'Breakin' Up is Breakin' My Heart'/'Wait'	London HLU 10015	MGM 13446
February 1966	'Let the Good Times Roll'/ 'Distant Drums'	Not released	Monument 906
March 1966	'Twinkle Toes'/ 'Where is Tomorrow'	London HLU 10034	MGM 13498
June 1966	'Lana'/ 'Summersong'	Not released	Monument 939
June 1966	'Lana'/'House Without Windows'	London HLU 10051	Not released

August 1966	'Too Soon to Know'/'You'll Never be Sixteen Again'	London 10067	MGM 13549
September 1966	'Communication Breakdown'/'Going Back to Gloria'	Not released	MGM 13634
September 1966	'There Won't be Many Coming Home'/'Going Back to Gloria'	London HLU 10096	Not released
February 1967	'So Good'/'Memories'	London HLU 10113	MGM 13685
June 1967	'Cry Softly, Lonely One'/'Pistolero'	London HLU 10143	MGM 13764
October 1967	'She'/'Here Comes the Rain Baby'	London HLU 10159	MGM 13817
January 1968	'Born to be Loved by You'/'Shy Away'	London HLU 10176	MGM 13889
July 1968	'Walk On'/'Flowers'	London HLU 10206	MGM 13950
September 1968	'Heartache'/'Sugar Man'	London HLU 10222	MGM 13991
April 1969	'My Friend'/'Southbound Jericho Parkway'	London HLU 10261	MGM 14039
August 1969	'Penny Arcade'/'Tennessee Owns my Soul'	London HLU 10265	MGM 14079
October 1969	'Break my Mind'/'How Do You Start Over'	London HLU 10294	Not released
January 1970	'She Cheats on Me'/'How do You Start Over'	Not released	MGM 14105

April 1970	'So Young'/'If I Had a Woman Like You'	London HLU 10310	MGM 14121
August 1971	'Last Night'/'Close Again'	London HLU 10339	MGM 14293
September 1971	'Ooby Dooby'/ 'Devil Doll'	Sun 6094001	Not released
February 1972	'God Love You'/. 'Changes'	London HLU 10358	MGM 14358
April 1972	'Remember the Good'/'Harlem Woman'	Not released	MGM 14413
May 1972	'Remember the Good'/'If Only for a While'	Not released	MGM 14413
September 1972	'Memphis Tennessee'/'I Can Read Between the Lines'	London HLU 10388	MGM 14441
February 1973	'Blue Rain'/'Sooner or Later'	Not released	MGM 14552
September 1973	'I Wanna Live'/ 'You Lay so Easy on My Mind'	Not released	MGM 14626
September 1974	'Sweet Mama Blue'/'Heartache'*	Mercury 6167014	Mercury 73610
April 1975	'Hung Up on You'/'Spanish Nights'	Mercury 6167067	Mercury 73652
June 1975	'It's Lonely'/ 'Still'	Not released	Mercury 73705
July 1975	'Oh! Pretty Woman'/'It's Over'	Monument SMNT 1054	Not released
February 1976	'Only the Lonely'/ 'It's Over'	Monument SMNT 3965	Not released

May 1976	'Belinda'/'No Chain at All'	Monument SMNT 4247	Monument 258 8690
September 1976	'(I'm a) Southern Man'/'Born to Love Me'	Monument SMNT 4797	Monument 45-200
April 1977	'Drifting Away'/ 'Under Suspicion'	Monument SMNT 5151	Monument 45-215
June 1977	'Dream Baby'/ 'Blue Angel'	Monument SMNT 5265	Not released
February 1978	'Oh! Pretty Woman'/'It's Over'	Monument SMNT 5971	Not released
March 1978	'Only the Lonely'/ 'Dream Baby'	Monument SMNT 5972	Not released
March 1978	'Ooby Dooby'/ Curtis Lee Track	Charly CYS 0143	Not released
June 1979	'Tears'/'Easy Way Out'	Asylum K 13153	Asylum E46048
September 1979	'Warm Spot Hot'/'Lay it Down'	Asylum K 12391	Not released
September 1979	'Poor Baby'/'Lay it Down'	Not released	Asylum E46541
July 1980	'That "Lovin' You" Feelin' Again' (with Emmylou Harris)/Craig Hundley Track	Warner Brothers K17649	Warner Brothers WBS 49262
May 1982	'Running Scared'/ 'In Dreams'	Monument SMNT 7076	Not released
June 1985	'Wild Hearts'/ Instrumental	ZTT ZTAS9	Not released

August 1985	'Ooby Dooby'*/ 'Cryin''*	ZTT ZTAS9	Not released
August 1985	'Wild Hearts'/ Instrumental/ 'Ooby Dooby'/ 'Wild Hearts'*	ZTT 12ZTAS9	Not released
August 1987	'In Dreams'*/ 'Leah'*	Virgin ROY 1	Virgin 7-99388
June 1988	'Cryin''* (with k.d. lang)/'Falling'*	Not released	Virgin 7-99434
November 1988	'You Got It'/'The Only One'	Virgin VS1166	Virgin
January 1989	'You Got It'/'The Only One'/'Cryin'' (with k.d. lang)	Virgin VST1166	Virgin
February 1989	'She's a Mystery to Me'/'Cryin'' (with k.d. lang)	Virgin VST 1173	Virgin
February 1989	'She's a Mystery to Me'/'Cryin'' (with k.d. lang)/'Dream Baby'*	Virgin VST 1173	Virgin

SOLO ALBUMS

	UK	US
1961 *Lonely And Blue*: 'Only the Lonely'/ 'Bye Bye Love'/ 'Cry'/'Blue Avenue'/'I Can't Stop Loving You'/ 'Come Back to Me (My Love)'/'Blue Angel'/'Raindrops'/ '(I'd Be) a Legend in my Time'/ 'I'm Hurtin''/ 'Twenty-two Days'/'I'll Say it's My Fault'	London HAU 2342	Monument M4007/ SM 14002
1962 *Crying*: 'Cryin''/ 'The Great Pretender'/'Love Hurts'/'She Wears my Ring'/ 'Wedding Day'/ 'Summersong'/ 'Dance'/'Lana'/ 'Loneliness'/'Let's	London HAU 2437/ SAHU 6229	Monument M4007/SM 14007

Make a Memory'/
'Nightlife'/
'Running Scared'

1963 *In Dreams:* 'In Dreams'/'Lonely Wine'/ 'Shahdaroba'/ 'No-one Will Ever Know'/'Sunset'/ 'House Without Windows'/'Dream'/ 'Blue Bayou'/'(They Call You) Gigolette'/ 'All I Have to do is Dream'/'Beautiful Dreamer'/'My Prayer'	London HAU 8108/ SHU 8108	Monument MLP 8003/ SLP 18003
1964 *The Exciting Sounds Of Roy Orbison* (UK)/*Roy Orbison At The Rockhouse* (US): 'This Kind of Love'/'Devil Doll'/ 'You're my Baby'/ 'Rockhouse'/ 'You're Gonna Cry'/'I Never Knew'/'Sweet and Easy to Love'/ 'Mean Little Mama'/'Ooby Dooby'/'Problem Child'	Ember NR 5013 (reissued in 1980 on Charly CRM CRM 2007)	Sun LP 1260 (reissued in 1969 as *The Original Sound of Roy Orbison* on Sun 6467 005)
1964 *Oh! Pretty Woman*: 'Oh! Pretty Woman'/'Yo te	London HAU 8207	Not released

amo Maria'/'It's
Over'/'Indian
Wedding'/'Borne
on the Wind'/'Mean
Woman Blues'/
'Candy Man'/
'Falling'/'Mama'/
'The Crowd'/
'Distant Drums'/
'Dream Baby'

1965	*There Is Only One Roy Orbison*: 'Ride Away'/'You Fool You'/'Two of a Kind'/'This is Your Song'/'I'm in a Blue Blue Mood'/ 'If You Can't Say Something Nice'/ 'Claudette'/ 'Afraid to Dream'/ 'Sugar and Honey'/'Summer Love'/'Big as I Can Dream'/ 'Wondering'	London HAU/SHU 8252	MGM E/SE 4308
1966	*The Orbison Way*: 'Crawling Back'/'It ain't no Big Thing'/ 'Time Changed Everything'/'This is My Land'/'The Loner'/'Maybe'/ 'Breakin' up is Breakin' My Heart'/'Go Away'/ 'A New Star'/	London HAU/SHU 8279	MGM E/SE 4322

'Never'/'It Wasn't
Very Long Ago'/
'Why Hurt the One
Who Loves You'

1966 *Orbisongs*: 'Oh!	Monument	Monument
Pretty Woman'/	LMO 5004/	MLP 8035/
'Dance'*/'(Say)	SMO 5004	SLP 18035
You're My Girl'/		
'Goodnight'/		
'Nightlife'*/Let		
the Good Times		
Roll'/'(I Get So)		
Sentimental'/'Yo te		
amo Maria'/		
'Wedding Day'/		
'Sleepy Hollow'/		
'Twenty-two		
Days'/'(I'd be) A		
Legend in My		
Time'		
1966 *The Classic*	London	MGM E/SE
Roy Orbison:	HAU/SHU	4424
'You'll Never be	8318	
Sixteen Again'/		
'Pantomime'/		
'Twinkle Toes'/		
'Losing You'/'City		
Life'/'Wait'/		
'Growing Up'/		
'Where is		
Tomorrow'/'(No)		
I'll Never Get		
Over You'/'Going		
Back to Gloria'/'Just		
Another Name for		
Rock 'n' Roll'/		
'Never Love Again'		

1967 *Roy Orbison's Greatest Hits*: 'The Crowd'/'Love Star'/'Cryin''/ 'Evergreen'/ 'Running Scared'/ 'Mama'/'Candy Man'/'Only the Lonely'/'Dream Baby'/'Blue Angel'/'Uptown'/ 'I'm Hurtin''	Monument LMO/ SMO 5007 (reissue MNT 64663)	Monument MLP 4009/ SLP 14009 (reissue MLP 8000/ SLP 18000)
1967 *Roy Orbison Sings Don Gibson*: '(I'd Be) A Legend in My Time'*/'(Yes) I'm Hurtin''/'The Same Street'/'Far Far Away'/'Big Hearted Me'/ 'Sweet Dreams'/ 'Oh Such a Stranger'/'Blue Blue Day'/'What About Me'/'Give Myself a Party'/ 'Too Soon to Know'	London HAU/SHU 8318	MGM E/SE 4424
1968 *Cry Softly, Lonely One*: 'She'/ 'Communication Breakdown'/'Cry Softly, Lonely One'/'It Takes One to Know One'/'Girl Like Mine'/'Just Let Me Make Believe'/	London HAU/SHU 8357	MGM E/ SE4514

'Here Comes
the Rain Baby'/
'That's a No No'/
'Memories'/'Time
to Cry'/'Just One
Time' ('Just One
Time' not on
MGM album)

1968 *The Very Best Of*   Not released   Monument
Roy Orbison: 'Only   MLP 8045/
the Lonely'/'Cryin'   .   SLP 18045
'/'Running Scared'/
'It's Over'/'Candy
Man'/'Oh! Pretty
Woman'/'Blue
Angel'/'In
Dreams'/'Dream
Baby'/'Mean
Woman Blues'

1968 *The Fastest Guitar*   London   MGM E/SE
Alive: 'Whirlwind'/   HAU/SHU   4475
'Medicine Man'/   8358
'The River'/'The
Fastest Guitar
Alive'/'Rollin' On'/
'Pistolero'/'Good
Time Party'/
'Heading South'/
'Best Friend'/
'There Won't be
Many Coming
Home'

1968 *Early Orbison*:   Monument   Monument
'The Great   LMO/   MLP 8023/
Pretender'/'Cry'/'I   SMO 5013   SLP 18023
Can't Stop Loving
You'/'I'll Say It's

My Fault'/'She
Wears My Ring'/
'Love Hurts'/
'Bye Bye Love'/
'Blue Avenue'/
'Raindrops'/
'Come Back to
Me (My Love)'/
'Summersong'/
'Pretty One'

1969	*More Of Roy Orbison's Greatest Hits*: 'It's Over'/ 'Blue Bayou'/ 'Indian Wedding'/ 'Falling'/'Working for the Man'/'Pretty Paper'/'Mean Woman Blues'/ 'Lana'/'In Dreams'/ 'Leah'/'Borne on the Wind'/ 'What'd I Say'	Monument LMO/ SMO 5014	Monument MLP 8024/ SLP 18023
1969	*Roy Orbison's Many Moods*: 'Truly Truly True'/'Unchained Melody'/'I Recommend Her'/ 'More'/'Heartache'/ 'Amy'/'Good Morning Dear'/ 'What Now My Love'/'Walk On'/ 'Yesterday's Child'/'Try to Remember'	Not released	MGM SE 4636

1970 *The Big O*: 'Break My Mind'/'Help Me Rhonda'/'Only You'/'Down the Line' (i.e. 'Go! Go! Go!')*/'Money'/ 'When I Stop Dreaming'/ 'Loving Touch'/ 'Land of a Thousand Dances'/ 'Scarlet Ribbons'/ 'She Won't Hang Her Love Out (On the Line)'/'Casting My Spell'/'Penny Arcade'	London HAU/SHU 8406	Not released
1970 *The Great Songs Of Roy Orbison*: 'Breakin' Up is Breakin' My Heart'/'Cry Softly, Lonely One'/ 'Penny Arcade'/ 'Ride Away'/ 'Southbound Jericho Parkway'/ 'Crawling Back'/ 'Heartache'/'Too Soon to Know'/'My Friend'/'Here Comes the Rain Baby'	Not released	MGM SE 4659
1971 *Hank Williams: The Roy Orbison Way*: 'Kaw-liga'/ 'Hey Good Lookin''/	Not released	MGM SE 4683

'Jambalaya'/'I
Heard You Crying
in Your Sleep'/'You
Win Again'/'Your
Cheatin' Heart'/
'Cold Cold Heart'/
'Mansion on the
Hill'/'I Can't Help
It'/'There'll be No
Teardrops
Tonight'/'I'm so
Lonesome I Could
Cry'

1972	*Roy Orbison Sings*:	London	MGM SE
	'God Love You'/	SHU 8435	4835

'Beaujolais'/'If
Only for a While'/
'Rings of Gold'/
'Help Me'/'Plain
Jane Country
(Come to Town)'/
'Harlem Woman'/
'Cheyanne'/
'Changes'/'It
Takes All Kinds
of People'/
'Remember
the Good'/
'Yesterday's Child'
('Yesterday's
Child' not on
MGM album)

1973	*Memphis*:	London	MGM SE
	'Memphis	SHU 8445	4867

Tennessee'/'Why a
Woman Cries'/
'Run Baby Run'/

'Take Care of Your
Woman'/'I'm the
Man on Susie's
Mind'/'I Can't Stop
Loving You'*/
'Run the Engines
Up High'/'It Ain't
No Big Thing' (not
the same song as
that of the same
title on *The Orbison
Way*)/'I Fought
the Law'/'The
Three Bells'/
'Danny boy'

1973 *The Great Roy Orbison*: 'Only the Lonely'/'Leah'/'In Dreams'/'Uptown'/ 'It's Over'/'Cryin''/ 'Dream Baby'/'Blue Angel'/'Working for the Man'/ 'Candy Man'/ 'Running Scared'/ 'Falling'/ 'Claudette'/'Ooby Dooby'/'I'm Hurtin''/'Mean Woman Blues'/ 'Lana'/'Blue Bayou'/'Oh! Pretty Woman' (double album)	Monument MNT 45159160 (import)	Silver Eagle SE 1046
1974 *Milestones*: 'I Wanna Live'/'You Don't Know Me'/	Not released	MGM SE 4934

'California
Sunshine Girl'/
'Words'/'Blue
Rain'/'Drift Away'/
'You Lay so Easy
on My Mind'/
'The World You
Live In'/'Sweet
Caroline'/'I've Been
Loving You Too
Long'/'The
Morning After'

1975 *The Monumental Roy Orbison*: 'Oh! Pretty Woman'/'All I Have to do is Dream'/'Yo te amo Maria'/'Dance'/ '(They Call You) Gigolette'/'I Can't Stop Loving You'/ 'Paper Boy'/'Borne on the Wind'/ 'Today's Teardrops'/ 'Distant Drums'/ 'Loneliness'/'Here Comes That Song Again'/'Blue Avenue'/'Let's Make a Memory'/ 'With the Bug'/ 'The Actress'	Monument MNT 69147	Not released
1975 *The Monumental Roy Orbison Volume Two*: 'Sunset'/ 'Dream'/'My	Monument MNT 69188	Not released

Prayer'/'Pretty
One'/'No-one Will
Ever Know'/'(Say)
You're My Girl'/
'Indian Wedding'/
'Let the Good
Times Roll'/'Lana'/
'House Without
Windows'/'Bye Bye
Love'/'Cry'/
'Sleepy Hollow'/
'Nightlife'/
'Wedding Day'/
'What'd I
Say'

1976	*I'm Still In Love With You*: 'Pledging my Love'/'Spanish Nights'/'Rainbow Love'/'It's Lonely'/ 'Heartache'*/ 'Crying Time'/ 'Still'/'Hung Up on You'/'Circle'/ 'Sweet Mama Blue'/'All I Need is Time'	Not released	Mercury SRM 1-1045
1976	*The Best Of Roy Orbison*: 'Oh! Pretty Woman'/ 'Borne on the Wind'/'Today's Teardrops'/'The Crowd'/'Cryin''/ 'Evergreen'/ 'Candy Man'/'Blue	Arcade ADEP 19 (K-Tel)	Not released

Angel'/'Uptown'/
'Only the Lonely'/
'It's Over'/'Lana'/
'Leah'/'In Dreams'/
'Pretty Paper'/'Blue
Bayou'/'Running
Scared'/'Falling'/
'Goodnight'/
'Dream Baby'

1977	*Regeneration*: '(I'm a) Southern Man'/ 'No Chain At All'/ 'Old Love Song'/ 'Can't Wait'/'Born to Love Me'/'Blues in My Mind'/ 'Something They Can't Take Away'/ 'Under Suspicion'/ 'I Really Don't Want You'/ 'Belinda'	Monument MNT 81808	Monument MG 7600
1979	*Laminar Flow*: 'Easy Way Out'/ 'Love is a Cold Wind'/'Lay it Down'/'I Care'/ 'We're Into Something Good'/ 'Movin''/'Poor Baby'/'Warm Spot Hot'/'Tears'/'Friday Night'/'Hound Dog Man'	Asylum K 53092	Asylum 6E 198
1980	*The Sun Years*: 'Ooby Dooby'*/ 'Tryin' to Get to	Sun CDX 4	Not released

You'/'Ooby
Dooby'/'Go! Go!
Go!'/'You're my
Baby'/'Rockhouse'/
'Domino'/'Sweet
and Easy to Love'/
'Devil Doll'/'The
Cause of it All'/
'Fool's Hall of
Fame'/'A True
Love Goodbye'/
'Chicken Hearted'/
'I Like Love'/
'Mean Little
Mama'/'Problem
Child'/'I Was a
Fool' (with Ken
Cook)/'Tryin' to
Get to You'*/'This
Kind of Love'/'It's
Too Late'/'I Never
Knew'/'You're
Gonna Cry'*/
'Mean Little
Mama'*/'You Tell
Me'/'I Give Up'/
'One More Time'/
'Lovestruck'/'The
Clown'/
'Claudette'*/
'Jenny' (with Ken
Cook)/'Find my
Baby For Me'
(with Sonny
Burgess)/'Ooby
Dooby'* (double
album)

1981 *Golden Days*: 'Oh! Pretty Woman'/ 'Running Scared'/ 'Falling'/'Love Hurts'/'Mean Woman Blues'/'I Can't Stop Loving You'/'The Crowd'/ 'Blue Bayou'/ 'Borne on the Wind'/'Lana'/'Only the Lonely'/'It's Only'/'Cryin''/ 'Pretty Paper'/'All I Have to do is Dream'/'Dream Baby'/'Blue Angel'/ 'Working for the Man'/'Candy Man'/ 'In Dreams'	Monument MNT 40-10026	Not released
1983 *Big O Country*: identical tracks to *Hank Williams The Roy Orbison Way* (1971) with three extra tracks: 'Too Soon to Know,' 'I Can't Stop Loving You' and '(I'd Be) A Legend in My Time'	Decca TAB 72	Not released
1984 *Problem Child*: 'Problem Child'*/ 'This Kind of Love'*/'I Never Knew'*/'You're	ZU ZAZZ Z 2006	Not released

Gonna Cry'*/'It's Too
Late'*/'Chicken
Hearted'*
(instrumental)/
'Tryin' to Get to
You'*/'Problem
Child'*/'Mean
Little Mama'*/
'This Kind
of Love'*/
'Claudette'*

| 1987 | *In Dreams: The* | Virgin | Virgin |
| | *Greatest Hits*: | VGD 3514 | 90604-1 |

'Only the Lonely'*/
'Leah'*/'In
Dreams'*/
'Uptown'*/'It's
Over'*/'Cryin''*/
'Dream Baby'*/
'Blue Angel'*/
'Working for the
Man'*/'Candy
Man'*/'Running
Scared'*/'Falling'*/
'I'm Hurtin''*/
'Claudette'*/'Oh!
Pretty Woman'*/
'Mean Woman
Blues'*/'Ooby
Dooby'*/'Lana'*/
'Blue Bayou'*

| 1988 | *For The Lonely*: | Not released | Rhino |
| | | | R1 71493 |

'Ooby Dooby'/
'Go! Go! Go!'/
'Rockhouse'/
'Devil Doll'/
'Uptown'/'I'm

Hurtin''/'Only the
Lonely'/'Blue
Angel'/'Cryin''/
'Candy Man'/'The
Crowd'/'Dream
Baby'/'Running
Scared'/'Leah'/
'Working for the
Man'/'In Dreams'/
'Falling'/'Mean
Woman Blues'/
'Oh! Pretty
Woman'/'Blue
Bayou'/'Pretty
Paper'/'It's Over'/
'(Say) You're My
Girl'/'Goodnight'

1988 *The Greatest Hits*:   Telstar   Not released
'Oh! Pretty   STAC 2330
Woman'/'Only the
Lonely'/'Love
Hurts'/'Lana'/
'My Prayer'/
'Goodnight'/
'Falling'/'Blue
Angel'/'All I Have
to do is Dream'/
'The Great
Pretender'/
'Running Scared'/
'Borne on the
Wind'/'Mean
Woman Blues'/
'Pretty Paper'/'The
Crowd'/'It's Over'

1989 *Mystery Girl*: 'You   Virgin   Virgin
Got It'/'In the Real V2576

World'/'(All I Can
Do is) Dream
You'/'A Love so
Beautiful'/
'California Blue'/
'She's a Mystery
to Me'/'The
Comedians'/'The
Only One'/
'Windsurfer'/
'Careless Heart'

1989	*The Big O. – The Early Years*: 'Ooby Dooby'/'Fool's Hall of Fame'/'One More Time'/ 'Rockhouse'/ 'Devil Doll'/'I Like Love'/'It's Too Late'/'Tryin' to Get to You'/'This Kind of Love'/ 'Claudette'/'Go! Go! Go!'/'You're my Baby'/'You're Gonna Cry'/'Sweet and Easy to Love'/ 'Lovestruck'/ 'Mean Little Mama'/'Chicken Hearted'/'The Cause of it All'/'I Never Knew'/ 'Domino'/'The Clown'/'Problem Child'/'A True Love Goodbye'	Pickwick TWK107	Not released

1989 *Our Love Song*: 'Our Love Song'/ 'Indian Wedding'/ 'Borne on the Wind'/'Evergreen'/ 'Lovestar'/'Mama'/ '(Say) You're My Girl'/'Goodnight'/ '(I Get So) Sentimental'/'Yo te amo Maria'/ 'Sleepy Hollow'/ 'Born to Love Me'	Monument MNT46341 71	Monument
1989 *Best Love Standards*: 'Distant Drums'/'I Can't Stop Loving You'/'No One Will Ever Know'/ 'Beautiful Dreamer'/'Let the Good Times Roll'/ 'Dream'/'The Great Pretender'/'Bye Bye Love'/'(I'd Be) A Legend in My Time'/'All I Have to do is Dream'/ 'Cry'/'What'd I Say'	Monument MNT46341 31	Monument
1989 *Rare Orbison*: 'Paper Boy'/'With the Bug'/'Here Comes That Song Again'/'The Actress'/'Wings of Glory'/'Drifting	Monument MNT46341 81	Monument

Away'/'Today's
Teardrops'/
'Belinda'/'No
Chain at All'/
'Pretty One'/'Blues
in my Mind'/'Only
With You'

CLASS OF '55

SINGLES

1985 'Birth of Rock 'n' Roll'/'Rock 'n' Roll (Fais Do-Do)'	Not released	Smash 884 760-7
1985 'Class of '55'/ 'We Remember the King'	Not released	Smash 888 142-7
1985 'Sixteen Candles'/'Rock 'n' Roll (Fais Do-Do)'	Not released	Smash 830 934-7

ALBUMS

1985 *Class of '55*: 'Birth of Rock 'n' Roll'/'Sixteen Candles'/ 'Class of '55'/ 'Waymore's Blues'/"We Remember the	Smash 830-002	Smash AR-LP-10 01

King'/'Coming
Home'/'Rock 'n'
Roll (Fais
Do-Do'/'Keep
my Motor
Running'/'I Will
Rock and Roll
With You'/'Big
Train From
Memphis'

1985	Interview album: includes interview with Roy Orbison	Not released	Smash AR-LP-10 01 (mail order only)

THE TRAVELING WILBURYS

SINGLES

September 1988	'Handle With Care'/'Margarita'	WEA 927 732-7	WEA
September 1988	'Handle With Care'/'Handle With Care'*/ 'Margarita'	WEA 921081-2 (compact disc)	WEA

ALBUMS

September 1988	*The Traveling Wilburys Volume One*: 'Handle With Care'/ 'Dirty World'/ 'Rattled'/'Last Night'/'Not Alone Any More'/ 'Congratulations'/ 'Heading for the Light'/'Margarita'/ 'Tweeter and the Monkey Man'/'End of the Line'	WEA 925 796-1	WEA

NOTE TO DISCOGRAPHY

All recordings have been listed in order of release rather than the order in which they were recorded. An asterisk (*) indicates an alternative version to that first released. On record labels and sleeves, there are variations in the spellings and renderings of titles. For example, 'Only the Lonely' is often followed by '(Know How I Feel)' while 'Cryin'' has more often been printed as 'Crying' since its original release. Some of the singles up to 1960 were first available at 78 rpm. There are many 'Various Artists' albums containing Roy Orbison tracks first issued on either Sun or RCA. Among the most common of these are *Roy Orbison Sings* (Allegro ALL 778, 1964), *Roy Orbison And Others* (Ember Famous Artistes FA 2005, 1965), *Special Delivery* (RCA Camden CDN 5118, 1969), *Little Richard And Roy Orbison* (RCA Camden CDS 1077, 1970), *The Exciting Roy Orbison* (Hallmark SHM 824, 1974). Some of these have been reissued several times. Rarer is a cassette – *Younger Days* (Charly ZCSUN 18057, 1979) – which includes the Je-Wel version of 'Ooby Dooby'.

Of the film soundtrack albums issued, the US-only *Zig-Zag* (MGM ISE-21-ST) contains one Orbison track ('Zig-zag') while *Less Than Zero* (UK – DEF JAM 460449; US DEF JAM C44042) contains 'Life Fades Away.'

Other important album compilations include *Focus On Roy Orbison* (London FOSU 15/16 – double, 1976) which concentrates on the later MGM material and the TV-advertised *The Roy Orbison Collection* (Monument MNT 10041). An EP – the aptly-titled *Rarities* – was a free gift with this collection. This contained the previously-unissued 'Darkness', 'How are Things in Paradise', 'Yes' and 'Party Heart'.

A number of other extended play discs had already been issued in Britain. However, these were strictly either album chasers or hits collections – with the exceptions of *Hillbilly Rock* (London RES 1089, September 1957) which was the first time any of Roy's Sun recordings were released in the country – and two Ember offerings of 1964, *Sweet And Easy To Love* (EP 4546) and *Tryin' To Get To You* (EP 4563), which also brought previously-unissued Sun items to the UK. The other EP's were *Only The Lonely* (London REU 1274, September 1957), *Roy Orbison* (London REU 1354, March 1963), *In Dreams* (London REU 1373, June 1963), *It's Over* (London REU 1435, August 1964), *Oh! Pretty Woman* (London REU 1437, December 1964), *Roy Orbison's Stage Show Hits* (London REU 1439, February 1965), 'Devil Doll' – from *The Exciting Sounds of Roy Orbison* – (Ember EP 4570, 1965) and *Love Hurts* (London REU 1440, June 1965). In December 1976, another EP – also entitled *Roy Orbison* – was released by Charly (CEP 111). This contained items from the Sun catalogue.

The German record company, Bear Family, have also put out some interesting Roy Orbison material – such as *The RCA Sessions*. This compact disc album – which also includes tracks by Sonny James – contains not only both the 1958–9 singles but also the rejected 'Paper Boy' plus 'With the Bug' (alternate take) and 'I'll Never Tell.' 'Double Date', however, remains in the vaults.

A more recent Bear Family release – *The Sun Years, 1956–8* (BCD 15461) – has unearthed a different take of 'The Clown'.

Lest we forget, there was, in 1962, a German language single by Roy Orbison of 'Mama'/'San Fernando' (London DL 20 726) as well as a different mix of 'Memphis Tennessee'

(London MSC 8474 T2 1L) which turned up in Europe around 1972.

Roy Orbison has also appeared as guest vocalist/instrumentalist on miscellaneous recordings by other artists. When signed to Sun, he sang backing harmonies on discs by Ken Cook, Sonny Burgess and others. Though it was likely that Roy himself could not have recalled all the records on which he appeared since then, among those on which his presence is most evident are:

> 'You've Got Love' by Johnny 'Peanuts' Wilson (US Brunswick 9-55039);
>
> 'I'm In a Blue, Blue Mood' by Conway Twitty (US MGM K13011);
>
> 'I Belong to Him' by Jessi Colter (with Waylon Jennings – US Capitol 4472);
>
> 'Indian Summer' by Larry Gatlin and the Gatlin Brothers (on the LP *Smile* – Columbia FC 40068 – produced by Barry Gibb);
>
> 'Leah' by Bertie Higgins (on the LP *Pirates And Poets* – Columbia FZ 38587);
>
> 'Beyond the End' by Jimmy Buffett (on the LP *Last Mango In Paris* – MCA 5600).
>
> 'Runnin' Down a Dream' by Tom Petty (on the LP *Full Moon Fever* – MCA MC66253).

Many limited editions – sometimes of less than one hundred copies – have been issued by the Roy Orbison International Fan Club, Schutterlarn 43, 5632 JF, Eindhoven, Holland. Most of these recordings feature Roy in concert, alternate takes, Coca-Cola commercials in which he was involved, and the rarer singles. *Roy Orbison Returns* – a mini-album – has further German language versions of his songs while *The Connoisseur's Roy Orbison* – in two volumes – mixes concert performances (including 'What'd I Say' with the Everly Brothers) with both sides of the Je-Wel disc, different versions of 'This Kind of Love' and 'Almost Eighteen' and Orbison-composed instrumentals by Jerry Byrd. Among the recordings of complete concerts is *Big O Live At*

The SNCO from a Dutch army camp in September 1972. This contains versions of the biggest Orbison hits – as do the majority of the few extant Roy Orbison bootlegs – which defy every known copyright law. Perhaps the best of these illicit recordings is a cassette of Roy's last British show. The fidelity is rather low at times but it captures the celebratory atmosphere of a memorable occasion.

As well as those mentioned in the text, there have been numerous cover versions of most of Roy Orbison's hits. Below is a list of some of the songs and the more notable artists concerned:

> 'Claudette': the Four Pennies, the Compton Brothers, Kris Jensen, Jack Launey (French version) and Robert Johnson;
>
> 'Uptown': Robert Gordon, Chase Webster, Ian Crawford and Johnny Seaton;
>
> 'Only the Lonely': Sonny James, Kitty Wells, Arlene Harden, Glen Campbell, J. Frank Wilson and his Cavaliers, the Flamingoes (Swedish version), Johnny Tillotson, Prelude and Roger Whittaker;
>
> 'Blue Angel': Denny Martin, Ronnie Shaw and Bogdan Kominowski (who took over from P. J. Proby in the title role of the London West End musical, *Elvis*, in 1979);
>
> 'I'm Hurtin': Arlene Howard;
>
> 'Running Scared': the Fools, Peter Ringle, Peggy March, Bob Luman, Jay Black, the Four Pennies, the Indians, the Lettermen, Glen Campbell, Ted Herold (German version), Paul Rich, Del Shannon and Neil Brian;
>
> 'Cryin'': Jay and the Americans, Lynn Anderson, Ronnie Milsap, T. Ford and his Boneshakers, Glen Campbell, Floyd Cramer (instrumental), Freddie and the Dreamers, Waylon Jennings, the Lettermen, Gene Pitney, Del Shannon, B. J. Thomas, Bobby Vinton, Don McLean (Spanish and Italian versions), Jeanne de Roy (German version), Little and Large and Suzi Stevens;
>
> 'The Crowd': Arlene Harden, Frank Ifield and Waylon Jennings;

'Working for the Man'; Sherwin Linton;

'Leah': the Canadian Beetles, the Delltones, Martin Denny (instrumental), the Federals, Tony and the Initials, Fred Jasper (in Dutch), Gert Timmerman (in Dutch), Ronnie Mason, Grant Tracy and Billy Stack;

'In Dreams': Tom Jones, Spencer King, Alf King, Les Carle, Vince Hill, Carl Gibson, Wayne Newton, Tiny Yong (in French), Marty Wilde, Sandalwood, Peter London and John Otway;

'Falling': Darryl Ford, Ray Pilgrim and Tim Reynolds;

'Blue Bayou': Glen Barber, the Hillsiders, Hargus 'Pig' Robbins, Towa Carson (in Swedish), Frank Ifield, Marielle Mathieu (in French), Dick Rivers (in French), Paola (in German), Linda Ronstadt (in Spanish as 'Lago Azul'), Mike Roland (in German), Floyd Cramer (instrumental), Bert Weedon, the Tielman Brothers, Barry Crocker, Jodi Vaughan, Billie Jo Spears, Nana Mouskouri, Frank Chacksfield and Slim Whitman;

'It's Over': Gene Pitney (in medley), Jerry Tawney, Arlene Harden, Jack Bedient and his Chessmen, Terry Brandon, Bubblerock, Karel Gott (in Czechoslovakian), Hal Prince, the Tramps (instrumental), Peter Kamp (in German as 'Wie Damals'), Dalida (in French as 'Je t'aime'), Cocki Mazzetti (in Italian as 'La Fine di Tutto') and Terry Brandon;

'Oh! Pretty Woman': the Newbeats, Tony Kaye, Arlene Harden (as 'Lovin' Man'), Andy Kim, Geno Washington and the Ram Jam Band, Jerry Allen (instrumental), Die Tommies (in German), Count Basie Orchestra (vocal by Leon Thomas), Gerd Bottcher (in German), Al Green, Peter Holm (in Swedish), the Lifeguards (instrumental), the Mercey Brothers, the Nutty Squirrels, Real Pascal et les Rockatones, Ray Pilgrim and his Beatmen, Benny Quick (in German), Roy's Boys (instrumental), Laurent Rossi (in French), Del Shannon, Wayne Thomas, Sylvie Vartan (in French), the Ventures (instrumental), Dick Rivers, Jan Hammer (instrumental), Johnny Carroll, I Campioni (in Italian as 'Sei la Sola'), Out of the West, Leroy Van Dyke,

    Blue Steel, Graeme 'Shirl' Strachan, Bruce Channel
    and John Spencer.

Perhaps the most intriguing version of 'Oh! Pretty
Woman' was the 'Fish in the Sea' (see text) rendition by
Curtis Byrd and the Joe-Ray Singers – released well before
Roy's hit. Less fascinating are the multitude of orchestral
recordings of Roy Orbison hits on budget labels by the likes
of the Sunset Strings, the Big Ben Hawaiian Band and the
Nashville Brass.

Finally, there are the multitudinous compositions by Roy
Orbison that were given away to other artists. Other than
those mentioned in the text, the following list of titles (with
performers concerned) contains those known – at the time
of writing – to have been released on disc:-

'Valley of the Roses' (Jerry Byrd), 'Time and Again' (the
Velvets), 'Suzie' (Sue Thompson), 'Spring Fever' (Velvets),
'Sugar Love' (Don Gant), 'So Long I'm Gone (Jerry Lee
Lewis, Warren Smith, Jay Brown), 'See Ruby Fall' (Johnny
Cash, Lester Flatt), 'Sad Eyes' (Don Gant), 'When the Blue
Hour Comes' 'Wings of Glory' (Bobby Bond). 'The Run-
around' (Bobby Goldsboro), 'Rita' (Roddy Crowell), Curtis
and Del), 'The Puppet' (Gene Thomas), 'Peace of Mind'
(Gene Thomas), 'Once Again' (Dannie Dexter), 'Another
Lonely Girl' (Mark Dinning), 'Baby's Gone' (Bobby Wright),
'Bad Boy' (Sue Thompson), 'Cast Iron Arm' (Shakin'
Stevens, Johnny Devlin), 'Long Time no Love' (Ronny
Smith), 'Bobby and the Boys' (Gene Thomas), 'Can't Forget'
(Mark Dinning), 'No-one Really Cares' (Joe Melson, Kris
Jensen), 'Memories of Maria' (Jerry Byrd, Buddy Merrill),
'Lovestruck' (Terry McGill), 'Lavender Lace' (Nellie
Rutherford), 'Daydream' (Don Gant), 'Fancy Dan' (Boots
Randolph), 'Hey!' (Don and Eddie), 'I've Had my Moment'
(David Box, Colin Cook) and, recorded by both Bobby Barker
and Gene Thomas, 'The Last Song'.

As told to Sam Hutt
Hank Wangford, Volume III, The Middle Years £7.99

This is the Story of Three People inextricably entwined. A story of passion and lust, greed and envy, doctors and nurses, Country and Western. The eternal triangle is given a UNIQUE twist, one that will wrench your heart from your chest cavity and leave you gasping for more.

HANK WANGFORD – the gap toothed Country and Western Super Star. The MAN who wears his heart on his sleeve with pride. The MAN who put Whisky on his Guitar and taught us to Jog with Jesus. The MAN with 10 ex-wives, whose mother told him not to mind how many affairs he had, as long as they were legal. The MAN who has tried marriage Sunny side up and Divorce over Easy. The MAN who guided us through the A-Z of C&W on Channel 4. But above all the man who really brought True Sincerity to Britain. THE LEGEND LIVES ON . . .

SAM HUTT – The gap toothed doctor, with the uncanny resemblance to Hank, his best friend and inseparable companion. The man who wrote his own sick note to the Social Security certifying to his schizophrenic condition – the HIPPIE fool, the idealistic doctor, the child of the sixties. Now SAM becomes HANK'S biographer, and keeps finding his own story getting in the way.

COL. FRANK WANGFORD (no relation) is the man who turned SINCERITY into the SINCERE TRUST. The Man behind HANK, the man who hired SAM, the MAN who knows as much about generosity as he does about humanity, the MAN who lets HANK keep HALF of everything he earns. More than just a business man, more than just a Svengali – HE is paying me to write this blurb.

This book contains VISIONS of COUNTRY MUSIC, VISIONS of AMERICA, VISIONS of LOVE and PASSION, VISIONS of HARLEY ST.

'SEX, DRUGS, MUSIC, RELIGION, PUBLICITY, in fact the whole of life is to be found in these simple pages. All this for just a snack. Enrich your life, and make an old man very happy, BUY THIS BOOK.'
COL. FRANK WANGFORD

Gerri Hirshey
Nowhere to Run
the story of soul music £4.99

'If you've ever been touched by the magic of Aretha, Otis, Marvin,
Little Stevie, Curtis, James, Smokey or by *any* soul record of the
1960s, or by the music's power to excite, uplift, warm, sadden,
illuminate or provoke, you'll certainly enjoy this . . . essential for the
soul music buff!' TIME OUT

All Pan books are available at your local bookshop or newsagent, or can be ordered direct from the publisher. Indicate the number of copies required and fill in the form below.

Send to: **CS Department, Pan Books Ltd., P.O. Box 40, Basingstoke, Hants.   RG21 2YT.**

or phone: 0256 469551 (Ansaphone), quoting title, author and Credit Card number.

Please enclose a remittance* to the value of the cover price plus: 60p for the first book plus 30p per copy for each additional book ordered to a maximum charge of £2.40 to cover postage and packing.

*Payment may be made in sterling by UK personal cheque, postal order sterling draft or international money order, made payable to Pan Books Ltd.

Alternatively by Barclaycard/Access:

Card No. ⬚⬚⬚⬚⬚⬚⬚⬚⬚⬚⬚⬚⬚⬚⬚⬚

Signature:

Applicable only in the UK and Republic of Ireland.

While every effort is made to keep prices low, it is sometimes necessary to increase prices at short notice. Pan Books reserve the right to show on covers and charge new retail prices which may differ from those advertised in the text or elsewhere.

NAME AND ADDRESS IN BLOCK LETTERS PLEASE:

....

Name ⸺⸺⸺⸺⸺⸺⸺⸺⸺⸺⸺⸺⸺⸺⸺

Address ⸺⸺⸺⸺⸺⸺⸺⸺⸺⸺⸺⸺⸺⸺

⸺⸺⸺⸺⸺⸺⸺⸺⸺⸺⸺⸺⸺⸺⸺⸺

⸺⸺⸺⸺⸺⸺⸺⸺⸺⸺⸺⸺⸺⸺⸺⸺

⸺⸺⸺⸺⸺⸺⸺⸺⸺⸺⸺⸺⸺⸺⸺⸺

3/87